CHRISTIANITY CONFRONTS MODERNITY

Christianity
Confronts Modernity

A Theological and Pastoral Inquiry
by Protestant Evangelicals and Roman Catholics

Edited By
Peter Williamson and Kevin Perrotta

SERVANT BOOKS
Ann Arbor, Michigan

Copyright © 1981 by *Pastoral Renewal*

Book design by John B. Leidy

Published by Servant Books
    Box 8617
    Ann Arbor, Michigan 48107

Printed in the United States of America

ISBN 0-89283-100-6

Contents

Contributors

Donald Bloesch is professor of theology, Dubuque Theological Seminary, University of Dubuque, Iowa. He is author of *Essentials of Evangelical Theology*, *The Invaded Church*, and many other works.

Edith Black is a doctoral candidate in ancient Near Eastern languages, University of California at Berkeley.

Stephen Board is the editor of *Eternity* magazine.

Stephen B. Clark is overall coordinator of The Word of God, Ann Arbor, Michigan, and author of *Man and Woman in Christ*.

I. John Hesselink is president and professor of theology, Western Theological Seminary, Holland, Michigan.

James Hitchcock is professor of history, St. Louis University, and president of the Fellowship of Catholic Scholars. His books include *Catholicism and Modernity* and *The Loss of the Sacred*.

Peter Hocken, a Roman Catholic priest, is a former professor of moral theology, Oscott College, England.

Kenneth S. Kantzer is editor of *Christianity Today* magazine.

Mark Kinzer is senior elder of the Free Church Fellowship, The Word of God, Ann Arbor, Michigan. He is author of *The Self-Image of a Christian*.

Kerry Koller is the director of the Center for Christian Studies, South Bend, Indiana.

Dr. Richard Lovelace is professor of church history, Gordon-Conwell Theological Seminary, South Hamilton, Massachusetts.

James I. Packer is professor of historical and systematic theology, Regent College, Vancouver, British Columbia.

Kevin Perrotta is managing editor of *Pastoral Renewal* and program coordinator of the colloquy.

Daniel Sinisi is chairman and associate professor, department of theology and philosophy, University of Steubenville, Steubenville, Ohio.

Russell Spittler is assistant academic dean, Fuller Theological Seminary, Pasadena, California.

Paul Vitz is associate professor of psychology, New York University, and author of *Psychology As Religion: The Cult of Self-Worship*.

Dale Vree is editor of the *New Oxford Review*. His books include *On Synthesizing Marxism and Christianity*.

Peter S. Williamson is editor of *Pastoral Renewal* and chairman of the colloquy.

Michael J. Wrenn is director of the graduate program in religious education, New York Archdiocesan Catechetical Institute, Yonkers, New York.

Preface

The essays and responses published here are the product of an unusual meeting. In October 1980 a group of eighty evangelical Protestant and Roman Catholic scholars and pastoral leaders convened in Ann Arbor, Michigan, for a colloquy on the challenges which contemporary society presents to Christians of all traditions. It was the first time that such a large number of evangelicals and Roman Catholics have met for theological and pastoral discussion on this subject. Evangelicals, who are participants in the most vital movement of Protestantism today, have not engaged in discussions of this sort with Roman Catholics before. Roman Catholics, for their part, have in the past entered into dialogue with representatives of particular theological traditions—with Anglicans and Lutherans, for example—or with the World Council of Churches, which represents liberal Protestantism more than evangelicalism. Neither Catholics nor evangelical Protestants have extensively sought such contacts with one another.

The meeting was made more unusual by its broad mix of evangelicals and Roman Catholics. Among the evangelicals there were theologians such as Donald Bloesch, Eugene Osterhaven, and James I. Packer; pastoral leaders and authors such as Larry Christenson, Robert Girard, Charles Simpson, and Howard Snyder; and leaders of various organizations, such as Calvin Malefyt, of the Ethics and Public Policy Center. There were participants in the charismatic renewal, Pentecostals, messianic Jews, black evangelicals—from twenty-five or so different denominations, and nondenominational churches. On the Catholic side there were, similarly, theologians such as Ronald Lawler and Frederick Jelly, ecumenists such as Peter Hocken, scripture scholars such as Benedict Viviano, and historians such as James Hitchcock, as well as clergy and lay pastoral leaders, even a Trappist monk. While common concerns

3

united them, the Catholics represented a diversity of experience and theological perspectives. The bishop of the local Roman Catholic diocese, Bishop Kenneth Povish, while not able to attend, gave his official approval to the meeting and undertook to be episcopal advisor for the organizers.

The presence of both academics and pastors made for wide-ranging discussion, and it allowed a sharing of views between two types of Christian leaders whose efforts are too often separated. The scholarly and pastoral dimensions of the meeting grew out of the character and concerns of the sponsoring organizations—The Word of God, an interdenominational Christian association in the Ann Arbor area; *Pastoral Renewal*, a journal for Christian leaders; and the Center for Christian Studies, a research group in South Bend, Indiana. Several academic participants commented that the colloquy helped meet a need for a pastoral context in which to carry on scholarly discussion, and pastoral leaders at the meeting reported that they found the colloquy a valuable opportunity to consider the larger intellectual and social situation of the Christian people.

Unlike the Vatican dialogues and others which have taken place between representatives of the Roman Catholic Church and Protestant traditions, the Ann Arbor meeting did not attempt to seek avenues to reunion or even to focus on areas of agreement and disagreement. Rather the purpose of the colloquy was to achieve a better understanding of the situation of all Christians vis-a-vis contemporary secular society. It was assumed that evangelical Protestants and Roman Catholics hold enough in common to make such an endeavor possible. The colloquy, then, was an exercise in collaborative rather than dialogic ecumenism.

Although participants' different theological commitments did not constitute the subject of the discussions, they surfaced during the meeting. The differences became evident, for instance, at points when Roman Catholics made reference to church teaching on birth control and divorce, and in evangelicals' comments on biblical inerrancy. Such differences, and the larger ones which underlie them, were respected without becoming the focus of the proceedings. It was clear that despite such areas of difference, the participants had much in common.

While unity was not the goal of the colloquy, the discussion of common problems and sharing of insights gave rise, as a by-product, to rapport with one another. The Holy Spirit seems always to want to use meetings such as this to deepen participants' brotherly love and respect for one another as men and women committed to the cause of Christ.

Each essay is followed by a pair of responses, one by a Catholic, one by a Protestant. When the essay is written by a Protestant, the Catholic's response follows first. When the essay is by a Catholic, the Protestant's response follows first. A note is in order regarding the essay by Dale Vree. Dr. Vree was unable to attend the colloquy, and a paper was read for him which was published at the time of the colloquy in the *National Catholic Register*. The paper takes a different ecumenical approach from that of the other essays but, by considering the impact of political ideologies on Christian thinking, makes a valuable contribution on the whole. At the colloquy itself only one response, John Hesselink's was given; a second, by Kevin Perrotta, has been added in this volume.

The essays and responses are published here substantially as they were presented at the colloquy, except for minor changes by their authors, and the omission of some material from some of the responses because of the limitations of space.

We who organized the colloquy counted it a privilege to participate in the beginnings of such a significant encounter of evangelical and Catholic leaders, which will hopefully point the way toward further exploration together of the historic challenges to Christianity posed by modernity.

THE EDITORS

Introduction

The confrontation of Christianity and modernity is not exactly new. If we take modernity to mean the changes in technology, social structure, and ideology which have transformed the world since the mid eighteenth century, it is plain that Christianity has been confronting modernity for a long time.* The history of the last couple of centuries is full of the consequences of the encounter; for example, the secularization of much of Europe and North America, the successful use of new missionary opportunities, the reinterpretation of the Christian message in terms of classical liberalism, existentialism, and political liberation.

But understanding the confrontation of Christianity and modernity is no mere historical or academic exercise. The confrontation goes on: modern social changes and ways of thinking continue to challenge Christian life and thought, and Christians still need to make basic adjustments in order to meet the challenge. In fact, some of us who have observed the course of

---

* In the discussion that follows and throughout this book, "modernity" refers to the set of changes in social structure and consciousness which have accompanied the rise of technological societies since the mid eighteenth century. The term is sometimes elsewhere used to mean the underlying assumptions of modern thought and life; Thomas Oden, for instance, uses "modernity" in this sense in *Agenda for Theology* when he writes, "By *modernity* I mean the overarching ideology of the modern period, characterized as it is by autonomous individualism, secularization, naturalistic reductionism, and narcissistic hedonism, which assumes that recent modes of knowing the truth are vastly superior to all older ways." Without arguing with Oden's distillation of the ideology of the contemporary period of history, it is important to understand that in this volume "modernity" means something broader than ideology—the complex of technical, social, and intellectual changes which presents Christians with both problems and opportunities.

7

events among evangelical Protestants and Roman Catholics during the last fifteen years have come to belive that for these Christians the confrontation with modernity has recently become or will soon become acute.

What is it about social and intellectual changes in our time that makes it particularly challenging for Christians? Social historians and others have been pointing out for some time that the world today is radically different from the world at any time in the past. Writers such as Peter Berger, Jacques Ellul, Marion Levy, Robert Nisbet, and Edward Shorter have attempted to analyze how modern technological change has transformed society root and branch. I have found especially helpful Marion Levy's sketch of some of the key differences in his book, *Modernization: Latecomers and Survivors.* His list, under the heading "How Peculiar Are the Modernized," makes interesting reading. He cites these points and others:

—"One of the most extraordinary things that we take for granted is education for an unknown future." Whereas today we expect substantial change every two or three decades, most people in the past grew up expecting that their world would be like their fathers' and their grandfathers'.

—People in modernized societies are used to having many fleeting encounters with strangers—on the roads, in stores, in business. But "almost to a person, nonmodernized people assume that the overwhelming majority of all their contact with other human beings will be contacts with people previously well-known."

—Most people in the past have been accustomed to dealing with other people in small social settings—family, village, urban quarter, guild. In these groupings personal life mingled with business. Today we all deal with large numbers of people in a huge range of organizations, from stores to schools to international corporations. In these places personal concerns are generally separated from the tasks at hand. Levy comments that humankind may very well be considerably less well-adapted to these kinds of relationships.

—The family has lost much of its educational function for young people after the age of five or six. And that is not all. Almost always before, in almost every society, boys after their first five years or so would be under the supervision of their fathers, joining them in work and recreation. Now, "the overwhelming majority both of little boys and little girls continue[s] under the direct domination and supervision of ladies until they [reach] maturity. This has never happened before in history. . . . Most of us have not even noticed this change, nor do we have any idea of its radicality."

These points from Levy's list only begin to identify the ways our modern societies are different from the ones that went before. To his list of social changes we could add technological ones; for example, the enormous amounts of energy required to sustain our modern way of life. Political developments could be cited, such as the centralization of power in national governments. Ideological developments could be described, such as the appearance for the first time of secular plans for completely restructuring society, as in the various brands of socialism.

We are living in a period of history which presents us with unique opportunities and problems. This is something we should give careful thought to. Many of the natural aspects of human life that used to help people maintain Christian values and relationships are being broken down. The qualities which make our world modern make it very different from any other social setting that Christian have ever had to deal with. It becomes clear that as the social restructuring of modernization advances, Christians need a pastoral strategy that deals with it.

This brings us back to the state of the churches, especially the state of things in evangelical Protestantism and the Catholic Church. There are signs that the kinds of social changes mentioned above, with the modern intellectual developments which have accompanied them, are making it increasingly difficult for evangelicals and Catholics to live out the Christian life and are endangering their faithfulness to Christian teaching.

In the Catholic Church the signs have become well-known. When Pope John XXIII and the Second Vatican Council opened some windows in the Church in the early 1960s, the Catholic Church entered a time of turbulence and upheaval. In many cases genuine renewal was marred by an undiscerning openness to secular influences, by confusion and weakening of confidence. By now we are all familiar with the decline in American Catholics' church attendance, the massive defection of priests and nuns, and the great rise in divorce and remarriage among Catholics. Almost as widely known have been the activities of theologians pressing for changes in the way the Church relates to scripture, in its understanding of dogma, and in its moral teaching. None of these developments were the intention or direct result of the actions of the Catholic popes or bishops; they have followed from a confluence of many factors, such as the influence of secular values transmitted through the mass media and the academic world.

The fall in church attendance, the exodus of priests, the rise in divorce—these are just some of the most prominent signs of a serious disturbance in Catholic life, signs of a weakening of Catholics' ability to maintain a way of life distinct from the surrounding secularized culture. In the theological controversies, a fundamental question has emerged. Unintentionally, the Second Vatican Council triggered the buildup of pressures for change which now seek to move the Catholic Church into deeper and deeper assimilation to modern culture. The struggle has reached the level of questioning what, if anything, is basic and fixed in Christianity. The issue has become how the Catholic Church can update itself without losing its identity.

Among those who have analyzed this situation has been James Hitchcock, author of *Catholicism and Modernity*, a book which, in my opinion, merits more attention than it has received. In Hitchcock's view, the teaching of Vatican II was not successfully communicated within the Church. The faithful were released from various customs and laws previously held inviolable, and the changes were administered without adequate explanation. In effect, the message that rippled outward from Vatican II was change itself, and openness to the modern world.

The result was that, at many levels of church life below the official level, Catholic teaching began to be shaped by what was acceptable to the modern mind. Aspects of Church teaching incompatible with contemporary thought were questioned or ignored; the Church suffered a weakening of its eternal perspective, of its active belief in the supernatural nature of the Christian religion. Catholicism's traditionally strong positions regarding personal, especially sexual, morality were questioned and rejected, even by those who did not express disagreement with basic dogma.

A mentality related to consumerism began to form the perspective of many Catholics, a mentality which seeks to be pleased and fulfilled rather than to be saved or to live up to any standard of behavior except that of one's own devising. This mentality reacts against traditions, moral restrictions, and other limitations to the satisfaction of what has been called "the imperial self."

The media have promoted these changes in the Catholic Church. During and after the Vatican Council, most American Catholics were flattered by the attention the media gave their Church. However, as the media interpreted the proceedings of the Vatican Council to Catholics, more and more Catholics began to see the Church from the secular media's perspective. Hitchcock argues, as have others, that in the modern world, a genuine pluralism—a pluralism that allows Christians to keep an outlook on life that is distinctive from those around them—requires the existence of communities with firm boundaries which are able to sustain them in Christian thinking that is independent of secular presuppositions.

Seeing the pattern of assimilation which is threatening the Catholic Church, some of us have become troubled by signs of the early stages of that process in evangelical Protestantism. Although the evangelical movement displays growth and vitality, the appearance of these signs is a matter of concern. In today's world things change quickly, as the experience of the Catholic Church in the last twenty years illustrates. The Catholic Church has shifted abruptly from a state of confidence, uniformity, and what some saw as rigidity, to a state of disarray as outspoken dissenters openly oppose the leadership of

Church authorities. Among evangelicals the signs of secular influence do not appear in striking reductions of basic truths such as the deity of Christ and his bodily resurrection, as have surfaced in the Catholic Church. The shift has begun in the areas of practical teaching and morality.

There are signs in the area of sexual morality, for example, of changing views and practices. Some evangelicals have begun to defend homosexual behavior—a position taken by Letha Scanzoni and Virginia Ramey Mollenkott in *Is the Homosexual My Neighbor?* and by other evangelicals. Here the secular gay liberation movement has developed a wing within evangelicalism. Attitudes toward divorce are also changing, and the incidence of divorce is rising—a sign that evangelicals, like Catholics, are increasingly vulnerable to the influence of secular patterns in their personal relationships. A widely publicized poll of 200 previously married and now single members of a large evangelical church in California showed that the great majority thought that sexual abstinence was unrealistic for them, and that only nine percent of the men and twenty-seven percent of the women said they had not had sexual relations in the past year.

The values of secular humanist psychology can be seen in the approaches which some evangelicals are taking to personal growth and maturity. One author writes that the breakup of his marriage was a sad but "healthy new beginning for each of us in our own way," as he was called by faith like Abraham to leave the security of marriage to embark on a spiritual pilgrimage toward emotional authenticity. Another writes, "I hope my wife will never divorce me, because I love her with all my heart. But if one day she feels that I am minimizing her or making her feel inferior or in any way standing in the light that she needs to become the person that God meant her to be, I hope she'll be free to throw me out even if she's one hundred. There is something more important than our staying married, and it has to do with integrity, personhood, and purpose." Here evangelicals are being shaped by the prevailing secular exaltation of the individual rather than Christian teaching about commitment, faithfulness, and perseverance in marriage.

Another sign of the pattern which I have observed is the tendency of some evangelicals to become preoccupied with political concerns and social issues. This happens to evangelicals whose political views are on the right as well as on the left. Their theology becomes affected, an identification of Christianity and their politics takes place, and finally they tend to read their Christianity in light of their politics.

A while ago I was in the home of Russell Hitt, retired editor of *Eternity* magazine and long time observer of American evangelicalism. We were discussing some of the observations I have made here, and I asked him if it was his impression that there has been a significant shift in evangelicalism in the last ten years or so. He agreed quite strongly that there has been a radical change, pointing out that in the past it would have been inconceivable that a book like Scanzoni's and Mollenkott's advocating permanent homosexual relationships would have been accepted as a possible opinion for discussion among evangelicals. The implicit theological consensus of the evangelical movement, he agreed, has begun to disintegrate.

Many of the developments which I have cited among both Catholics and evangelicals originate in a desire to correct an imbalance or distortion. For example, the church's failure to adequately deal with problems of the poor or women or people with homosexual difficulties gives rise to a reaction which seeks to right this imbalance. The reaction, however, quickly adopts the perspectives and agenda of a secular movement concerned with the same issue. The movement within the church then mirrors what is happening in the secular movement, only with a lag of a few years and in a way that is toned down somewhat because of its different constituency. The movement within the church seeks the same goals as the secular one, and even holds the secular movement as a model that Christians ought to learn from.

Liberal Protestants and secular observers are sometimes better able to recognize this process than the Catholics and evangelicals involved in it. These observers applaud the secular goals which the Catholics and evangelicals are pursuing, but are amused at their insistence that they are proceeding in a way that is consistent with Catholic or evangelical views of scripture. For example, this kind of observation was made by Robert Price in a *Christian Century* article entitled "A Fundamentalist Social Gospel?" (Nov. 28, 1979). The author noted that "a certain hermeneutical naivete mars the otherwise admirable consciousness-raising that is now occurring among evangelicals." A portion of his comments is worth quoting at length:

> Most conservative evangelicals have been taught that personal opinions and cultural views are worthless unless they can make direct appeal to a biblical warrant of some sort. Many of the current "young evangelical" writers grew up in the 60s, and could not resist the perceived cogency of certain cultural trends—for instance, racial and sexual equality, or nonviolence. Their religious upbringing provided no basis or authorization for espousing such views, however. . . . Some renounced their religious backgrounds. Others sought to accommodate their new liberalized stance to the evangelical ethos. The main strategy was an appeal to the Bible that I call "hermeneutical ventriloquism."
>
> The young evangelical approaches the problem like this: "Feminism [for example] is true; the Bible teaches the truth; therefore the Bible *must* teach feminism." Now it is far from obvious that the Bible explicitly *teaches* feminism, yet the young evangelical will feel that he or she has no right to be a feminist unless "the Bible tells me so." Thus the primary task of the reform-minded evangelical is to make the Bible teach feminism in the most plausible way.
>
> I think it is rather revealing in this regard to examine the intrafeminist dialogue in young-evangelical publications. There we find at least two competing approaches. Sharon Gallagher, Aida Spencer, Letha Scanzoni and others maintain that *rightly understood* the plain sense of the text has always been feminist in nature. For instance, 1 Timothy 2:12, read in the light of Assyrian, rabbinic or Hellenistic texts, seems suddenly to mean that women should not teach only if they happen to be heretics, orgiasts, etc. Or the "head-

ship" of Christ over the church and of husband over wife, in Ephesians 5:23, *really* connotes "source," not "authority," despite the context which would seem to suggest that "source" *implies* authority (e.g., Eph 1:22). Other writers— Virginia Mollenkott and Paul Jewett—admit that various biblical texts *do* inculcate male domination, but that such "problem texts" (problematic only to feminists, note) should be ignored in favor of the implicit thrust of other, egalitarian texts such as Galatians 3:28. The agreed-upon goal is that the Bible is to support feminism. The debate is over the best way to arrive at this predetermined goal exegetically! The Bible *must* support the desired social position; otherwise how can the young evangelical believe it, much less persuade fellow evangelicals?

So far, I have proposed that many activist evangelicals have really come to hold their social views on the basis of cultural osmosis or legitimate political argumentation. But they need to believe that "biblical mandates" are the reason for their conviction. The real reason has been hidden, even from themselves.

By quoting Price I am not implying that all the evangelicals and Catholics who are concerned about the status and role of women are simply following the *zeitgeist*, the spirit of the age. I do think that Price puts his finger on a real problem, which he describes as "hermeneutical ventriloquism." The problem is one of unconsciously absorbing secular positions and then looking in scripture and theology for ways to support them. Evangelicals and Catholics who operate in this mode are opening themselves to cultural assimilation and loss of Christian identity. The process is not as advanced among evangelicals as it is in the Catholic Church; but it is my opinion and that of others that we are witnessing the early stages of the process.

What I have said about the impact of modern social changes and ideologies on Christians today leads to the conclusion that we must make both an offensive and defensive response. We are in need of new pastoral strategies that will support and strengthen Christian life together in a world of constant change; and we need a firmness about Christian teaching which maintains its distinctiveness. We must be faithful to the revelation entrusted to us. We need an approach which does not fearfully seek to flee from the encounter with modernity but which develops ways to live its life and carry out its mission in the modern world.

It was toward the accomplishment of these twin goals that we aimed in sponsoring the colloquy from which the essays in this volume come. The colloquy, by bringing together a wide range of people concerned about these issues, was a significant step forward. It opened with an analysis by Mark Kinzer of some of the characteristics of modernity from a pastoral perspective. There followed examinations of the confrontation with modernity in Christians' thinking about politics (Dale Vree), in their operational assumptions in Church work (James Hitchcock), in the field of psychology and counseling (Paul Vitz), and in the study of scripture (Steve Clark). In conclusion, Donald Bloesch called for an alliance of evangelical Protestants and Roman Catholics around the kinds of theological and pastoral issues which the colloquy addressed.

PETER WILLIAMSON

CHAPTER ONE

Christian Identity and Social Change in Technological Society

Mark Kinzer

We are examining the confrontation between Christianity and modernity. Much of our discussion focuses on the ideological confrontation—the penetration of secular and non-Christian ideas into the basic intellectual framework of the Christian people. This is certainly a critical point of confrontation. However, as a Christian pastor I devote even more attention to the way this confrontation between Christianity and modernity finds practical expression in the daily lives of Christians. Just as we are obliged to approach matters of doctrinal truth with a thoroughly and distinctively Christian mind, guided by revelation and wisdom and discerning clearly between the true and the false, so we are obliged to live a thoroughly and distinctively Christian way of life, incarnating Christian truth in the concrete details of our daily tasks and relationships.

Therefore, it is understandable that my topic leads me to a pastoral and sociological analysis of the confrontation between Christianity and modernity. Such a perspective reveals the practical implications of filling our churches with Christians who think in a non-Christian way. It also clarifies some of the sociological and historical roots underlying many of our thorniest theoretical problems. The interaction between thought and life works both ways—faulty Christian thinking produces flawed Christian living, but a disordered and confused pattern of life also produces a confused intellectual viewpoint. Therefore, a pastoral and sociological analysis of Christianity's confrontation with modernity can prove to be of vital interest and importance.

In facing the modern world, Christianity is challenged to adapt itself and apply itself to a drastically new environment. This is not the first time Christianity has been so challenged. In the early centuries of the church, an essentially Jewish band of disciples living a Jewish way of life and proclaiming a Jewish message of salvation marched the highways of the Roman Empire and brought a pagan empire to faith in the God of Israel. In the process, this Jewish church needed to adapt itself and apply itself to an entirely new intellectual and social environment. In every great missionary endeavor and in the transition to every new historical epoch, the church has received the same challenge to new adaptation and application. And every successful response has been guided by the same simple principle: adapt whenever possible to the thought and habits of the new environment in order to apply and preach the gospel, but never compromise essential Christian truths.

Though Christianity has been challenged before by new environments, it has probably never faced a challenge as great as it faces today. This challenge and threat is unique for three main reasons. First, it comes at a time when the Christian people are confused about their precise identity and how they should relate to the society in which they live. We will examine the historical reasons behind this confusion in just a moment; it is enough to note here that this uncertainty regarding the boundaries separating the church from the surrounding society has contributed greatly to the vast infusion of non-Christian currents of thought and life into the Christian people. Second, the new social environment, technological society, has an unparalleled capacity for shaping and influencing the lives of its members. This has also gravely exposed the Christian people to a formation in patterns of life and thought contrary to essential Christian truth. Finally, the sheer novelty of the new environment has posed a unique challenge. The church must now adapt itself and apply itself to a society that is in many ways unlike any that has ever existed before, a society in which change is the norm, and which therefore poses a slightly different challenge today than it did yesterday, and which will pose a new and unprecedented challenge tomorrow.

In the remainder of this paper I will look at the first two of these reasons which explain the uniqueness of our current predicament. I will then proceed to point out some of the practical consequences of the Christian people's vast exposure to non-Christian influences. In conclusion, I will sketch in a few principles that should guide our pastoral response to the confrontation between Christianity and modernity. In all that follows, the focus will be pastoral and sociological—examining the actual life of the Christian people as it encounters modernity.

Christian Identity and Christian Social History

Christian social history can be conveniently divided into three main periods: diaspora Christianity, Christendom, and the modern period. This distinction sheds much light on the special dilemmas faced by Christians in the modern world as they relate to the secular society around them. We must understand this historical background if we are to fully grasp the profound Christian identity conflict of the twentieth century.

The first era of Christian social history, diaspora Christianity, is the period from 30 A.D. to 312 A.D., from the death and resurrection of Christ to the conversion of Constantine. In this period the Christian churches consisted of tightly knit pockets of believers scattered throughout the Roman and Persian Empires. These early Christian communities were a controversial minority group, attractive to some (as seen by their continuous growth in numbers) and repellent to others (as seen by the sporadic outbursts of violent persecution directed against them). They were disciplined bodies of people with their own leaders and their own way of life.

Two social features of disapora Christianity are especially important for our purposes. First, there was a clearly recognizable boundary between the Christian community and the outside world. It was clear who was in the community and who was not in the community. The church in this period evolved elaborate procedures for initiating new members (the catechumenate), disciplining repentant wrongdoers (public penance), and excluding the unrepentant (excommunication). The identity of the Christian people was visible alike to both believer and unbeliever. Second, the members of the diaspora church coupled evangelistic zeal and charity toward their unbelieving neighbors with a healthy mistrust for pagan teaching and the pagan way of life. Though the early Christians acknowledged that some truths were accessible to the pagans, they looked not to the outside world but instead to their own scriptures and traditions and teachers for the only reliable knowledge of what to think and how to live. Thus the diaspora church adapted itself and applied itself to its surrounding environment, speaking the same language and following many of the same customs; but it had enough social distance to swim against the current when necessary and maintain the truths of the gospel in a relatively pure form.

The second era of Christian social history begins in 312 A.D. with the conversion of the Roman Emperor Constantine (the king of Armenia was converted at around the same time). This era extends to approximately 1700 A.D. In this period the Christian church, once a minority group in the empire, became first a majority and then virtually identical with the entire society. The Islamic invasions of the seventh century eventually plunged many eastern churches back into a diaspora situation, but the majority of Christians during this period lived in a society that was at least nominally a Christian society. This is the era of Christendom.

Many Christians disagree in their evaluation of this transition from diaspora Christianity to Christendom. For some (like Constantine's contemporary and friend, Bishop Eusebius of Caesarea) the conversion of Constantine and the Christianization of the Empire is seen as a great triumph for the cause of Christ, providing the peace and security in which the church could develop its liturgy, art, and theology, and opening up countless avenues for the preaching of the gospel and its application to all of human life. For others (like the sixteenth century Anabaptists) the emergence of Christendom is the greatest and most tragic disaster in all of church history, subjecting the Christian community to centuries of political intrigue, moral scandal, and theological compromise. My purpose here is not to evaluate this transition one way or the other, but to merely describe it as an important phase of Christian social history apart from which many of our current dilemmas are incomprehensible.

The era of Christendom thus witnessed an erasing of the boundary line between Christianity and society. Church leaders became prominent political figures. All dominant intellectual movements had to at least superficially find their mooring in Christian truth. Any attempts at reforming the church were also attempts at reforming all of society. A decisive change in the social history of the church had occurred, and it affected the entire life of the Christian people.

The third main period in Christian social history is the modern era, beginning sometime around 1700 A.D. and continuing to the present. The crucial transition point here, less datable than Constantine's conversion but of equal significance, is the beginning of the movement to de-Christianize Christendom. The seventeenth and eighteenth century Enlightenment began this process which has only neared completion in the twentieth century. In the modern era, Western Christendom repudiated its cultural heritage and integrated its life instead around new secular ideologies and technologies. No longer would the dominant architects of culture attempt to build on an explicit foundation of Christian truth.

Fourteen hundred years of Christendom had left the Christian churches unprepared to deal with a largely non-Christian society. The church was so identified with society as a whole that it could not conceive of returning to its ancient diaspora form of life. Therefore, the de-Christianization of society was accompanied by the de-Christianization of the church. The lack of distinct identity—clear walls and boundaries—exposed the Christian people to the strong secular winds of doctrine blowing through society at large. Many Christians in the modern era thus think and live much like their non-Christian neighbors.

The problem of Christian identity in the modern world is complicated by the fact that the church does not merely face another overt form of paganism as it did in its confrontation with the Roman Empire. This modern non-Christian system has learned from Christianity. Sometimes it has even passed off its new ideas and ways of life as true Christianity (as in Thomas Jefferson's watered-down deistic version of Christianity). It at least borrows many of its most appealing ethical principles from the Christian tradition (as in the Marxist concern for the poor). The end result is certainly not genuine Christianity. However, it sounds close enough to Christianity to make Christians uncomfortable about repudiating it root and branch. The Christian people are thus put in a difficult and ambiguous position. What and where is Christianity? What and where is the church? How does one discern between the church and the surrounding non-Christian society?

Some bodies of Christians temporarily escaped these nagging questions of identity. In particular, this is true of those Christian bodies who suffered over the centuries as harried minorities and who thus learned to live a type of diaspora life even in the midst of Christendom. This is also sometimes true of immigrant peoples and oppressed nations who recognize in some form of traditional Christianity their only means of retaining a national and cultural identity. There are also some Christian churches which have maintained a clear identity by taking strong doctrinal stands and resisting contemporary trends. However, the de-Christianization of Western society affects these groupings today as well, because of forces at work in technological society that will be described later in this paper.

The Christian churches have not totally floundered over the past two centuries. The nineteenth century showed many signs of powerful evangelism and revival. The twentieth century can also claim its share of martyrs, heroes of faith, and lively spiritual movements. However, beneath these apparent signs of vigor lay many unsolved intellectual and social dilemmas that have risen prominently to the surface over the past few years. As Christians grapple with a society that grows ever more visibly hostile to Christian truth, they experience with greater intensity the need to draw some line between that which is consistent and that which is inconsistent with their faith. Yet the ambiguities inherent in the third stage of Christian social history make this simple line-drawing a surprisingly arduous and confused task.

The Great Formative Influences of Mass Technological Society

Even if the walls of the Christian people stood strongly in place, they would still be challenged by the formidable forces that batter against them in mass technological society. Those Christian bodies which were relatively unaffected by the de-Christianization of Christendom face a stiffer challenge in this new type of society. The remainder of the Christian churches, already confused, have been thrown into an even greater crisis of identity. The immense modern forces of influence and social control have had an impact on the Christian churches that must not be underestimated.

The shift from traditional to technological society that has occurred in the past two centuries in the West forms an essential background for understanding the challenge facing the church in the modern world. Such astute sociological observers as Jacques Ellul, Peter Berger, Marion J. Levy, Peter Laslett, Robert Nisbet, and Edward Shorter have commented extensively on the revolutionary changes that result from this new phase of social history. Ellul's volume entitled *The Technological Society* has become a semi-classic. Stephen Clark's recently published work, *Man and Woman in Christ*, also includes a penetrating analysis of technological society. In what follows I will presume a basic familiarity with the nature of this radical social change, and concentrate specifically on those aspects of technological society which exercise a powerful secularizing influence on the daily life of the Christian people.

There are five aspects of life in modern technological society that especially weaken the Christian people's ability to think and live in a distinctively Christian way. They are as follows: (1) The breakdown of natural groupings, (2) the specialization of knowledge and expertise, (3) the pervasiveness of the media, (4) mass education, and (5) the collectivization of labor. We will now take a brief look at each of these features of life in technological society.

1. *The breakdown of natural groupings.* The formation of the modern nation-state and the establishment of a modern technological society have resulted in the partial or total breakdown of natural groupings. This fact has been noted by such sociological observers as Jacques Ellul, Peter Berger, and Robert Nisbet. The term "natural grouping" (borrowed from Ellul) refers to social bodies of small to moderate size which are based on stable, cohesive personal relationships.[1] The relationships are personal: they involve the entirety of people's lives, not simply one or two aspects, such as work or school. They are stable: they are enduring relationships, built for time, and thus not tolerant of widespread individual mobility. They are cohesive: they call for a recognition of group authority and a personal loyalty to fellow members. The conjugal family is the main natural grouping still in existence; in the past many other natural groups also flourished, such as the extended family, the local church or parish, the village, the town, the guild, and the traditional neighborhood. In fact the very structure of traditional societies usually consists of an interrelated network of natural groupings, each possessing its own identity, rights, customs, and social obligations.

In technological society, natural groupings are not totally eliminated. The existence of at least some natural groupings seems to be a necessary requirement for human survival, providing essential personal support that cannot come from other sources. However, in technological society natural groupings are minimized in extent and importance. The structure of society rests instead on two basic types of units—the mass collective and the individual. The mass collective is a convenient term for the vast network of huge and impersonal institutions that largely dominate life in technological society. These institutions—whether political, military, industrial, commercial, educational, religious, or charitable—all depend on a flexible population of mobile, autonomous individuals who can serve within them. Thus the "liberation" of individuals from their traditional loyalty and subordination to natural groups frees them to serve the needs of the mass technological society.

This brings us to the great paradox of modern technological society. Collectivism and individualism need one another. They are opposed to one another in theory and ideology, but are indissolubly wedded in practice and social reality. This paradox becomes more striking when we look at the specific question of social control. The ideology behind technological society promises freedom from the personal authority found in natural groups. Technological society gives this freedom, but at the price of a new form of authority and control, what Jacques Ellul calls "propaganda." Ellul uses the term "propaganda" to refer to more than just direct political indoctrination. Subsumed under this term for him are all the subtle forms of mass influence, operative in both the West and the East, which shape attitudes, values, beliefs, and behavior:

> For propaganda to succeed, a society must first have two complementary qualities: it must be both an individualist and a mass society. These two qualities are often considered contradictory. It is believed that an individualist society, in which the individual is thought to have a higher value than the group, tends to destroy groups that limit the individual's range of action, whereas a mass society negates the individual and reduces him to a cipher. But this contradiction is purely theoretical and a delusion. In actual fact, an individualist society must be a mass society, because the first move toward liberation of the individual is to break up the small groups that are an organic fact of the entire society. In this process the individual frees himself completely from family, village, parish, or brotherhood bonds—only to find himself directly vis-a-vis the entire society. (p. 90, *Propaganda*)

Propaganda can be effective only in an individualist society, by which we do not mean the theoretical individualism of the nineteenth century, but the genuine individualism of our society. . . . In individualist *theory* the individual has eminent value, man himself is the master of his life; in individualist *reality* each human being is subject to innumerable forces and influences, and is not at all master of his own life. As long as solidly constituted groups exist, those who are integrated into them are subject to them. But at the same time they are protected by them against such external influences as propaganda.

An individual can be influenced by forces such as propaganda only when he is cut off from membership in local groups. Because such groups are organic and have a well-structured material, spiritual, and emotional life, they are not easily penetrated by propaganda.[2] (p. 91, *Propaganda*)

Thus, in technological society, individualism is not what it appears to be. It appears to be freedom from the constraints of authority. Instead it turns out to be merely an exchange of the direct personal authority of natural groups for the indirect and impersonal social control of the mass collective.

This rather involved sociological analysis has great consequences for the Christian community. The Christian people has always relied on natural groups to provide the foundation of its communal life and the primary vehicle for the teaching and training of its members. The conjugal and extended family supported by the community of the local church have traditionally provided Christians with the environment in which they live out their Christian lives. With the steady weakening of natural groups in technological society, Christians and non-Christians alike are individualized and subjected to the new authority of the secular mass collective. Even the dedicated Christian now finds it difficult to have his mind and his life formed by Christian truth rather than by the potent secular currents to which he is constantly exposed.

2. *The specialization of knowledge and expertise.* The effectiveness of propaganda and social control in technological society de-

pend in part on the popular societal attitude toward knowledge. From its very beginnings, modern society has derived much of its distinct personality from its reliance on science and technology. Along with the great material successes in the West over the last two centuries has come a mammoth knowledge industry that has produced an unprecedented number of universities, scientists, scholars, libraries, books, periodicals, and novel ideas. As in every other burgeoning industry, the obvious path of expansion has been the way of specialization. As the data in each field increases and the effort required to master that data similarly increases, it becomes more and more difficult for even a professional academician to master many areas of human knowledge. For the ordinary man or woman, the task is hopeless from the outset.

This brings us to another of the many paradoxes of modern technological society: the astronomical growth in the knowledge industry, even with its accompanying system of mass education, actually *reduces* people's confidence in what they know. True, I may know more about the functions of the human body than a learned physician of six centuries past. But compared to what my family doctor knows today, and even more strikingly compared to what medical researchers know today, my freshman physiology course flickers as a feeble light indeed. The obvious consequence is that I must regularly look outside myself to the professional knowledge producers and distributors if I am to be confident that my thoughts and my life line up with current truth.

If this sense of ignorance and the need for enlightenment only touched upon such technical disciplines as the natural sciences and computer engineering, then the modern problem with the knowledge industry would not be very grave. However, the same numinous authority attached to experts in these fields is attached by extention to other experts with less proven skills and more popularly relevant theories. I am speaking primarily of the behavioral scientists. I would not recommend that we dismiss all the findings or the methods of behavioral science; however, we should recognize three major problems with this type of expertise.

The first problem is that the behavioral sciences are especially susceptible to non-scientific ideological influences. Human behavior cannot be studied solely with objective, quantitative tools; the role of subjective judgment is crucial in the process. Thus the language and data in behavioral science may look objective, but the conclusions are often guided by unstated beliefs and values. A second problem is that behavioral science has considerable impact on most people's daily lives. Behavioral scientists are the reigning experts on marital adjustment, childrearing, personal relationships, and psychological health. When people look for an expert opinion in one of these areas, they usually look to someone in the caring professions, which all involve extensive training in the behavioral sciences. The media are also replete with alluring self-help recipes for a happy and successful life, all advanced by men and women who stand firmly on their psychological or sociological credentials. Social historian Christopher Lasch severely criticizes this growing influence of the behavioral sciences in his insightful study of family life entitled *Haven in a Heartless World*. A third problem is that many of the principles disseminated by behavioral scientists contradict or undermine basic Christian truths. Paul Vitz demonstrates this point in his book *Psychology As Religion*, and his paper in the present colloquy should further elaborate on this topic. Thus, I conclude that though the behavioral sciences can sometimes contribute to the improvement of human life, their authoritative expertise also serves to inculcate the secular values and behavior patterns of mass technological society.

The general receptivity to the counsel of behavioral science affects Christians as much as it does non-Christians. Christians often place uncritical trust in professionally trained experts. In place of a truly Christian approach to their daily lives, many Christians thus receive a secular mentality and a secular formula for ordering their daily lives.

3. *The pervasiveness of the media*. The breakdown of natural groups exposes individuals to greater outside control, and the exploding knowledge industry inclines individuals to look to trained secular experts for practical advice; but the main agents

who actually shape people's lives, who give daily application of the values and perspectives of technological society, are the media, the schools, and the work site.

The media pervade technological society like arteries and veins in a human body. They facilitate the constant flow of information and entertainment so essential to the survival of a modern technological culture. Given the speed of the revolutionary innovations in the media over the past fifty years, it is remarkable that so few people recognize how powerfully the new media influence their lives. Individuals deal daily with magazines, newspapers, books, radios, record albums, tapes, the television, and the cinema. They are bombarded with facts and opinions and stimuli, and have neither the time nor the expertise to sort out the good from the bad.

One of the relatively recent media innovations that alone has had an incalcuable impact on our culture is the television. The average American sits before his TV twenty-five to thirty hours per week. That equals about one-fourth of most people's waking life. And this does not merely affect non-Christians. I was in England several months ago while a particular American television special was being aired. Eighty to ninety percent of England was watching that program, including many Christians that I met during my stay. The program was a topic of lively conversation wherever I went. How can this type of media exposure fail to shape the lives of people in technological society? For most Christians today, the products of secular television are clearly a more potent influence than Sunday sermons or traditional Christian teaching.

4. *Mass education.* Before the nineteenth century, mass education was nonexistent. Today it is a presumed fact of life. The very nature of technological society demands a highly trained work force and a means of socializing youth into the patterns of a mass culture. The modern educational system attempts to meet these needs.

Schools play an important role in shaping the lives of modern youth. Young people spend much of their first eighteen years of life going to school, and many continue on for two to ten years afterwards. Of course, the schools are notoriously ineffective at accomplishing fully what they set out to do. Nonetheless the total environment—peer-group, teacher, course material—inhabited by the student for ten to twenty of his most formative years is destined to leave a deep mark on his life. He may not always learn to read and write proficiently, but he usually assimilates a fair amount of secular humanist ideology—agnosticism, feminism, sexual permissiveness, disrespect for authority, and moral autonomy.

Most Christian youth attend these public educational institutions. Some others attend private religious schools, but most of these institutions today are very similar to their secular counterparts. They are also difficult to sustain financially. The consequences are clear: Christians and non-Christians alike have their early lives shaped by a secular organ of mass technological society.

5. *The collectivization of labor.* Productive labor, like education, once occurred mainly within natural groupings. Lawyers, physicians, craftsmen, merchants, farmers—all worked in their homes or near their homes, within the context of stable, cohesive personal relationships. In contrast, productive labor in technological society occurs mainly in large institutional work settings such as office buildings, shopping malls, and factories. As soon as the student graduates from one mass institution, he must seek employment in another.

The impersonal, dehumanizing influence of the technological work setting is often noted. One less often hears a discussion of the educative and formative role played by this collective work environment. As in the school system, the entire environment is the educator. One learns ways of relating, talking, acting, and thinking by observing and interacting with the people who constitute the environment. As in the school system and in the media, the patterns of thinking and living that are fostered in the work setting are not usually Christian patterns. Therefore, Christians encounter in their jobs another powerful secular influence attempting to shape their lives.

The point of discussing these five aspects of technological society is not mainly to encourage nostalgia for the good old days. The pre-technological age had its own set of problems and challenges. My aim instead is to examine some of the sociological factors that show why the Christian people has such a difficult time trying to live a distinctively Christian way of life in the modern world. An understanding of Christian social history and the formative influences of technological society can help us to understand and respond to the grave challenges now facing the Christian church.

The Consequences: Losing a Distinctively Christian Way of Life

My experience as a pastor has convinced me that there are many important areas of daily living in which Christians are more influenced by the secular world than by genuine Christian truth. There are five areas which show particularly strong secular influence: family life, sexuality, personal relationships and emotions, entertainment, and finances and possessions. I am not so ambitious or foolish as to attempt here either a thorough discussion of how modern Christians approach these areas or a thorough presentation of the genuine Christian approach to them. However, I would like to point out some of the main ways that non-Christian patterns in these areas get adopted by Christians. I will then conclude this paper with a few recommendations as to how we should respond *pastorally* to the confrontation between Christianity and modernity.

The first and perhaps the most important area of secular influence is the family. The family in the past two centuries has gone through many convulsions and, as Edward Shorter's *The Making of the Modern Family* shows, one does not want to identify the family of the nineteenth or early twentieth century with the traditional family or the model Christian family. Still, regardless of the deficiencies in the models of family life which we have grown up with, it is clear that the most recent Western trends are no improvement. In fact, these recent trends have brought the family to a point of crisis. We now see a serious loss of parental discipline in the rearing of children, and a corresponding decrease in the young's respect for age and authority. We now witness a loss of the concept of "raising" children, of deliberately teaching them and forming them according to a clear standard of Christian character, and the introduction of a concept of "facilitating" their growth into what they themselves want to be. We now see a breakdown in the role differentiation between men and women, with male "house-husbands" and female breadwinners and democratic decision-making. We now see the ideal of husband-wife companionship exalted, replacing the view that children are in any way essential to marriage or the family. We now witness the spread of concepts such as "contractual marriage" and "nonbinding commitments" which limit the obligations each marriage partner has to the other. We witness the widening of the concept of the family to include homosexual and lesbian marriages, with children. Finally, we see the breaking of the onus tied to divorce and the subsequent skyrocketing of the divorce statistics. These trends should be of great concern to Christians who understand the importance of the family to the life of the Christian people.

My reason for describing these trends in family life is not mainly to file a grievance against Western society in the second half of the twentieth century. I only list these trends because they also seriously undermine the *Christian* family. For example, the divorce rate among confessing Christians has risen parallel to the divorce rate in the surrounding society. One can also see among Christian families a developing breakdown in role differentiation among men and women and parental discipline of children. One can also see among Christians many other perspectives on marriage and family adopted directly from the outside world. Clearly, the loss of boundaries between the Christian and secular world and the immense formative power of technological society lead to Christian assimilation of secular trends. The Christian churches face here a serious pastoral challenge.

The second significant area of worldly influence on the church is sexuality. Shorter's *The Making of the Modern Family* again provides a helpful historical framework for evaluating the most recent cultural trend. According to Shorter, the first great modern period of sexual liberation began at the end of the eighteenth century. At this time in Western Europe, the illegitimacy rate rose dramatically, and the ideal of romantic/ sexual love became firmly embedded in the Western view of marriage. Sexual activity and sexual preoccupation thus increased generally. Shorter believes that a second great revolution has begun in the last two decades and is still continuing. In this new movement, sex is divorced from marriage and the ideal of romantic love, and is valued on its own as a private pleasure.

Over the past two decades we have seen growing acceptance and practice of homosexuality, couples living together outside of marriage, exotic forms of intercourse (e.g., anal and oral), and general promiscuity. We have also seen our society, once obsessed with "marital fulfillment" (the legacy of the first sexual revolution), now obsessed with pure sexual fulfillment. We have also witnessed a loosening of legislative restrictions on pornography, and a subsequent rise in the number of adult book stores, art movie studios, and more than explicit sexual stimuli on ordinary television and movie screens. Perhaps most alarming of all, we see what appears to be a vast rise in sexual promiscuity at lower age levels, particularly among young teenagers. This youthful sexual activity is fostered by the custom of "dating," that curious, historically unique but now culturally universal custom which brings young men and women together as couples in a sexually provocative environment, unsupervised and unchaperoned, at an age when they are least adept at controlling their newly budded impulses, and certainly unprepared for marriage. The "traditional" pattern of dating which evolved during the post-war era has recently been changing into a more informal pattern of indiscriminate male and female companionship, sometimes called "hanging around together." These customs lead many teenagers to view sexual activity as enjoyable recreation connected in no essential way to the formal act of courtship and the institution of marriage. Margaret Mead spoke of this Western cultural pattern forty years ago in *Male and Female* as ludicrous and nonsensical, and the custom has only become stranger as the years have passed.

Once again, the point here is not to deplore Western decadence but to insist that these patterns of decadence are reflected in today's church. Most Christians still perceive the unique value of marriage, but many have become very open to the validity of homosexual unions, premarital sex within a loving relationship, and the ideal of sexual fulfillment. Also, many Christians view the ideal of celibacy, encouraged in the scriptures and valued by Christians over the centuries, as a neurotic sign of psycho-sexual maladjustment. This suspicion of celibacy permeates the Christian churches in the West, Roman Catholic and Protestant alike. Perhaps the most destructive patterns adopted by Christians from the surrounding culture are "dating" and "hanging around together." I have often seen Christian youth groups torn to pieces or seriously weakened by the pairing off of young men and women at an age when neither were ready for or interested in marriage. Along with this Christian view of dating often goes the odd notion that sexual activity short of coital penetration is acceptable for Christians outside of marriage.

A third area of daily Christian living affected considerably by the secular world is the area of personal relationships and emotional life. The modern world has made emotional authenticity and expression the chief criterion of relationships and behavior. As Lionel Trilling points out in *Sincerity and Authenticity*, the axiom of Polonius, "This above all, to thine own self be true," is interpreted in the twentieth century West as enjoining total fidelity to one's fluctuating internal states. Thus it is hypocritical to act in a loving way toward a person for whom one feels no affection or attraction. One is not being "real." Similarly, true intimacy in human relationships can be obtained only through baring one's heart and sharing one's deepest feelings. Of course, there is a grain of truth in this teaching. A true friendship cannot develop without some measure of freedom in self-expression. However, the modern approach to emotions leads to more than just a measure of freedom in self-expression; it leads also to a subjective, introspective focus in every area of one's life, and to a mode of conduct based not on revealed truths and objectively-based norms of behavior and the actual demands and challenges of human personal relationships but based instead on the transient, protean internal states that supposedly constitute what and who I am.

This view of emotions and personal relationships is very common among Christians today. Many Christians think of agape-love as an emotion. Many think of shared emotions as the epitome of love and personal union rather than seeking personal union through service, generous self-giving, and grateful receiving. Many Christians think of spiritual experience and Christian piety solely in terms of internal emotional states. This is no place for a thorough teaching on emotions and personal relationships, and I am afraid I cannot do adequate justice to this topic any more than to the others. Nonetheless, it should be clear that the modern Christian approach to this area is formed more by the trends of the surrounding secular world than by genuine Christian truth.

A fourth area in which the world exerts great influence on Christians is the area of entertainment. The predominant forms of modern entertainment are media related—television, movies, popular novels—but many other forms are also common, such as concerts, plays, games, participatory and spectator sports, dancing, singing, and dining. None of these forms of entertainment are inherently evil. Many of them have tremendous potential for good. Perhaps the electronic media are most questionable as forms of entertainment because of the passivity required of the spectator. However, the critical factor is not so much the form of the entertainment as the content. Dancing is a healthy human form of entertainment, but what about disco dancing? Movies can be used for Christian purposes, but what about the more common modern fare found at the local theater and drive-in? Games are relaxing and enjoyable, but what about serious gambling? My conclusion here is not that all forms of modern entertainment are evil, but that much that fills these forms today is in fact of little Christian value and is often destructive of Christian life.

The point to be made here about Christians and modern entertainment is actually very simple: too often one cannot distinguish what Christians do for entertainment from what non-Christians do. They both attend many of the same questionable movies, dance many of the same questionable dances, and read many of the same questionable novels. Christians are probably more chary of entertainment that is explicitly pornographic or illegal, but aside from this there is little distinction. This is both a sign of the lack of discrimination exercised by most modern Christians in the way they shape their lifestyle, and also an influence that further secularizes their ways of thinking and living.

A fifth and final area of world influence on Christians is the area of finances and possessions. I actually have in mind here all of the broader lifestyle questions raised by modern Western materialism. The extraordinary technological success of our society has allowed many people in the West to live out or at least strive for an ideal of maximum material consumption and self-gratification. The new world cherishes as its highest values material security, prosperity, and comfort. A new material value has also emerged in the past century and has quickly captured the hearts of modern men and women: the value of convenience. Many people are willing to spend much of their money to avoid simple inconveniences like dragging their golf cart, lifting their garage door, or washing their dishes. New technological contrivances constantly fill the market with tempting devices that promise to steamroll the rough patches of daily life. Thus it would be fitting for modern man to replace the classic revolutionary slogan "Liberté, Fraternité, Egalité" with a less grandiose summons to "Comfort, Consumption, and Convenience."

Admittedly the Christian teaching on all questions of lifestyle is not perfectly clear. Many good Christians disagree on significant points. I would certainly not want to promote legislation forbidding all Christians from owning a dishwasher. However, this much should be clear to us all: the Christian approach to finances, possessions, and lifestyle looks at the material goods of this world in a very different way than does the approach of the modern world. These material benefits are gifts from God to be enjoyed, but they are subordinate to the far higher goods of a right relationship with God and a right relationship with our neighbor. Material goods are also to be used shrewdly to advance the kingdom of God, as illustrated by Jesus' parable of the unrighteous but prudent servant. Therefore, one would expect Christians to contribute generously to their churches, to the needy, and to Christian outreach work. One would also expect them to be less concerned about comfort, convenience, and consumption, grateful when they have an abundance but ready to endure privation with joy, able to be abased and to abound. Is this the portrait of the ordinary modern Christian? I think not. The lifestyle of most Christians looks more like the lifestyle of their non-Christian neighbors than like this brief sketch. Once again, Christians have had their daily lives more formed by the surrounding secular society than by the truths of the kingdom of God.

Such examples of secularized Christianity as I have described here, if accepted as accurate pictures of the state of the Western church, could lead one to a severe chastisement of the Christian people for their infidelity to the Christian way of life. This is not my main purpose here. Instead, let us look at these examples of Christian assimilation to the ways of secular society as indicative of the dilemmas raised by this third period of Christian social history and accentuated by the powerful controlling forces of technological society. If any one group of Christians should assume responsibility for the present failure of the church to live fully the Christian life, it is the pastors and teachers of God's people. The leaders of the church have been confused and divided in the face of one of the greatest pastoral challenges in Christian history. The borders have been left unguarded and have been easily penetrated. The pastoral task that now lies before us is immense, the stakes great.

A Pastoral Response to the Christian Confrontation with Modernity

Once we acknowledge the pastoral and theological crisis facing the church in the modern era, we inevitably encounter a temptation. This is the temptation to merely *react* to the modern aberrations, rather than respond to them with constructive solutions. Many Christians recognize that something is wrong, but have no positive alternative other than a return to the life of thirty, fifty, one hundred, or seven hundred years ago. The Christian past is an essential source of practical counsel in our effort to respond to the Christian present, but we cannot merely duplicate yesterday's solutions to today's problems. The Christian way of life must be adapted and applied to each new environment in which it is lived. Therefore, our perception of the breakdown of a distinctive Christian way of life should not lead us to advocate a type of restoration of Christian boundaries which shuts its eyes to the twentieth century world and pretends that this world does not exist. A more constructive response is required, one which refuses to succumb to either reaction or accomodation.

In the space remaining, I can hardly hope to offer a thorough pastoral plan for responding constructively to the challenge of modernity. However, I do want to sketch in a few of the main pastoral priorities that should guide us in such a response.

1. *The first pastoral priority is to build and strengthen natural groupings within the Christian people*. These groupings are essential for living and passing on the Christian way of life, and also for providing necessary insulation against the cultural norms of the surrounding society. Without such groupings based on stable cohesive personal relationships the distinctive Christian pattern of life dissolves.

The most important natural grouping in the Christian community is the family. Therefore, one of our chief pastoral objectives should be the strengthening of family life according to genuine Christian principles. These principles include differentiation of sexual roles, parental discipline of children, and responsible paternal involvement in the family (especially in the rearing of the older sons).

Whenever possible, we should also build or strengthen natural groupings outside the family. For example, a group of Christian families that are friends and have a common vision for their Christian lives might decide to move into the same neighborhood together. Their children could play together, and they could all support one another in their daily Christian lives. This would be a way of restoring part of the traditional neighborhood grouping. If moving together is not an option, these families might still have regular activities together and build their lives together in such a way that they form something like a natural grouping. In some situations it is even possible to form a full Christian community with stable bonds of mutual commitment extending over a large number of people. I live in such a community myself. It is very difficult to build Christian communities like these, and not all Christians can live in them; however, some type of restored natural grouping outside the family is very important for supporting a Christian way of life.

The most urgent pastoral need today is not merely the pastoring of individuals, but the forming of environments, the fostering of committed Christian personal relationships—in short, the strengthening and building of natural groupings. In former days Christian pastors could take natural groupings for granted and mainly direct their efforts to the support of individuals. In modern technological society this is no longer the case. The effective pastor today must be more than just a preacher or confessor or counselor—he must be a leader of men and women, adept at ordering and forming the life of a people.

2. *The second pastoral priority is to provide people with teaching and counsel on practical aspects of daily Christian living.* I am not advocating here a trendy, "relevant" kind of presentation of Christian teaching which ignores the great eternal realities of the faith. We *must* teach about the incarnation, crucifixion, resurrection, and ascension of Christ and the other "massive objectivities" of Christian truth. However, pastors can often lose their heads in the airy mists of Christian theology and fail to address those issues which press most insistently on the daily lives of the man and woman in the pew. How should I relate to my wife? How should I raise my children? How should I handle my finances? How should I relate to my job? These are the issues that Christian pastors must address in their teaching and counseling if they are to provide a Christian alternative to the pervasive teaching of the world.

It is not easy to provide this type of teaching and counsel.

Most Christian pastors cannot answer these difficult daily life questions on their own. They need to seek help from Christian writers, teachers, publishers, and pastoral leaders, who have a special responsibility to encourage the development and dissemination of reliable Christian teaching materials that offer practical guidance for daily living.

3. *The third pastoral priority is to equip Christians to deal with the powerful formative influences of mass technological society.* The few hours per week that a pastor has with his people are often rendered ineffective by the twenty to thirty hours per week the people spend being subtly indoctrinated by their television, radio, newspaper, and news magazine. Pastors need to teach their people how to be less credulous and more critical before the secular media and the secular "experts." They also need to teach about how much exposure to the media is reasonable, and how much is too much. They need to teach their people to recognize work and school environments as non-Christian environments, and to guard themselves accordingly. As long as Christians have their lives shaped so dramatically by the surrounding secular world, they can never recognize, understand, and live out the fullness of Christian truth.

4. *The fourth pastoral priority is to restore processes of initiation and discipline to the local church community.* The church today needs to learn again from its ancient experience as a diaspora community. If the boundaries between the church and the surrounding non-Christian society are to be distinct, if the church is to live its own way of life, then we must again learn how to effectively initiate new members into the community life and discipline members who are unfaithful to that life. Initiation must be more than just a transmission of information or the evocation of an initial commitment; it must be the movement from one way of life to another, the transferal from one kingdom to another. Church discipline should be administered justly, firmly, and in love. It should be possible to exclude members from the church on account of serious offenses. Only so can a genuinely Christian way of life be preserved in the midst of a non-Christian society.

Essentially, the church today needs to have a fresh awareness of its distinctiveness, of its separation from the secular world. It needs to return to a type of diaspora form of life. This emphasis on the separation of the church from the surrounding society is not popular among Christians today. Christian leaders more commonly stress involvement in the world. There is great fear of an escapist or ghetto mentality. These concerns should be taken seriously. Christian thinking and living must be adapted and applied to its environment, for the church's raison d'etre is to bring God's word and God's love to the world. However, the church has nothing distinctive to bring to the world if it merely conforms to every worldly pattern. The church must live as an integrated community following its own way of life if it is to make the contribution that only it can make.

I have focused in this paper on Christian living rather than Christian thinking. Obviously the distinction is an artificial one. Thought is one part of life. The two cannot really be separated. Nonetheless, I have made and used the distinction in order to stress that the confrontation between Christianity and modernity is not merely an academic affair involving a few learned (or not so learned) professors, nor merely a "doctrinal" affair affecting a few important but isolated credal formulas. Instead this confrontation implies a basic challenge to the way of life of the Christian people. The nature of our response to this challenge, both theological and pastoral, will determine whether the next generation will have ample opportunity to encounter that holy people whose life is *in* the world but not *of* it.

Response

Kerry Koller

Mr. Kinzer reminds us of an absolutely crucial point, namely, that the forms of social organization have a fundamental and architectonic influence upon our lives and our thought. A few weeks ago, I was out in California, which is for the United States one of the advancing edges of the wave of modernity. If you want to see modernity happen you can visit California. I lived a good portion of my childhood and adult life there, but on this visit I saw the state as something of a laboratory of the very thing Mr. Kinzer discusses in his paper. What I saw among the Christians I know there was an increasing inability to deal with life in a human and Christian way. The image occurred to me of people hanging on the edge of a cliff and slowly slipping off. That is to say, they were struggling to understand and to deal with their situation but were increasingly unable to. As time goes on the influence of the modern secular society as described in Mr. Kinzer's paper causes them to slip farther and farther into the abyss.

There are two ways of analyzing situations like this. The first—which I consider the standard approach—consists of examining the ethical and religious values and practices of the people. This kind of analysis is not sufficient. These people have high ethical and religious values, and they are practicing Christians. With all of that, however, their Christian lives continue to be eroded. What is needed in order to understand situations like this is, I think, the kind of analysis suggested by Mr. Kinzer. One needs to look at the social structure, at natural groupings, the mass collective, the effect of the media—all the various ways in which the social organization of modernity undercuts the lives of Christians.

It is unfortunate that many of us who are concerned for Christian renewal often ignore this kind of analysis. Too often we engage simply in the analysis of values and practices, assuming that the strategies appropriate to the social structure of Christendom and preindustrialized society will work as we move toward the twenty-first century.

A caution is, however, in order here. The radical historicizing of Hegel, Marx, Dilthey, and others has given us the aphorism of the barely educated that "everything in our world is totally unlike anything that came before." It is perhaps in response to this that many Christians make the equally serious mistake of maintaining that nothing is different. Well, very much has changed and we are very different from those who came before us but—here's the paradox—we are also very much like them. Many of the essential dimensions of our experience were essentials of theirs also. There is a common cultural heritage in the West, and we can move back and forth through the ages listening to men and women from the past speak to us through their art, their music, their literature. We can understand them. We can recognize them as fellow human beings dealing with many of the same human realities with which we have to deal.

But, on the other hand, there are ways in which these human relatives from the past are like people from another planet. Their experiences, their expressions, their expectations, the social fabric of their lives, are totally different from ours in many ways, and we have to work very hard at times to understand even a little bit of them and their world. What is going on when Odysseus slays all those suitors? Is he just a blood-thirsty savage? What is the nature of the relationship between Jesus and his Father? Is it like a modern father-son relationship, built on feelings of tenderness and looking for each other's self-actualization? Why does the analogical and allegorical exegesis of the Church Fathers seem so foreign to us? The point is: there are differences. There is a hermeneutical problem. In many ways, you can't go home again.

This leaves us, I think, in a difficult spot. On the one hand, we must defend the continuity between ourselves and the past. Historic Christianity, Christian tradition, and for Catholics, the teaching magisterium, provide the basic linkage. If we relinquish these, all will be lost. On the other hand, we must be aware that there are profound differences in our situations, and if we are going to bring Christianity to life in our times, we must have some answers to the problems posed by modern social structures.

There are aspects of the contemporary social structure, as pointed out by Mr. Kinzer, which make it almost impossible to maintain a Christian life. Christianity is a social religion. We are members of a kingdom, of a city, of an organic body. If we try to erect Christian life and thought on social structures which are inimical to that thought and life, we will not succeed. Mr. Kinzer reminds us of this fact and, I think, gives us more than a reminder. He gives us an analysis which is the beginning of a pastoral strategy. Personally, I find his analysis and strategy valuable.

There is, however, one thing which gives me pause. It haunts the entire discussion, but does not come to expression until the final sentence of the paper, namely, "being in the world, but not of it." I think more than giving us answers to that question, Mr. Kinzer sets it before us as the primary pastoral problem. Surely, Christians need to get some distance from some aspects of contemporary social structures, but just as surely, as Mr. Kinzer points out, Christianity is not going to be rebuilt in our time by a wholesale return to pretechnological and preindustrial social forms. That will not work. It would be possible for small enclaves of Christians to live this way, and they might do a profound work for the kingdom of God in our time. They will not, however, be the model for all other Christians. We cannot retreat from the twentieth century. We want to be in the world, not only for evangelistic reasons, but also because there are many good things which God wants to provide for us through the world and, I think, through some of those things which are uniquely modern in the world. On the other hand, we do not want to be of it. Unless we can give some precision to that formula in a way which articulates the forms of social organization which we want to see in twentieth-century Christianity, we will not, I think, succeed in bringing the modern world to Christ.

I would like to make a second point. This is more theoretical, and it has to do with the connection between social reality and the meaning of words. A good deal of modern philosophy and theological reflection has to do with trying to revivify Christian language or religious language or, as it is sometimes called, "God talk." The argument rages back and forth in the journals whether or not religious language in fact has a meaning, whether in fact it's meaningless, whether it makes any sense at all, whether it is verifiable or not verifiable, and so forth and so on. Many Christians, many sincere Christians, believe that in order to reinstate Christian life in our time we must first reinstate the meaning of Christian language. They maintain that we need to transfuse Christian terminology and concepts from the meaning-rich plasma of philosophy. If people find Christian terminology meaningful at the conceptual level, it is argued, they will be able to build some sort of revivified Christian life and Christianity will come alive again.

Wittgenstein, Holmer, and others have shown that this approach is largely wrongheaded. Wittgenstein, in his later writing, was concerned to show that language was a form of life. He wished to show that language functions successfully in the context of its use in life and that philosophical and theological problems arise with the language only when it becomes inappropriate to the social reality. As the social structures of modernity erode the distinctive aspects of Christian living, Christian language becomes more and more meaningless. It has less and less relationship to the lived experience. To the practitioner of philosophy and theology this looks like a problem to be solved by conceptual methods. But this is a serious mistake. The problem does not lie with the language; it lies with the lives of those who use the language. If their lives were to be rechristianized, the language would once more come to life, not vice-versa. The fundamental issue lies not in philosophy and theology, or with language, but rather in the daily lives of people attempting to live as Christians.

It follows from this that the role of social structure is of crucial importance. If we are going to have a philosophical and theological account of Christianity, that account has to be grounded in the lives of Christians. Paul Holmer in his *Grammar of Faith* points out repeatedly that many of the philosophical and theological issues which surround Christianity in the modern world have their roots in the lack of a vital Christian life. He argues, for example, that the search for new theological foundations becomes a reasonable search only when our theology is so removed from life as to be able to stand on its own. And what that means, of course, is that once this theological problem becomes significant, the language has been severed so completely from lived Christianity that it makes very little difference whether you can solve the conceptual problem or not. The real problem lies in the quality of Christian living, not in the nuances of theological discourse.

The import of these remarks, then, is this: as Mr. Kinzer points out, social-structural principles are crucial to the renewal of the Christian life at the pastoral level, that is, at the practical level. The point of this second comment of mine is to show that the pastoral practical issues lie also at the heart of a revitalization of Christian philosophy and Christian theology. It cannot be, I think, the other way around. We will not revitalize Christianity by dealing only with the philosophical and theological issues. Language is a form of life. Its meaning depends on and is deeply rooted in the social realities within which those words and those concepts are used. Philosophy and theology do not give Christian language its meaning. Christian life gives Christian language its meaning. Philosophy and theology thrive, as Wittgenstein says, when language goes on a holiday, that is, when language no longer has its home in its proper social and lived context.

This, I think, is perhaps the achievement of Mr. Kinzer's paper, that it points out the key role which social forms have for us in the confrontation between modernity and Christianity. As was said at the outset, this is not often noted by writers and those in pastoral ministry who are attempting to deal with the situation of the church in today's world. This is an invaluable suggestion on the part of Mr. Kinzer and, it seems to me, forms the basis of any winning strategy for dealing with modernity and the inroads that it has made into Christianity. Still, Mr. Kinzer has not solved the problem that lies before us, which is to discover and create the pastoral forms of life which will revitalize Christianity in the twentieth century. He does give us an analysis, and he does give us the beginnings of a strategy. This is a great help, but the task remains to be done, and in my estimation, everything hangs in the balance.

Response

Kenneth Kantzer

I gratefully appreciate Mr. Kinzer's thoughtful analysis of the problem of Christian identity in the midst of the extremely rapid changes we are experiencing in our modern technological society. He has picked up the things that I think are bad and forthrightly labeled them bad. I like that. I note also that his focus on the practical aspect of these issues, rather than on the ideological, is not due to any intent to dismiss ideas as unimportant. Rather, he insists that ideas, too, are integral to a genuinely Christian identity. He chose to concentrate on the practical because of his own background and special expertise, and that is good. In his method of handling the problem of Christian identity he was influenced also by pressure from the modern mind set. Somehow to late twentieth-century humans, practical issues seem to be more important and relevant than theoretical ones. Our computerized age certainly makes it easier for us to come to grips with the enormity of the problems relating to broken homes, divorces, abortion, sexual deviation, and TV programs when we are able to reduce them to technological data; and technological data, as Mr. Kinzer reminds us, are vastly revered in our day.

As an academic person, I confess, I might have focused more sharply on the theoretical so as to confront ideas: God and no God, rational and irrational, moral absolutes and moral relativism, supernatural and miracle, human responsibility and uninhibited freedom, the urgency of the immediate and the urgency of final judgment. But, with Mr. Kinzer, I share a tradition that goes back to Aurelius, Augustine, and beyond. I too, therefore, insist that both the practical and the theoretical are relevant, indeed essential, to anything I recognize as Christianity. With

Augustine, moreover, we hold that the amount any individual possesses of either the practical or the theoretical conditions the amount he can attain of the other. Truth does serve as the guide for right action. Right action leads to greater potential for truth. Loss of truth opens one to control by blind irrational forces or by designing minds who reduce persons to things for the achievement of their own goals. Failure to act is destructive of our capacity for truth. In short, there is no Christian armchair theology. This would be a contradiction in terms. And so, also, there is no pure activism that deserves the name of Christian. Such would be a contradiction in terms.

Mr. Kinzer draws his picture of the contemporary scene with broad strokes. Fortunately he bases his study on acute observations of the social scene. I do not find his analysis superficial or manipulative. He drives us to his interpretation by data which cannot be gainsaid. With Mr. Kinzer's basic analysis of the problem, therefore, we must agree—or so it seems to me.

Mr. Kinzer's solution to the problems he raises gives me greater pause. In his constructive response I have a faint sense of deja vu. Let us whip ourselves sharply, redouble our exertions, and push on more enthusiastically in the same right direction we have taken during the past century. But on this point I cannot criticize him with as clear a conscience as I should like, for I cannot come up with much better.

I do not dare deny, even should I wish to do so, the dreadful seriousness of the plight into which Western Christendom, and American Christianity in particular, have fallen; yet I should like to point out a few factors that help us to understand our modern world better, and, perhaps, just because they shed light on darkness, throw a slightly more optimistic caste on the whole of the human scene. At the very least, they may palliate the gloom so as to preserve us from despair.

Two principles are evident from the religious movements of Western Christendom, and particularly of the United States, over the last two centuries. The first is a pattern traceable also in the history of the ancient church, and the second is clearly spelled out in the Bible.

The first principle, crucial to our understanding of the

American church, and especially of Protestant churches, stems from a very simple fact. In two centuries, the American church has grown from less than 10 percent of the total population to over 70 percent. During the lives of many of us, the American church has increased from less than 50 percent to over 70 percent. We should not be surprised, therefore, to observe once again what is often described as "the Constantine effect" on the churches: the church has added members faster than it has discipled them. In its eagerness for growth, the church has accepted millions of the unconverted and the half-converted—especially in the Protestant churches. The Roman Catholic Church did not suffer so much at this point as the Protestant churches because its growth tended to rise more from a higher birth rate and, therefore, from within family influences and rearing, and also more from immigration of real or nominal Catholics. In any case, the church needs to recognize that its task of discipling is immense—greater than at any period of its history since the time of Constantine. And we ought not to be too badly discouraged at the warping influence of the modern world upon a membership drawn so rapidly from the world into the church. In one sense, this is only the price of success.

At the same time another trend becomes clearly observable. The impact of Christianity on Western society has eroded in startling fashion over the last decade or two. Within the nominal church, it is scarcely necessary to point out the devastating departure from biblical Christianity. It began with the erosion of biblical authority (I'm betraying my Protestant background there) and spread to the person of Christ as the God-man, on through basic theism and the possibility of supernatural intervention by God in the structure of the universe. Ultimately it leads to the loss of a rational universe, of ethical norms, and of ultimate meaning. What more precise illustration could we find for chapter one of the book of Romans! Indeed, the book of Romans, especially 1:18 through 3:20, is the key to our rational understanding and emotional acceptance of all this.

As Albert Outler reminds us, we need to read the book of Romans with an open daily newspaper in our hand. He writes: "St. Paul's catalog of the immorality of his own age can be matched, one by one, in ours. . . . But what is distinctive in St. Paul is his diagnosis: the demoralization of the human [when he loses God]." (See his paper, "The Loss and Recovery of the Soul," presented at the Notre Dame Colloquy on the Loss of the Sacred, November, 1979.) God's response to man's failure to recognize him is wrath and, even worse, abandonment; and divine abandonment leads inevitably to immorality and the loss of all human goodness and dignity. God gives mankind up. Ephesians 2 sums up the process: without Christ, without God; and without God, without hope in this world. But even this wrath of God is not to be divorced from his goodness. Through his wrath, the good plan of divine grace and redemption is furthered. Human beings who have come to the end of their own strength have no recourse but to throw themselves upon the mercy of God, who alone brings hope and meaning and true righteousness.

In our modern world, this step-by-step rejection of biblical religion can be traced right within the bosom of the church. So here, I trust, I shall not have to document it. What is necessary is only to point out its effects on the life of the church. There can be no real doubt that the decline in the church has paralleled at least to some degree the influence of secularism in our world and of modern theological liberalism within the church. Membership statistics are very interesting at this point. The yearbook of the American churches tells us that the United Church of Christ has lost half a million members during the last twenty years. The American Lutheran Church, the United Presbyterian Church, the Episcopal Church, and the Christian Church (Disciples) are also down a half a million or more. And the United Methodist Church is down a million one hundred thousand.

Of course, some churches have grown. But they are not the churches that are especially noted for having been infiltrated with theological liberalism. In this same period, for example, the Southern Baptist Convention increased its membership by three million two hundred thousand. The Lutheran Church Missouri Synod likewise has grown by one hundred seventy thousand. . . .

Just the other day I picked up a copy of the September-October issue of *Harvard Magazine*. There I found something that helped me understand what is happening to dropouts from the church. I discovered a lengthy article by one of our leading biochemists, Dr. Lewis Thomas. It was the Annual Phi Beta Kappa Oration for June, 1980. He wrote:

> Today an intellectually fashionable view of man's place in nature is that there is really no great problem: the plain answer is that it makes no sense, no sense at all. The universe is meaningless for human beings. We bumbled our way into the place by a series of random and senseless biological accidents. The sky is not blue: this is an optical illusion—the sky is black. You can walk on the moon if you feel like it, but there's nothing to do there except look at the earth; and when you've seen one earth, you've seen them all. The animals and plants of the planet are at hostile odds with one another, each bent on elbowing any nearby neighbor off the earth. Genes, tapes of polymer, are the ultimate adversaries and, by random, the only real survivors. This grasp of things is sometimes presented as though based on science, with the implication that we already know most of the important knowable matters and this is the way it all turns out. It is the wisdom of the twentieth century, contemplating as its only epiphany the news that the world is an absurd apparatus and we are stuck with it and in it. In the circumstances, we would surely have no obligations except to our individual selves, and of course to the genes coding out the selves (p. 20).

But Dr. Thomas doesn't buy that. He recognizes it as a sort of standard "scientific" view of the latter part of our twentieth-century world. But he demurs:

> I cannot make my peace with the randomness doctrine: I cannot abide the notion of purposelessness and blind chance in nature. And yet I do not know what to put in its place for the quieting of my mind. It is absurd to say that a place like

this place is absurd, when it contains, in front of our eyes, so many billions of different forms of life, each one in its way absolutely perfect, all linked together to form what would surely seem to an outsider a huge spherical organism . . . I like this thought, even though I cannot take it anywhere, and I must say it embarasses me. I have that nagging hunch that it is a presumption, a piece of ultimate hubris. . . . We talk—some of us anyway—about the absurdity of the human situation, but we do this because we do not know how we fit in, or what we are for (p. 21).

Here a great modern scholar, by the sweep of his own broad logic in response to the total universe in which he finds himself, illustrates the teaching of holy scripture: without God, without hope in this world. He has come to the end of his intellectual and emotional tether. For him, as for Pascal, the eternal silence of these infinite spaces fills him with dread; and he finds it unacceptable. He is searching, and you and I know what happens to him who truly and sincerely persists in his search for truth. . . .

Matthew Arnold wrote "Dover Beach" in 1853, but it rings much more authentically in 1980. In the years since the turn of the century, it could be duplicated many times over in our modern poets.

The sea of faith
Was once, too, at the full, and round earth's shore
Lay the folds of a bright girdle furled.
But now I only hear
Its melancholy, long, withdrawing roar,
Retreating to the breath
Of the night-wind down to the vast edges drear
And naked shingles of the world.

The world which seems
To lie before us like a land of dreams,
So various, so beautiful, so new,
Hath really neither joy, nor love, nor light,

Nor servitude, nor peace, nor help for pain;
And we are here as on a darkling plain,
Swept by the confused alarms of struggle and flight,
Where ignorant armies clash by night.

But despair can often be only the other side of the coin from hope. In "The Hound of Heaven" a despairing soul, flotsam upon the sea of life, finds a lifeline flung to him from his heavenly father.

O world invisible, we view thee
O world intangible, we touch thee
O world unknowable, we know thee
Inapprehensible, we clutch thee.

Does the fish soar to find the ocean
The eagle plunge to find the air—
Do we ask of the stars in motion
If they have rumour of thee there?

Not where the wheeling systems darken,
And our benumbed conceiving soars!—
The drift of pinions, would we harken
Beats at our own clay-shuttered doors.

The angels keep their ancient places,
Turn but a stone and start a wing.
T'is ye, T'is your estranged faces
That miss the many splendoured thing.

But when so sad thou canst not sadder,
Cry; and upon thy so sore loss,
Shall shine the traffic of Jacob's ladder
Pitched between Heaven and Charing Cross.

Yea, in the night, my soul, my daughter
Cry—Clinging Heaven by the hems;
And lo, Christ walking on the water
Not of Gennesareth, but Thames.

And so as the dark night of unfaith grows darker and darker and the light of hope grows dimmer and dimmer, I confess to hope for the church. And that hope is in the Morning Star with the promise of a new day and a new hope for the church—whether the reprieve of another earthly day with new opportunities for the gospel or the apocalyptic day of the second coming of Christ, we don't know. We don't need to know.

CHAPTER TWO

Ideology versus Theology: Case Studies of Liberation Theology and the Christian New Right

Dale Vree

The Church . . . does not need to have recourse to ideological systems. —Pope John Paul II

Liberation theology and the Christian New Right in America are two leading examples of how political ideology can invade Christian theology. Both serve as object lessons on how *not* to do Christian social ethics.

Liberation theology comes in all shapes and sizes, but the brand that is of interest to us is the standard brand that speaks the idiom of Marxist ideology. The primary spokesman for this brand is, as all agree, Fr. Gustavo Gutiérrez, the Peruvian Roman Catholic theologian. The key problem in Gutiérrez's thought is his understanding of salvation and the way he relates it to political liberation for Latin Americans (by which is meant liberation from poverty, domestic capitalism, and U.S. hegemony). He makes liberation an integral part of salvation; indeed, for him, liberation is part of a "single salvific process."[1]

Since the Second Vatican Council, the Catholic Church has been willing to say that political action (or liberation) has something to do with the Kingdom of God (or salvation), although she has refused to specify exactly what the relationship is, and has insisted that political goals cannot be identified or equated with the Kingdom. Were one to say that the Kingdom *is* political liberation and that liberation is the product of human action—which is what a Marxist would be happy to see a Christian say—one would all too easily fall into the classical Pelagian heresy—that man is saved by good works, not grace, and that man can save himself. To say that is to deny the salvific significance of Christ's atoning sacrifice on the cross and his Second Coming. It is to deny that redemption is God's miracle and ultimately not of this world and this time. Hence, it is impossible for a Christian to equate liberation with salvation.

Yet, Gutiérrez is unhappy with the recent Catholic position that political action has some (unspecified) relation to the Kingdom. Said he: "It is not enough to say that Christians should not 'shirk' their earthly responsibilities or that these have a 'certain relationship' to salvation."[2] Although Gutiérrez wants to relate eschatology to politics by uniting liberation and salvation into a single process, he also wants to keep liberation and salvation separate—for fear of sliding into Pelagianism. Traditionally, orthodox Christians have said that salvation, the Kingdom, is an act of God, is his gift. According to official Catholic theology, the Kingdom "will be the effect solely of divine intervention."[3] The problem for any theology of liberation is to talk of salvation as a gift without inducing passivity and indifference to politics. Hence, Gutiérrez's problem is to conceive of political liberation as part of a salvific process which finds fulfillment in God's Kingdom—without opening the door to Pelagianism and without contradicting himself.

Gutiérrez sees man "assuming conscious responsibility for his own destiny." The result will be "the creation of a new man and a qualitatively different society."[4] And yet he also says that, "The Bible presents liberation—salvation—in Christ as a total gift."[5] But how can the integral "salvific process" be a product of both men's "conscious responsibility" as well as a "total gift" from Christ? It is unclear at this crucial point whether Gutiérrez is revealing himself to be a Pelagian or just plain confused.

Perhaps, however, Gutiérrez wants to say that man must initiate his liberation while God will have to finish it by turning liberation into salvation. This is the most generous interpretation I can give his position. Said Gutiérrez, "Without liberating historical events, there would be no growth of the Kingdom. But the process of liberation will not have conquered the very roots of oppression and the exploitation of man by man without the coming Kingdom, which is above all a gift."[6] Gutiérrez is trying to protect man's autonomy and free creativity as well as God's sovereignty. But Gutiérrez actually succeeds in truncating man's autonomy (because man cannot finish what he has started) and compromising God's omnipotence (because God cannot start what he alone can finish). For Gutiérrez, salvation is obviously contingent on man's prior action. Gutiérrez wants to affirm that the coming Kingdom is above all a gift, but one must conclude from what he has said that the coming Kingdom (which he describes as the "complete encounter with the Lord" which will "mark an end to history[7]) is first and foremost a product of human action. Enter Pelagius! Enter Thomas Muentzer and a whole host of heretical chiliasts whom Friedrich Engels correctly identified as forerunners of Marxism.

By making liberation an indispensable part of the salvific process, Gutiérrez has managed to bring Marxism into the drama of Christian salvation. Marxists are actually doing God's work. And by liberating man, they are quite literally freeing God's hands so he can usher in the Kingdom. Hence, Marxists become Christians incognito.

Gutiérrez says he believes in salvation for everyone—believers and nonbelievers alike. This universalism, which allows him to collapse evangelization into liberation, constitutes a radical rupture with orthodox Christianity. At Puebla, the Third General Conference of Latin American Bishops warned that since human beings "can close themselves to him [God] and even reject him, he also judges them and sentences them to eternal life or eternal death."[8] Because of his universalism,

Gutiérrez is freed from the responsibility of presenting the Christian message to Marxists, and can sit back and let them evangelize him.

Curiously, while there is no doubt in Gutiérrez's mind that God will grant salvation to Marxists, there seems to be some doubt that all Christians will be saved. Gutiérrez may be a universalist, but he *does* believe in divine judgment: "we will be definitively judged by our love for men, by our capacity to create brotherly conditions of life."[9] And Gutiérrez does not doubt that many, perhaps most, Christians are not measuring up to that standard. So his best pastoral advice to Christians would be to join with Marxists, who are presumed to be actively creating brotherly conditions of life. Not only do Marxists—unknowingly—hold the keys to the Kingdom of God, but they turn out to be spiritually gifted. Since Marxists are very adept at loving mankind, and since loving mankind is the "only way" to have a "true encounter with God,"[10] and since a "knowledge of God" is actually a "necessary consequence" of loving mankind,[11] one is forced to conclude that Marxists are remarkably religious people. Never mind that Marxists don't seem to be aware of their spiritual gifts. Father Gutiérrez is aware of them and that seems to be what counts.[12]

Lest one think I am picking on Gutiérrez and finding fault for its own sake, I cite the words of Alfredo Fierro, a rigorously logical Spanish liberation theologian who happens to be both a Marxist materialist and an honest Pelagian. Said Fierro: "Time and again Gutiérrez points out that liberation is primarily a gift. . . . On the other hand Gutiérrez also affirms . . . that it is man who liberates himself. . . . Now it is obvious that these two propositions, if taken on the same level, are contradictory."[13] It must be emphasized that the two propositions are indeed on the same level, and that this level is *not* that of the mystery of divine election, where both human free will and God's predestination are held in paradoxical tension. For the Church clearly teaches—contrary to the Pelagian side of Gutiérrez—that man cannot build the Kingdom of God on earth by himself. As Pope Paul VI said, the "proper growth [of the Kingdom] cannot be confounded with the progress of civilization, of science or of human technology."[14] It is one thing to say, as the Church does, that human action has some unspecified "foreshadowing" relationship to the Kingdom[15]; it is quite another to say that it is both *wholly* a gift of God and yet *wholly* an act of man. The Church's condemnation of Pelagianism completely rules out the latter proposition, but that latter proposition is indispensable to any liberation theology that is to have any credibility with Marxists. One gets the impression from all this that if Gutiérrez is not simply confused, he is trying to reinterpret the Second Coming of Christ as political revolution. The result would then be, as Fierro says, a theology that is "merely rhetorical."[16] Theology then becomes a mythology that is employed to mobilize guillible pre-scientific masses for purely secular purposes.

There is not enough space to detail the thought of other liberation theologians, but it would be well to identify other themes in liberation theology that run counter to Christian orthodoxy.

Most fundamentally, there is the issue of authority. The object of liberation theology's desire is *political* liberation. Whatever stands in the way—even the Bible and Church tradition—are regarded as of secondary importance to *"praxis"* (i.e., revolutionary action). *Praxis* is given revelatory status. The traditional distinction between sacred history and profane history—a distinction the Church makes in order to affirm *both*—is collapsed, and the former is reduced to the terms of the latter. Here the imperatives of political action become quite literally idolatrous. Hence, José Miguez Bonino, an Argentine Protestant theologian and one of the six Presidents of the World Council of Churches, says in tones that characterize liberation theology, that "to do justice *is* to know Yahweh," indeed it is the "only" way to know Him.[17] Faith here is blatantly reduced to works. Even Robert McAfee Brown, a major American interpreter and defender of liberation theology, recognizes the one-sidedness of this approach. Yet, he falls back on the (very lame) excuse that, well, *"all* Christians read the Bible 'selectively.'"[18] Brown, a prototypical modernist Protestant, inadvertently reveals here the debilitating subjectivism of both his own theology and that of liberation theologians.

And yet, it isn't subjective at all. *Praxis* is really a euphemism for revolutionary action *as prescribed by Marxist categories*. Yes, liberation theologians are "on the side of the poor[19]—that is, the poor as defined by Marxist intellectuals to fit their own ideological preconceptions of how the poor *ought* to behave. If the poor are not engaged in Marxist-style class struggle, then the liberation theologians will *not* be found on their side. Liberation theologians use the exalted concept of *praxis* to demolish the theological absolutes of Scripture and tradition, only to turn around and subordinate *praxis* to the *theory* of Marxism. For liberation theologians, theology is supposed to be a reflection on *praxis*, but it winds up being a reflection of Marxism. What is accomplished is the reduction of theology to ideology.

This is not to say that the Church cannot learn from *praxis*, from the events that take place during her pilgrimage on earth, for we must take note of the "signs of the times." As Bonaventure Kloppenburg put it, "it is perfectly acceptable . . . to say that liberating or revolutionary historical praxis may be a means of discovering new demands or dimensions of faith, just as any other human situations (suffering, joy, etc.) may be. . . . [But] this does not turn praxis (or any other situation) into a theological source in the proper sense. . . ."[20] Hence, we must always distinguish between the signs of the times" and the Spirit of the Age or Zeitgeist, which would claim for itself revelatory status. For if the Zeitgeist or the world is allowed to set the agenda for the Church, to recall the formulation of the 1975 Hartford Appeal for Theological Affirmation, then we have no need of a Church.

"That liberation theology is a heresy," said Evangelical theologian Kenneth Hamilton, "I believe to be beyond question." But he added that, "in the history of the Christian churches, heresy has always paved the way for a better definition of orthodoxy."[21] The challenge of Marxism and of liberation theology has forced the Church to sharpen her understanding of the proper relation between the faith and politics. The result is most clearly seen in the progression of the social teachings of the Catholic Church, stretching from Leo XIII's *Rerum Novarum* in 1891 right up to the conclusions of the Puebla conference in 1979 and Pope John Paul II's utterances in Brazil in May-June 1980.

The phenomenon of liberation theology calls for discernment. As Bishop Alfonso Lopez Trujillo, the Secretary-General of the permanent secretariat of the Latin American hierarchy, said, "The problem is not in elaborating a theology of liberation, which seems valid and necessary, but in the manner in which it is done."[22] The Catholic Church is not afraid of a liberation theology, but (unlike the World Council of Churches) she insists that it be uncompromisingly Christian and authentically liberating. The Catholic Church has identified herself with aspirations for social justice on the part of industrial and farm laborers. She has clarified and developed her position on socialism to the point that, while rejecting Marxist philosophy and violent class struggle, she recognizes the right of workers to strike and to have decision-making roles in businesses. While she is keen on protecting the dignity of the individual and freedom of worship (and is therefore opposed to *total* state ownership of the economy), she has allowed for situations where private productive property may be expropriated and publicly owned. Ever since Pope John, the Church has sought to disentangle herself from capitalism and from appearing to be the ideological buttress of big business, and she has sought to distance herself from not only the philosophical materialism of the East but also the practical materialism of the West. At a time when Communism glares at us with an "inhuman face" and when social democracy and secular liberalism are in disarray throughout the world, the social teachings of the Catholic Church, grounded as they are in the Gospel of Jesus Christ, offer attractive guidelines for social justice and human development.

While the Catholic Church teaches that the Christian must show preferential (though not exclusive) love for the poor,[23] liberation theologians want that love to be exclusive—and to politicize that love so as to validate Marxist notions of violent class struggle. Although the Church has sided with workers and peasants in actual class struggles—even in the United States—the Church cannot give "a blank check" to the concept. This is so because, as Fr. Arthur F. McGovern said, "Morality is not subordinate to class struggle."[24] As the Nicaraguan bishops recently declared, "We think that class struggle as part of social dynamics is a positive factor that can lead to just transformation of structures. But class hatred, which is addressed against particular persons in contradiction to the commandment to love your neighbor, is a different thing."[25] More than that, as the Catholic Church has made clear time and again, the *primary* mission of the Church is not political liberation, but evangelization—the preaching of the Gospel to every man, woman, and child throughout the world.[26] Yes, it is very hard for the rich man to make it into Heaven, but for God all things are possible. Moreover, there *is* a Heaven and a Hell, realities that liberation theologians tend to neglect.[27]

Moreover, our eternal destiny is far more important than our temporal destiny. As inescapable as class struggle may be, that is not the ultimate struggle; it must always be kept subordinate to the struggle of the Church to bring the light of Christ to every creature. As Samuel Escobar, an Evangelical from Argentina, has said, "acknowledging the fact of oppression in society and the fact that there are oppressors and oppressed, the Christian does not give to that alignment the almost ontological character that Marxism gives to it. For the gospel the line that divides men is a different one. . . . men under the lordship of Christ and men in rebellion against the One who should be their Lord."[28] Liberation has ties to salvation, but as the Latin American bishops stated at Puebla, the former remains "subordinate" to the latter.[29] Reiterating the teaching of *Gaudium et Spes*, they note that social progress has a "foreshadowing" relationship to the Kingdom of God, yet the former cannot be equated with the Kingdom, as liberation theologians are wont to do.[30]

Socialism could be established worldwide, and the poor might gain the whole world—and yet they could lose their souls and their eternal bodies. They could also lose their temporal bodies—for a transformed social structure full of people whose hearts have not been transformed is hardly a formula for human liberation. A liberation theology that ends with human death is neither Christian nor liberating, for our true liberation is our oneness with Jesus Christ in his Kingdom—both now and forever more.

One of the great themes of liberation theology—as of all modernist theology—is the imperative to be "relevant" to modern man *as he is*. On June 17-19, 1978, 200 Christians met in New York City under the auspices of the Alternative Theology Project in the Americas to seek to apply liberation theology to North America, or in the words of participant Sergio Torres, "to contribute to a theology . . . that will be *relevant* to this country."[31] Subsequent speakers crafted theologies of black liberation, Native American liberation, women's liberation, etc. But one wonders just how "relevant" these theologies are to the majority of American Christians. One might speculate that if the conferees *really* wanted to make theology relevant, they would address themselves to the cares of the millions of Christians who go to Billy Graham crusades, watch the television programs of Oral Roberts and Rex Humbard on Sunday mornings, and tune in to the Christian TV networks.

Not a chance of course. The liberationists no doubt consider these kinds of people invincibly irrelevant and as such not worth being relevant to. But while liberationists linger in their self-made ghettoes, a new liberation theology has arisen in America that promises to liberate people from spiritual maladies, the lure of cults and immorality, medical problems, and financial insecurity—as well as from high taxation, federal regulations, national humiliation, the Communist menace, and SALT II. This new liberation theology in America goes by the name of the "Christian New Right," and it caters to the tens of millions of sincere Christians who regard Billy Graham as a national hero. Its leading institutions are Christian Voice, Jerry Falwell's Moral Majority and "Old Time Gospel Hour," Pat Robertson's Christian Broadcasting Network and "700 Club," and Richard Viguerie's *Conservative Digest*. Its leading figures are, in addition to Falwell and Robertson, evangelist James Robison, Senators Orrin Hatch (R-Utah), Roger Jepsen (R-Iowa), Gordon Humphrey (R-New Hampshire), and Jesse

Helms (R-North Carolina), Congressmen Philip M. Crane (R-Illinois) and Robert Dornán (R-California); as well as Hal Lindsey (author of the best-selling book *The Late Great Planet Earth*, which has been made into a movie) and—until recently—Anita Bryant.

Now, a lot of the criticism leveled at the Christian New Right is patently hypocritical. The usual lament of modernist Christians, themselves deeply involved in social action and political lobbying, has been that the Christian New Right seeks to mix politics and religion and stir up "divisive issues." It takes one to know one, I suppose.

But the Christian New Right is itself afflicted with the same kind of double standard, but in reverse. It has emerged from the old ranks of Bible Belt fundamentalism and Evangelicalism. During the period of modernist ascendancy in American Protestantism—roughly since the Scopes Trial—fundamentalism has been on the defensive in America. But one of the fundamentalists' best arguments against the Social Gospel was that the latter politicized the faith and used it to promote purely secular political objectives. Now that fundamentalists and Evangelicals are on the ascendant, that position has been quietly dropped, and Christianity is being politicized with gusto—to the point of, in the case of Christian Voice, organizing national campaigns to get pastors to endorse political candidates from the pulpit.[32] Indeed, Christian Voice endorsed Ronald Reagan for president prior to the New Hampshire primary and formed a subsidiary called Christians for Reagan.

Jerry Falwell is honest about this flip-flop. Said he: "Back in the sixties I was criticizing pastors who were taking time out of their pulpit to involve themselves in the Civil Rights Movement or any other political venture. I said you're wasting your time from what you're called to do. Now I find myself doing the same thing and for the same reasons they did."[33] Indeed, Falwell has plunged so deeply into partisan politics that he met personally with Ronald Reagan in Detroit to offer his advice on the day Reagan won the Republican presidential nomination.

It is interesting that at a time when fundamentalist and Evangelical clergy are getting into partisan politics, the Roman

Catholic clergy are—thanks to firm guidelines from John Paul II—absenting themselves from partisan politics. The Pope's rationale is that partisan politics compromises the primary vocation of the minister—which is spiritual, evangelistic, and reconciling—and that priests must not usurp the proper vocation of the laity for partisan politics. Perhaps evangelist Rex Humbard made the point most succinctly when he said, "If I got into politics I'd be like a blacksmith pullin' teeth."[34]

The Christian New Right, like liberation theology, claims to speak for the oppressed. As New Right TV personality Pat Robertson articulates it, "The Bible tells us we are to lift the yoke of oppression, and in today's world we see the yoke of oppression has come down on about a billion people."[35] And the oppressed can also be found in America. The way the Christian New Right talks about taxes and federal regulations, there is little doubt that middle and upper-middle class taxpayers are numbered among the oppressed.

Like liberation theology, the Christian New Right also tends to have a distinctive eschatology. It is not the eschatology of the Catholic Church, nor of historic Christianity throughout most of its history. Rather, it is an eschatology which has precedents in the early Church but which is now concentrated among fundamentalists and Evangelicals in America—namely, apocalyptic premillennialism. The basic idea is that the Bible, especially its prophetic sections, teaches that we now live in the Last Days. The signs of the times—especially the reestablishment of the Jewish homeland in Zion in 1948, the reunification of Jerusalem in 1967, and now the moving of the Israeli capital to Jerusalem—are said to point unmistakably in this direction. There are a multitude of minor themes. For example, Pat Robertson said, "The fall of Iran (i.e., of the Shah) was clearly foretold in prophecy."[36] He also thinks that, according to Bible prophecy, war with the Soviet Union in the Middle East is inevitable. Robertson gives strong, virtually unqualified, support to Israel—just as liberation theologians have given similar support to Cuba, China, North Vietnam, and Allende's Chile. In April, Jerry Falwell and five other New Right-oriented Protestant ministers met with Menachem Begin in Washington,

D.C., to assure him of their support for Israeli settlement of the occupied West Bank.[37] And in order to more effectively support Israel, Robertson believes America must build herself up militarily.[38]

While Robertson is prolife in the sense that he is anti-abortion, his vehement "Better Dead than Red" posture makes him rather cavalier in his attitude toward life *outside* the womb. Asked he, "Is life so important, physically continuing life so important, that we would allow a world to be given over to slavery?"[39] Many feminists regard responsibility for children to be a form of slavery, and Robertson regards Communism as slavery, but both place a higher value on liberation from slavery than on life itself.

And much like the liberation theologians who are prone to excuse violence and defend doctrines of "just revolution," Robertson has his own doctrine of "holy war." Generally, among people like Robertson there is an assumption that the Battle of Armageddon is about to take place in the Middle East, and that after this battle Jesus Christ will return to establish his millennial thousand-year Kingdom on earth. But there is an undercurrent of Pelagianism to all this, for it almost seems to be assumed that Armageddon cannot be won by the Children of Light—and the Kingdom of God cannot be built on earth—without the military might of the United States assisting God's forces. Now, no one is *saying* as much, but the fervor and urgency with which many premillennialists are pushing for an American military buildup and for all-out American support for Israeli foreign policy leaves the impression that correct political action is indispensable to the successful outcome of eschatological events. According to strict premillennialist eschatology, it is *God* who will deliver Israel from her enemies. But in Robertson's scenario, God is to be helped by American military power. Hence, increased military spending becomes a divine imperative. And the resulting intensification of the arms race escapes moral censure. Now, I'm sure if Robertson were asked if he is for peace, he would say "yes." Who wouldn't these days? But I can't imagine Pat Robertson making a pilgrimage to the United Nations, as did Pope Paul in 1965, and pleading,

"No more war, war never again!"[40] It is hard to tell here whether eschatology is being used by the New Right to promote an American military buildup and an aggressive American foreign policy, or whether the latter are being used to promote the Kingdom of God. I am not sure whether we are dealing with an eschatologized politics or a politicized eschatology. Perhaps both.

Karl Barth was severely criticized by many American Christians for what they took to be a political double standard. Barth rallied Christians against Nazism, but largely fell silent after the Second World War on the Communism issue. There were many reasons for Barth's stance—an important one being that he felt Nazism, which presented itself as the defender of Christian civilization, constituted a tremendous temptation to Christians whereas Communism, which openly presented itself as materialistic and atheistic, was hardly tempting to Christians.

Although I do not equate the Christian New Right with Nazism, I feel somewhat akin to Barth in that the Christian New Right would seem to be both more attractive and a greater threat than liberation theology—at least at the level of the mass Christian public in America. Indeed, I would join with most orthodox Christians in applauding the Christian New Right's defense of the traditional family, and its opposition to pornography, prostitution, abortion, amoral sex education, "gay" liberation, salacious television, women's "liberation," the ERA, and secular humanism in the schools. Here, the program of the Christian New Right is strongly Christian. Liberation theology, on the other hand, is a pretty obvious prostitution of Christianity, and the Vatican has been quite explicit about where it goes haywire. But if there is something wrong with the Christian New Right, it is much harder to locate. First, the Christian New Right is largely a Protestant affair and there is no Magisterium to authoritatively draw boundary lines. Secondly, the Christian New Right comes out of the hyper-orthodox precincts of Protestantism and does not directly assault any cardinal tenet of Protestantism. Thirdly, in a time of moral collapse and national drift, it speaks strongly for traditional morality and a renewed national purpose—and as such taps profound anxieties and honorable longings on the part of tens of millions of orthodox Christians, including non-Protestants.

Yet, in addition to its weakness for a Pelagian-leaning eschatology, there is a fatal flaw in the position of the Christian New Right, namely, its fundamental working assumption that America has been chosen by God to carry out his purposes (a notion that certainly has implications for the eschatology described above). The view of America as a "redeemer nation" is not only basic to the Christian New Right, but to American civil religion generally—and it can be traced back to the settling of America, and beyond to the mingling of Enlightenment and Puritan thought in England. In the late sixteenth century, a feeling emerged that England was the "New Israel" in covenant relationship with God. The notion was popularized in John Foxe's *Book of Martyrs.* As Robert D. Linder and Richard V. Pierard tell it, Foxe asserted that, "From Wyclif to Henry VIII and his break with Rome to the first Elizabeth, England was guided by God's hand in defying antichrist, that is, the papacy. The day would come when England would fulfill its divine destiny, free the world from papal bondage and usher in the millennium."[41]

This notion of the "New Israel" came to America with the Puritans, and it is alive and well among the Christian New Rightists. The assumption clearly surfaced in the Washington for Jesus (WFJ) rally held on April 29, 1980. Pat Robertson was Program Co-Chairman of the rally, and the New Right was in on the organization of the rally right from the start. When the planned rally was heavily criticized for claiming Washington for right-wing politics instead of for Jesus, the leaders decided to soft-pedal their political agenda (causing some New Right leaders to refuse to attend the rally—notably, Jerry Falwell).

The governing text for the rally was II Chronicles 7:14: "If my people, which are called by my name, shall humble themselves, and pray, and seek my face, and turn from their wicked ways; then will I hear from heaven, and will forgive their sins, and will heal their land." The rally was therefore billed as "A National Day of Humiliation, Fasting and Prayer." The people who attended came to seek national forgiveness and national renewal on the assumption that America is the New Israel and that the locution, "my people," in II Chronicles now refers to Americans.

But an orthodox Christian would, I think, want to ask: on what authority may or must I believe that America is the New Israel? Since America is nowhere mentioned in the Bible, the source of revelation must be extra-biblical. If one scrutinizes the Catholic tradition of both the Western and Eastern Churches, one will nowhere find warrant for the belief. The best one could come up with is that if there is a New Israel, it is not America, but the Church of Jesus Christ (see Gal 6:16; I Pet 2:9; Rom 9).

The notion that America is the New Israel would probably have to be considered heretical. It is astounding that people who hold up the principle of *sola scriptura* could believe such a notion. Perhaps the lesson here is that people who lack a sense of the historic Catholic Church of the ages, and who have no ecclesiology to speak of, will be tempted to invent new ecclesiologies—in this case, by making the nation into the Church. Also, there is a danger that Christians who profess *sola scriptura*, but who perhaps feel the limitations of that position, will craft ersatz traditions—in this case, a tradition grounded in the experience of the Pilgrims and the Founding Fathers. For example, one frequently hears it said in the circles of the Christian New Right that the U.S. Constitution was "divinely inspired."

The originator of the rally and the Chairman of the WFJ National Steering Committee was the Rev. John Gimenez, pastor of the Rock Church in Virginia Beach, Virginia, the same town where Pat Robertson's Christian Broadcasting Network is headquartered. Gimenez said (in a news packet distributed by WFJ) that April 29 was selected to be the date of the rally because that is "the date in 1607 when the Jamestown settlers planted a cross at Cape Henry, in what is now Virginia Beach, and claimed this nation for God, as His vehicle for spreading the Gospel to every nation." But nowhere in the Bible is there any warrant for such a belief. The vehicle for spreading the Gospel has been and ever will be the Church. Pastor Gimenez

says a "covenant" exists between God and America, but cove-
nants are not established between God and a particular nation
by human fiat. Gimenez also claims that "the very foundations
of the American system" were "totally based on the Word of
God." This is vain, arrogant, and sectarian nonsense, and does
not even merit a reply.[42] Yet, one does wonder how many
Eastern Orthodox Christians in Rumania, how many Lutherans
in Norway, Catholics in Mexico, Anglicans in Uganda, Presbyterians in Korea, or Pentecostalists in Brazil he could find to
agree with him. Actually, any number of "Christian patriots"
can play the "New Israel" game—even liberation theologians.
According to Ignacio Ellacuria of El Salvador, "The Third
World [has] . . . a redemptive and saving mission, a mission
which it has to accomplish in history as did the oppressed
people of Israel."[43]

Gimenez also asserted: "Many see America today as the
'helpless giant'. . . . A congressman warned that by the mid-
1980s America will face internal subversion, bankruptcy, or
military defeat. Another senator asked us to pray that God
won't permit any enemy to strike this continent because we are
not able to defend ourselves." If political themes were soft-
pedaled at the rally, they were nonetheless visible and audible.
Speaker after speaker fretted about Communism, big government, and the Soviet peril. Now, maybe we should indeed be
worrying about these things, but not because America is God's
chosen nation or his instrument for world evangelization. The
anxieties that WFJ played on are real, but the rally's theological
assumptions were so patently nationalistic that one wonders if
the purpose of the rally wasn't basically to mobilize Christians
in a rightward political direction in an election year.

According to Joyce Ribbens Campbell, the segments of WFJ
"openly involved in political campaigns . . . have spoken out in
support of Reagan for President."[44] Back in August 1979, direct
mail wizard Richard Viguerie mapped out the political strategy
of the Christian New Right as follows: "Carter doesn't even
know what his base of support is. He thinks it is the blacks, the
union officials, the environmentalists, the McGovern liberals in
the Democratic Party. But when Brown and Kennedy announce

for President later this year, they will take three-quarters of this liberal-labor coalition with them. Then Carter will frantically look to the taxpayer, the born-again Christian, the moral major- ity American, who will have left him for someone else, like Reagan, Connally or Crane." The overall goal of the Christian New Right, said Viguerie, is "to remove liberals from power in America" within "the next six years."[45] The Christian New Right, which is theologically ecumenical—including Mormons, Orthodox Jews, and no doubt the Moonies—has a bottom line that is identical to that of the liberal ecumenists—namely, polit- ics. In the case of the Christian New Right, it is conservative politics. But like the liberal ecumenists, the conservative ecu- menists use theology and morality—especially morality—to run interference. Now, it is fine with me if Christians vote for Re- agan. Many will do so simply on the grounds that only he wants to change the moral tone of the country. But morality is *not* the bottom line of the Christian New Right. It is preaching the vir- tues of balanced budgets, reduced spending for domestic pro- grams, increased spending for military programs, and a tougher foreign policy as ends in themselves. The motif of WFJ was that if America doesn't repent of her sins, God will visit America with judgment via financial bankruptcy or military collapse. The ultimate concern here was not morality, but politics. Morality was a means to the end of restored national greatness.

That there is a considerable amount of disingenuousness in the Christian New Right's trumpeting of the morality and family issue is evident from their definition of "family" and "morality" issues. The Christian Voter's Victory Fund (of the National Christian Action Coalition) has devised a "Family Issues Voting Index" which rates the voting records of mem- bers of Congress. "In the Senate, votes for the separate Depart- ment of Education, a binding level on the 1980 federal budget and a limit on federal matching funds for state social-service programs are deemed anti-family. And the index condemns a House of Representatives bill which would provide additional financial assistance for medical services for children and preg- nant women. Another 'anti-family' bill calls for a three-year program to spend $65 million for grants to state and local efforts to prevent domestic violence and aid its victims."[46] The assumption is that *any* federal involvement in family life—even if designed to help the family—is *ipso facto* anti-family, except in the case of abortion. Here, government intervention—i.e., outlawing abortion nationwide—is winked at.

Christian Voice, the organization that endorsed Reagan early in the primary season, has also devised an index; this one allegedly measures the morality of the voting records of every member of Congress. According to Christian Voice, you are "moral" if you voted against a Department of Education, to lift economic sanctions against Rhodesia, to ban busing, to reinstate the 1955 defense treaty between America and Taiwan, and to support a constitutional amendment to balance the federal budget.[47]

The notion that America is the New Israel is not only idolatrous, but dangerous. America's enemies become God's enemies. The notion does not allow for the possibility that the foreign policy objectives of right-wing Americans could stand under the judgment of God. For the Christian New Right, there is no thought that America could be unfair and exploitative and hegemonic in her dealings with other nations. There is no sense that God might want America to give more of her bounty to the poor of the world, no sense that God might be more interested in our waging peace than in seeking nuclear superiority over the Soviets. The Christian New Right is prolife in the sense of being anti-abortion, but one hears no acknowledgment of the reality that, as the 1971 Synod of (Catholic) Bishops put it, "The arms race is a threat to man's highest good, which is life."[48] I'm not trying to say here that God favors a liberal foreign policy over a conservative one. The conservatives may well be right—but on simple *Realpolitik* grounds. But when theology is brought into the picture it is necessary to consider all the possible dimensions of God's will, and allow the Gospel to govern one's politics instead of letting one's politics govern one's theology.

A key figure in the Christian New Right is James Robison, probably the hottest young evangelist in America today. Speaking at the palatial home of the Forth Worth multi-millionaire industrialist, T. Cullen Davis, he exclaimed, "Has God turned against America? No, America has turned against God with its dependence on the federal government and its maze of regulations," adding that, "I'm for big business. I'm for small business. I'm for independent business. I'm for corporate business."[49] For over a century, Christians have been trying to live down Karl Marx's accusation that religion is a mere servant of capitalism, that religion is the "opium of the people," that preachers preach what the ruling class wants to hear. I can just hear Marx turning in his grave and muttering, "I told you so."

It is obvious that it is right-wing ideology more than Christian morality that is the governing principle of the Christian New Right. What bothers me is not so much the ideology as the way in which hardball-playing right-wing politicos are manipulating Christian morality and using sincere Christians to further their own power ambitions.

All in all, it appears that the pro-family forces in America are being commandeered by people with a very special political agenda. From a public relations point of view, the Christian New Right can be seen telling America that the people who are for family morality are also for the business elite, indifferent to the poor, and for more guns and less butter. The impression given is that orthodox Christians are simply a bunch of wild Neanderthals—greedy, belligerent, and on the make—just as the secular humanists always warned. The witness of the pro-life movement will be particularly damaged, for the people who are stressing the sanctity of life are seen to be the very same people calling for military confrontation with the Soviet Union, for more bombs and missiles, for the reinstitution of the draft, who are anxious to dismantle federal agencies protecting vegetable and animal life and the health and safety of workers, and who before long may be campaigning for a nation-wide reinstitution of the death penalty. As the cause of morality and family gets entangled in all sorts of extraneous causes, it will be the ultimate casualty.

In conclusion, I would urge all Christians to beware of external manipulation. Those who seek lasting peace and greater justice for the poor and less fortunate should be careful and avoid letting their theology collapse into the Marxist categories of liberation theologians. And likewise, those American Christians who are fed up with the moral depravity of this nation should avoid letting their indignation be corraled and channeled and exploited by the gods of nationalism and greed.

Notes

1. Gustavo Gutiérrez, *A Theology of Liberation* (Maryknoll, N.Y.: Orbis Books, 1973), p. x.

2. *Ibid.*, p. 46.

3. M.J. Cantley, "Kingdom of God," in *New Catholic Encyclopedia* (1967).

4. Gutiérrez, pp. 36-37.

5. *Ibid.*, p. x

6. *Ibid.*, p. 177.

7. *Ibid.*, p. 168.

8. "Message to the Peoples of Latin America" 325, in *Third General Conference of Latin American Bishops: Evangelization at Present and in the Future of Latin America: Conclusions* (Washington, D.C.: National Conference of Catholic Bishops, 1979).

9. Gutiérrez, pp. 198-99.

10. *Ibid.*, p. 202.

11. *Ibid.*, p. 206.

12. For a fuller treatment of Gutiérrez, see Dale Vree, "Political Transubstantiation," *Freedom at Issue*, no. 36 (May-June 1976), pp. 22-24.

13. Alfredo Fierro, *The Militant Gospel* (Maryknoll, N.Y.: Orbis Books, 1977), p. 326.

14. Paul VI, *Credo of the People of God* (New York: Paulist Press, 1968), p. 35.

15. "Gaudium et Spes" 39, in *Official Catholic Teachings: Social Justice*, ed. by Vincent P. Mainelli (Wilmington, N.C.: Consortium Books, 1978).

16. Fierro, p. 327.

17. José Miguez Bonino, *Christians and Marxists* (Grand Rapids, Mich.: Wm. B. Eerdmans, 1976), p. 35. See also Gutiérrez, pp. 202, 206.

18. Robert McAfee Brown, *Theology in a New Key: Responding to Liberation Themes* (Philadelphia: Westminster Press, 1978), p. 116.

19. See Brown, pp. 60-61.

20. Bonaventure Kloppenburg, *The People's Church* (Chicago: Franciscan Herald Press, 1978), p. 53.

21. Kenneth Hamilton, "Liberation Theology: Lessons Positive and Negative," in *Evangelicals and Liberation*, ed. by Carl E. Armerding (Nutley, N.J.: Presbyterian and Reformed Publishing Co., 1977), pp. 123-24.

22. Alfonso Lopez Trujillo, *Liberation or Revolution?* (Huntington, Ind.: Our Sunday Visitor, 1977), p. 27.

23. See Pope Paul VI's apostolic letter *A Call to Action* 23, and John Paul II's "Homily at the Basilica of Gaudalupe" 4, in *Third General Conference of Latin American Bishops*.

24. Arthur F. McGovern, *Marxism: An American Christian Perspective* (Maryknoll, N.Y.: Orbis Books, 1980), pp. 295-96.

25. "Nicaragua's Catholic Bishops Endorse Democratic Socialism," *New Oxford Review* 47 (January-February 1980), pp. 29-30.

26. See Pope Paul VI, *Evangelii Nuntiandi* 34, in *Official Catholic Teachings: Social Justice*.

27. See Pope Paul VI, *Credo of the People of God*, p. 30.

28. Samuel Escobar, *Christian Mission and Social Justice* (Scottdale, Pa.: Herald Press, 1978), pp. 53-54.

29. "Message to the Peoples of Latin America" 355, in *Third General Conference of Latin American Bishops*.

30. *Ibid.*, p. 475

31. Sergio Torres, "For a More Relevant Theology in the USA," in *Is Liberation Theology for North America?* (New York: Theology in the Americas, n.d.), p. 2.

32. See Ted Moser, "If Jesus Were a Congressman," *The Christian Century* 97 (16 April 1980), p. 445.

33. Interview with Jerry Falwell, in *Eternity* 31 (July-August 1980), p. 18.

34. Rex Humbard, quoted in "Stars of the Cathode Church," *Time* 115 (4 February 1980), p. 65.

35. Wes Michaelson, "An Interview with Pat Robertson," *Sojourners* 9 (September 1979), p. 20.

36. Michaelson, "Interview," p. 21.

37. Religious News Service dispatch, April 16, 1980.

38. See R.W., "Pat's Perspectives," *Sojourners* 9 (September 1979), p. 18.

39. Michaelson, "Interview," p. 22.

40. "Address of Pope Paul VI to the United Nations General Assembly, October 4, 1965" 5, in *Official Catholic Teachings: Social Justice*.

41. Robert D. Linder and Richard V. Pierard, *Twilight of the Saints* (Downers Grove, Ill.: InterVarsity Press, 1978), p. 54.

42. *Ibid.*, pp. 155-58.

43. Ignacio Ellecuria, "The Function of Economic Theories. . . .," in *Christianity and Socialism*, ed. by Johann-Baptist Metz and Jean-Pierre Jossua (New York: Seabury Press, Inc., 1977), p. 129.

44. Joyce Ribbens Campbell, "Washington for Jesus Rally: Report and Analysis—Part I," *Public Justice Newsletter* 3 (June-July 1980), p. 1.

45. Richard Viguerie, "Born-Again Christians: A New Political Force," *Conservative Digest* 5 (August 1979), p. 48.

46. Editorial, "Purity and Single-Issue Politics," *The Christian Century* 97 (9 April 1980), p. 395.

47. Moser, *op. cit.*, p. 445.

48. "Justice in the World," in *Official Catholic Teachings: Social Justice*, p. 286.

49. Religious News Service dispatch, June 19, 1980.

Response

I. John Hesselink

irst, it may be helpful to define our terms. I think it is safe to assume a common understanding of the word "theology," but when it comes to "ideology" we may not be as clear. "Ideology" in itself is not necessarily evil; commonly defined, it is simply a "body of ideas reflecting the social needs and aspirations of an individual, group, class or culture."[1] As I understand the term, it more often connotes those underlying, often subconscious presuppositions or prejudices we bring to any given subject. Some people would limit the meaning of ideology to political ideas, but this appears to me to be too narrow an understanding of the concept.

We are all subject to ideology whatever our theological positions may be, for we are affected by the opinions and thinking of those among whom we live and with whom we associate. Ideology, therefore, is not necessarily a pejorative concept. As James Smart observes in his book, *The Cultural Subversion of the Christian Faith*, "The truth about all of us, however, is that we are never as free as we think we are. Our whole existence, Christian or non-Christian, is webbed into a network of traditions that determine, far more than we ever realize, and feel and act. . . . In many instances even our interpretation of Scripture represents an unexamined and untested conformity with a tradition that we have inherited from the past."[2]

When ideology becomes dangerous and insidious, however, is when it subtly—and sometimes overtly—undermines the Christian faith and uses biblical concepts for its own ends. Dale Vree provides us with two current cases; liberation theology on the left and the so-called "Christian New Right" on the right. His choices, I feel, are happy ones because in both cases we have blatant examples of the ideological subversion of the Christian faith. This is not to say, however, that there are not legitimate concerns in both of these movements; and both can, with varying degrees of justice, appeal to the Bible for some of the notions and ideals which they espouse.

There is nothing new about such phenomena. All Christian theology, even at its best, represents to some extent an infiltration of biblical thought by current philosophical ideas. Augustine was influenced by neo-Platonism, Anselm by Roman law, Aquinas by Aristotle, Luther by the Nominalists, Calvin by Plato and stoicism, Brunner by Kierkegaard, Karl Barth by Kant, Jürgen Moltmann by Ernst Bloch, and W. Pannenberg by Hegel. It is not necessarily evil to utilize current thought; in fact, one must engage in dialogue with current thought and utilize some of its concepts if one is to be a relevant theologian. . . .

More recently, however, we have theological approaches which claim to be biblical but which are suspect from an evangelical perspective. We have before us in the paper of Dale Vree a case study of two very influential but highly diverse current phenomena. The main difference, apart from the fact that one represents a left-wing viewpoint and the other a right-wing position, is that Liberation Theology is of Latin American origin whereas the Christian New Right is a distinctly American phenomenon. Nevertheless, Liberation Theology has roots in some of the earlier theologies of revolution propounded by European and American writers,[3] and the Christian New Right can find antecedents in neo-Fascist and rightist movements in other parts of the world which often seek to pass themselves off as authentically Christian movements.[4]

I think we should also keep in mind the different spheres in which these left- and right-wing ideologies are most influential. Liberation theology and related theologies of revolution flourish primarily in academic circles in the United States, Europe, and Asia. (Some striking examples: the appointment of avowed Marxist theologians to positions in Japanese and Dutch university divinity schools, and the obvious sympathies with Marxism of a theologian like Moltmann.) In Latin America, however, such theologies/ideologies are rife among many clergy and laity of all stripes, not simply liberal types. There is also the World Council of Churches, which is strangely silent about the dangers of Marxism and revolutionary movements (and in fact occasionally aids and abets such causes) in its efforts to promote social, political, and economic justice in the Third World.

This is therefore no small isolated threat; but it does not affect most of us directly in a concrete way as does the Christian New Right. For most of us live in conservative middle class (or upper middle class) areas where politically oriented fundamentalist leaders such as Jerry Falwell and his Moral Majority have a tremendous appeal. It is an interesting coincidence that the week before I received my assignment to give this response *Newsweek's* cover story was on "Born-Again Politics" (September 15, 1980); and the week after I received Vree's paper I received in the mail (unsolicited) a book by Richard Viguerie with the unambiguous title, *The New Right: We're Ready to Lead.*[5] The latter provided ample evidence that *Newsweek's* concern was fully justified. The introduction is written by Jerry Falwell and much the same line is taken as that by Pat Robertson, John Gimenez, James Robison, and similar types, cited by Vree in his paper. If Viguerie is typical, then the reason for pulling out all the stops at this juncture is that these New Rightists are convinced that the coming election is "perhaps the most important presidential election in the twentieth century." Their theme is that a "godless minority of treacherous individuals . . . have been allowed to formulate national policy" (Jerry Falwell, Introduction); that "the left is old and tired. The New Right is young and vigorous" (pp. 1, 242); and that "the tide is turning" their way, which they equate with "freedom's way" (p. 243).

At the moment I find this more frightening and ominous than any Marxist-influenced theologies. As Vree astutely observes (p. 69), the situation is similar in some ways to the appeal of Naziism to the so-called "German Christians." In the long run, however, I am not sure whether Marxist-inspired liberation-revolution theologies are not a more serious threat. Liberation theology may be "a pretty obvious prostitution of Christianity"

(Vree, p. 69) to American evangelicals and upper and middle class conservatives, but it is not at all "obvious" to many Europeans, Africans, and Latin Americans!

This is a small caveat which does not diminish my general agreement with the thesis and thrust of Vree's paper, even though I regret the spirit in which it is written.[6] I also appreciate the parallels Vree discerns between these extremely different ideologies, e.g., both feel they represent the oppressed and both are engaged in a "holy war" (see p. 68). My task, however, is not simply to praise our author but to provide some critical analysis and thereby stimulate thought and discussion.

While basically affirming the position taken in this paper, at the same time I would raise some questions and make a few observations.

1. I find it curious that Vree constantly appeals to Roman Catholic sources in his critical remarks, whereas his most trenchant criticism of both left- and right-wing ideologies (as they affect the church) is their Pelagianism! As a convinced Calvinist I should rejoice in this, but I have two problems, apart from this interesting mix of theological approaches:

> A. Is Pelagianism peculiar to either liberation theology or the New Right? We Calvinists find Pelagianism almost as evident in most Baptist, Pentecostal, Wesleyan, liberal, and Roman Catholic theologies!
>
> B. Can we avoid the seeming dichotomy of saying on the one hand that liberation (or salvation) is primarily a gift (see Gutiérrez, see Vree, p. 58) and affirming on the other hand that one must work for his own liberation? (Granted, the tension is stretched too far when it is said that "it is man who liberates himself," as Gutiérrez allegedly does, p. 58.) Vree finds the same Pelagian strains in certain aspects of the New Right's ideology as well (see p. 69). I concur, but I do not think this is unique to either movement or the main reason for fearing them.

2. Secondly, I would urge more sensitivity to both the varieties of liberation theology and those who could generally be

labelled the Christian New Right and the valid biblical concerns which each extreme represents. Vree recognizes in passing the validity of many of the concerns of the New Right (p. 69), but he does not appear as appreciative of the matrix out of which liberation theology comes. For liberation theology represents a response to the anguish and terrible injustice experienced by the masses in Latin America, injustice which cries out for an answer and concerted action which traditional Western theology has not provided. Whatever the aberrations of most liberation theologies may be, the answer cannot be simply silence or fault-finding.[7]

3. Third, there comes the most difficult question of discerning the spirits. There is a legitimate place for united Christian involvement in political, social, and economic issues (recall the last chapter of Calvin's *Institutes* and the role of Abraham Kuyper in the Netherlands and his spiritual heirs), although the record of Christian action organizations, whether liberal, conservative, or neo-Calvinist, is not impressive. But better too much involvement than none at all! Rather than condemn all liberationists or rightists out of hand, we should listen to, and, on occasion, support, legitimate cries of outrage and injustice whether from oppressed peasants in Brazil, who may see in Marxism their "present help in time of need," or the conservative blue- and white-collar burghers in Grand Rapids who are sick and tired of having their dreams and goals eroded by an aggressive, decadent minority, whether they exercise undue power in the local university or the city hall.

What is required, I feel, is a more contextual approach (even though I eschew the more blatant forms of situation ethics as espoused by Joseph Fletcher). An overly doctrinaire approach cannot do justice to the dynamics and diversity of current ideological trends. As Henry Stob, emeritus professor of ethics at Calvin Seminary, observes in relation to Christian labor unions and Christian political parties in his own (Dutch Reformed) tradition, "If . . . the basis of fact and prudence is abandoned, and recourse is had to the principle of antithesis, and if, what is worse, the question is argued in terms of simple fidelity to Christ, the advocates of separate Christian organizations will not get the hearing they would otherwise deserve, and they will, I fear, do injury to their cause."[8] This warning should be taken seriously by all those Christians who are convinced that they have a biblical mandate to witness to society on behalf of the one who is not only the head of the Church but also the King of kings and Lord of lords.

4. Finally, echoing Vree's conclusion but in different terms, the concerns of those on the right and the left should *both* be taken seriously by *all* Christians. Most of us are guilty of an unbiblical bifurcation. That is, we tend to promote and get involved in only those causes which are dear to our hearts. If we are more conservative, the issues will be things like abortion and pornography; if we are more liberal, the issues are likely to be racial justice, hunger, and peace. If we are truly biblical, we will have both concerns—the social righteousness of the prophets and the personal righteousness of the apostles. If we maintain this biblical balance, neither a New Right nor a new left will ever get off the ground.

Notes

1. *The American Heritage Dictionary of the English Language*, ed. William Morris (Boston/New York: American Heritage Publishing Co. and Houghton Mifflin Co., 1970).

2. Subtitle: "Life in the Twentieth Century Under the Sign of the Cross" (Philadelphia: The Westminster Press, 1977), p. 95.

One of the leading Latin American liberation theologians, J.L. Segundo, maintains that the "biblical message itself is already impregnated with a certain ideological slant." The problem, he maintains, is that most Western Christians come to the Bible with their own ideological prejudices which run counter to those of the Bible. See J. Andrew Kirk's *Liberation Theology*. An Evangelical View from the Third

World (Atlanta: John Knox Press, 1979), pp. 71-72.

3. See Kenneth Hamilton's essay, "Liberation Theology: An Overview," in *Evangelicals and Liberation*, ed. Carl E. Armerding (Philadelphia: Presbyterian and Reformed Publishing Co., 1977), pp. 1-5. For its distinctiveness, however, cf. J. Andrew Kirk, *op. cit.*, Chapters One and Two and pp. 204-5.

4. "The totalitarian tendencies in the Moral Majority program lie in the attempt to foist the vision on those individuals no longer sharing its assumptions," "What's Wrong with Born-Again Politics?" a Symposium, *The Christian Century*, October 22, 1980, p. 1003.

5. Published by the Viguerie Company, Falls Church, Virginia. Viguerie, I am told, is a Roman Catholic layman, so we have here in the alliance of Viguerie and Falwell an interesting ecumenical alliance!

6. Contrast the much more balanced and charitable approach of the contributors to *The Christian Century* symposium cited in Note No. 4, or the article by Robert Zwier and Richard Smith, "Christian Politics and the New Right," in *The Christian Century*, October 8, 1980, pp. 937ff. Similarly, the evangelical critics of liberation theology such as J. Andrew Kirk (who lives in Argentina), cited in Note No. 2. The contributors to *Evangelicals and Liberation*—Kenneth Hamilton, Harvie Conn, and Clark Pinnock, among others—and John R.W. Stott (*Christian Mission in the Modern World*, pp. 92ff.) write in quite a different spirit from Vree.

7. Cf. the above references, especially Kirk's "Conclusions," *op. cit.*, pp. 204ff.; Harvie Conn's call for "a fully God-centered praxis" (the last word is a key concept for liberation theologians) in *Evangelicals and Liberation*, pp. 107ff.; and the last two chapters in the above volume: "Liberation Theology: Lessons Positive and Negative," by Kenneth Hamilton, and "A Call for the Liberation of North American Christians," by Clark Pinnock.

For an appreciative, yet critical evaluation of liberation theology by an American theologian in the liberal tradition see Schubert M. Ogden's *Faith and Freedom: Toward a Theology of Liberation* (Nashville: Abingdon Press, 1979). On the one hand, he criticizes traditional theology—whether orthodox, neo-orthodox, or liberal—as being primarily "the rationalization of positions already taken" (p. 121); whereas, on the other hand, his basic criticism of liberation theologies is their "exaggerated humanism, or homocentrism" (p. 103). Earlier in the book (pp. 32ff.) Ogden identifies four specific points where he finds theologies of liberation wanting.

8. "Social Strategy: Christian Power Organizations," in *Ethical Reflections* (Grand Rapids: Wm. B. Eerdmans Publishing Co., 1978), pp. 196-97.

Response

Kevin Perrotta

The purpose of these papers is to examine several fronts on which the boundaries between Christian and non-Christian thinking and behavior tend to become blurred in technological society. Dale Vree has given us a stimulating analysis of Christians' assimilation to secular perspective in the area of political engagement. He terms this the confrontation between theology and ideology. By ideology I take him to mean theoretical systems which involve sociopolitical programs and implications. It seems to me that he is not using the term to refer to the more fundamental sets of beliefs, values, and assumptions which shape the life of social groups. In this latter sense, Christianity itself contains at least many of the elements of an ideology.

Dr. Vree has illustrated Christians' tendency today not only to be insufficiently critical of secular ideologies but even to *identify* these ideologies with the Christian perspective on sociopolitical issues and, indeed, with the gospel itself. His choice of examples shows that this tendency is not confined to Christians of one particular tradition, part of the world, cultural background, or social class. The difficulty of maintaining a clear distinction between Christian and non-Christian thinking in the political realm is a universal challenge of the modern period. It is worth asking why this is so.

Part of the explanation, it seems to me, is that Christian thinking of the past does not answer our questions about what is the right Christian response to the disorder and inequities of the global technological society which have arisen in the last couple of hundred years. Thus Christians are particularly open to the political ideologies which have arisen in the modern period to answer these problems. Christianity entered the modern period unprepared to deal with the systemic poverty generated by capitalism, for example, or with the complex processes of social decay in advanced technological societies; but ideologies such as Marxism and political conservatism offer diagnoses and cures. This accounts for some of the allure of the political ideologies: they analyze problems that Christians are deeply concerned about and offer solutions designed to fit contemporary circumstances.

But what accounts for the confusion of these ideologies with the Christian message? How do they come to be seen as *Christian* approaches? The answer lies in the fact that these ideologies have learned from Christianity. Those on the left have derived a concern for the poor, a desire to see all members of society treated charitably; those on the right, a commitment to the integrity of the family and sexual morality. These attitudes seem to be Christian ones. In many cases, their source is the Judeo-Christian heritage of Western civilization. Thus Christians are faced with ideologies which, having adopted elements of Christian social thinking, are harder to distinguish from Christian positions than they would be if they plainly rejected goals that Christians cherish.

Dr. Vree's analysis should spur Christians to become more discerning of their christening of political ideologies of either the right or the left. His critique of liberation theology focuses, as he says, on the standard brand, not the only one. But his comments apply to the fundamental weaknesses of any left-leaning theology that loses an orthodox understanding of the relationship between the church and the world, the temporal and the eternal, sin and salvation, human experience and divine revelation, man's efforts and God's. Equally, his critique of the Christian New Right's identification of American national concerns with the cause of Christ, and conservative political programs with biblical righteousness should properly give Christians on the New Right pause. Dr. Vree is to be thanked for illustrating that similar dynamics are at work in the loss of the distinctiveness of the Christian message in Christians' allurement by both the left and the right.

In respect to Dr. Vree's criticism of Christians in the New Right, however, I think he has weighted their rhetoric too heavily and thus attributes to them some positions which they do not in fact hold. For example, if pressed for careful analysis, I believe, many of them would greatly nuance their statements which identify America as the New Israel. At least sometimes what they have in mind is that there is a parallel between America and Israel: America's origins and history have been marked by a significant Christian influence, and the nation has been blessed by God and will be judged by him if it does not repent.

Dr. Vree also sees more political and less religious motivation in Christians on the right than I do. For instance, I think there is no compelling reason to see as politically motivated their condemnation of all federal intervention in the family as anti-family. Perhaps I am revealing my own biases here, but it seems to me that the blanket condemnation is explainable as a reaction to the increasing intervention by government agencies whose policymakers are inspired by secular ideologies which have little sympathy with Christian morality or principles of family life.

My reservations detract nothing from the cogency of Dr. Vree's critique of the Christian New Right. Where he tends to see heterodoxy and political motivation I am more inclined to see an undiscerning mixture of scriptural faith and political ideology. Many Christians on the right have not carried out the process of discrimination between the two which Dr. Vree calls for. If my reservations are on target, Dr. Vree's analysis loses none of its importance; rather there is a greater likelihood that the Christians he is speaking about will be open to listening to his criticism.

Dr. Vree's paper raises the need for Christians to develop criteria by which to distinguish secular political ideologies from the Christian message. This is an important task because Christians will continue to confront aggressive political ideologies seeking to capture the enormous powers of modern government, and eager to co-opt Christians into support of their efforts. Many elements of modernity give rise to these movements—the destruction of mediating social groupings between the individual and the state, the revolution in expectations of improvement in material conditions, the very awareness that the technological instruments are at hand to reshape society according to ideological goals.

How might Christian criteria be developed? Revealed truth must be the source of such criteria. Human plans for government and society must be evaluated according to the purposes and standards which God has shown us he has for mankind. The development of criteria from revelation will lead us into areas where, as Protestants and Catholics, we are not in complete agreement. But certainly we have in common the core essentials which would make it possible to work together to develop criteria for distinguishing Christian faith from secular ideologies. This point is demonstrated, for instance, in the essays in this book, especially those by Stephen Clark and Donald Bloesch.

In learning to apply Christian criteria to political ideologies, it will be helpful to understand particular causes and programs in the context of their full ideological commitments. Christians should ask what views of ideal social structure, morality, and truth lie behind this political agenda? In what view of the world and the purposes of human existence did this program originate? What categories of thought are implied by this political analysis? Which of these assumptions are generally consistent with the Christian message and which are not? In what direction does this ideology tend to distort the true understanding of reality revealed in scripture? We should be attentive not only for points at which political ideologies are in flat contradiction to the gospel, but also to points at which they express different emphases, at which they place a priority on different aspects of the truth than scripture does. Distortions at these points can in the long run be as destructive of Christian thought and life as more apparent contradictions, as is illustrated by the way ideologies such as nationalism usurp the place of Christ, distort the Christian message, and replace Christian commitments with secular ones.

Christians who want to prevent secular political ideologies

from determining their understanding of the gospel and of the responsibilities of the Christian life must have a prudent suspicion of political ideologies. Rather than assuming that they can be accepted as "the signs of the times," Christians should exercise caution in adopting programs which have taken form outside the body of believers seeking to understand and apply God's word, that is, outside the church. As James I. Packer has remarked, ideas should be examined for their genetic makeup, to see what view of God, the world, and man they have inherited and give expression to. It is in giving impetus to this task that Dr. Vree's essay is most genuinely stimulating.

CHAPTER THREE

The Course of Radical Change in the Churches

James Hitchcock

At least in the Catholic tradition, heresy is sometimes defined not simply as error or denial of Christian doctrine (thus an atheist is not a heretic, nor is a Hindu) but as distortion of some belief which is authentic Christian doctrine, over-emphasis on one part of the creed at the expense of other parts. Heresy might almost be described as a cancer, an uncontrolled growth which threatens to devour all the other cells in the body.

Heresy in the formal sense of an outright denial of some Christian doctrine can almost always be traced to heresy in a subtler and less formal sense. For example, the Gnostics and Docetists of the early centuries denied Christ's humanity because they believed material creation was evil, the human soul merely imprisoned in the body. Attempts to refute formal heresy are almost always futile unless these less obvious assumptions about the nature of reality are first laid bare.

Heresy in a formal sense is quite widespread in contemporary Christianity—beliefs about Christ, for example, or about the nature of the scriptures, which are at odds with traditional Christian teaching. But in another sense contemporary heresy is extremely elusive. Many Christians, some of them in positions of influence in the churches, do not trouble themselves to deny official doctrine overtly because they regard it as so irrelevant as not to be worth the trouble. The categories of religious thought are often now formed without any regard for the way in which Christians have articulated their faith over many centuries, so that only people with a fair amount of formal theological knowledge can even detect discrepancies.

Seventy-three years ago Pope Pius X condemned a Roman Catholic heresy which he called Modernism. It is not necessary to delve into the specific doctrines of that movement. Rather it is the name which is interesting. At first glance one might say that it is not a very useful term, since every age of history is by definition modern in its own time, and every heresy can be called modern in that it reflects the cultural assumptions of its age.

However, the term is valid because it is perhaps only in the past century that religious thinkers have insisted on a specific duty of the Church to become modern. Only since the Enlightenment has it been urged that the Church has an obligation to conform itself to the spirit of the age in a conscious and deliberate way. No doubt theological shifts in earlier centuries always reflected cultural presuppositions to one degree or another. But not even the worst heretics of earlier centuries were prepared simply to canonize their times. The Arians taught a certain doctrine about Christ because they believed it to be true. It is impossible to imagine them accusing the orthodox of "failing to come to terms with the developments of the fourth century."

An adequate understanding of contemporary Christianity thus requires close attention to the spirit of the age, because that spirit seeks to govern not only in the general way which is almost inevitable but, more importantly, because there are influential people in the Church who regard it as their primary responsibility to bring the Church into conformity with that spirit. Ours is an age which has canonized itself.

It is important to recognize, however, that, like most heresy, contemporary distortions of Christian doctrine often take place for very good motives. Often, for example, the primary motive is the attempt to remove certain barriers which are thought to intrude between the Church and the unbelieving world. The motives are often consciously evangelical, in the sense of desiring to win the uncommitted to Christ. Unfortunately, some would-be evangelists do not stop to ask themselves how much of the Christian faith they end up sacrificing in their attempts to make it "relevant" to the non-believer.

I propose to discuss, not formal doctrinal errors, but rather underlying cultural attitudes which themselves usually go unexamined and which are mainly responsible for those doctrinal errors which do develop. I also propose to concentrate primarily on attitudes which have perceptible effects in the practical order, especially on moral belief and behavior or in the way in which Christians view the world. In each instance I wish to emphasize the fact that the heretical attitude, if we can call it that, has a kernel of truth and appropriateness in it. The error derives from its being overemphasized at the expense of other valid ideas. Finally, my catalogue of attitudes derives largely from my experience as a Roman Catholic and as a participant-observer in the wrenching changes which have occured in that church in the past twenty years. I strongly suspect, however, that the same catalogue has abundant applicability to many Protestant churches as well.

Contemporary-mindedness

As already noted, ours is perhaps the first age of history which insists on a kind of obligation to be "up to date." For evangelical purposes, there is certainly a lot to be said for this idea. First of all, religious belief and practice does, willy nilly, reflect to some extent the age in which it came into being. Christ certainly spoke in an idiom comprehensible to his listeners. And when the Church is often dismissed as a relic of the past, it is wrong to burden it with unnecessary historical accretions which seem to confirm that judgment. There is a certain approach to religion (sometimes, oddly enough, even found among non-believers) which treats it as a nostalgic refuge from the chaos of the present.

The crucial consideration, of course, is the ability to discriminate between what is merely historical accretion and what is the embodiment of eternal truth. A case in point might be liturgical worship or the language of scripture. In both instances strenuous efforts have been made to create idioms which are modern and devoid of anything archaic. However, it is valid to ask whether an idiom which is purely contemporary runs the risk of losing reverberations of eternity. Since all creeds, liturgies, and scriptures were formulated at some period in time, they reflect the culture of that time. Theoretically, therefore, it should be possible to translate their substance into the idiom of a later time. However, few arts are as difficult as the art of translation, and some contemporary religious idioms speak to the times but not adequately of the things of God.

Many contemporary Christians are understandably anxious not to cut themselves off unnecessarily from the culture around them. But, sometimes by imperceptible stages, they pass from a determination to remain in dialogue with the world to a tendency to accept almost everything which is characteristic of the world. Prevailing beliefs and practices come to have a normative character, not subject to judgment from a Christian perspective except in the most blatant instances. Much ingenuity and energy are expended in justifying contemporary practice in theological terms. (This tends to be true especially with regard to politics and sexuality, both of which will be discussed later.) The demands of modernity come to seem paramount, more authoritative and urgent than the demands of the Gospel itself.

The process by which this standard of worldliness comes to be accepted in a sense recapitulates in microcosm the various fallacies discussed throughout this paper. It includes at a minimum the following: a certain uneasiness at what are deemed to be distorted, corrupt, inhumane, or rigid elements in the religious tradition itself; the affirmation of the goodness of the world which God has made and which must therefore be seen as offering much that Christians can accept and affirm; a humility about one's own beliefs in the face of alternative beliefs; a determination to perceive God's grace at work in seemingly profane situations; a growing consciousness of the fact of historical and cultural change, so that stances which were appropriate to prior ages are no longer deemed so.

Ultimately there can take place what I have called elsewhere the "flight from eternity." By this I mean a tendency to interpret the meaning and value of Christianity in such thoroughly worldly and contemporary terms that the prospect of eternal life in the Kingdom of God is lost sight of. There is an instinctive fear that overt attention to the perspective of eternity will distract Christians from the present and from their duty to be in the world.

In innumerable ways modern culture conveys the message to people that it is impossible to resist history. Change is taken as the only predictable certitude. Those who resist change are regarded as doomed to a marginal place in society. This attitude has been imbibed deeply by many instinctively traditional-minded Christians. They may not like what the world seems to offer them, in terms of social customs, moral values, laws, etc., but they regard it as foolish to resist. Their main concern is how to make their accommodations to change as gracefully as possible. (It should be noted that all the attitudes catalogued here have their opposite equivalents, like excessive rigidity, which might have been dominant at other periods of history.)

Ecclesiastical Humility

In the past twenty years, Roman Catholics have been made very much aware of the sin of what is called "triumphalism." By this is meant an arrogant, domineering, even contemptuous attitude towards others not of the same faith, the belief that one has nothing to learn from others, that one's own Church is always right, that institutional self-aggrandizement is a proper ecclesiastical activity.

Humility, obviously, is a basic Christian virtue. While it is primarily a personal virtue, there is perhaps an appropriate ecclesiastical humility as well. The Church as an institution has been guilty of errors and sins throughout history, at least in the sense of the actions of its leaders or the collective actions of its members.

However, as with contemporary-mindedness, it is a relatively short step from this to an attitude in which the Church is constantly apologizing to the world practically for its very existence. Past sins are dwelt on with such obsessiveness that the kind of institutional self-hatred develops which Christianity is often accused of fostering in individuals. There is by now a quasi-official stereotype of historical Christianity which portrays it as a tyrannical, fanatical, obscurantist movement repeatedly suppressing human freedom while failing to recognize or encourage the constructive movements of history. Many Christians themselves share this view of their past.

There results from this a kind of psychic paralysis similar to the kind we are familiar with from individual pathology. If the past history of the Church is so bleak, if until the day before yesterday Christianity failed to embody even its own authentic teachings, why should anyone belong to the Church today, or what basis is there for a hopeful future? Evangelization is thwarted, because Christians cannot preach to the world with any sense of conviction, or without an acute sense of embarrassment.

Many Christians thus find themselves in the position of continually apologizing to the world and even seeking the world's absolution. Whatever might be thought of this from a moral standpoint, in practice it tends to mean seeking absolution on the world's terms. Christian teaching is subtly corrupted by the desire to excise whatever the world might find objectionable, or whatever might arouse memories of past excesses.

Genuine Christianity must teach with authority, as Christ taught with authority. Yet it is the point of much contemporary Christianity to eschew all authority whatever. In the end it prefers to speak of Christians being engaged in the common human search for meaning, possessing no truth and no authority which others do not have. Such a view is impossible to reconcile with the New Testament.

Secular Ecumenism

The word "ecumene" is, of course, from the Greek, meaning "the entire world." Although the tendency has been to restrict its use to religious relations, obviously the same impulse towards breaking down barriers, towards establishing relations of love, which obtains in the religious sphere has applicability to the larger world. Christians are commanded to love not only other Christians but all human beings. Furthermore, since God created the universe, what is in the universe is very good. Positive values must be recognized and responded to wherever they are found.

Beginning with these indisputable theological assertions, some contemporary Christians come to approach the world in largely uncritical ways, however, a tendency which is strongly reinforced by their inferiority complex about the Church, which was discussed previously. With memories of the Inquisition or of Cotton Mather in their heads, these Christians want at all costs to avoid a stance which would be unduly censorious of the world, or would fail to detect the good things emanating from worldly movements.

The uncritical stance is only part of the problem, however. Beginning with the principle that God works in and through the world, some Christians are constrained to be continually alert for evidences of his action. Thus they have a propensity for not only minimizing the sinful aspects of worldly movements but for seeing them positively and even sacrally. They come to conceive it as their duty to validate worldly movements in theological terms. Furthermore, since it must be assumed that God's action in the world is continuous, there is a strong imperative to find a new sign of that action even as the wave of the previous one is ebbing. In the past twenty years a host of such movements have served this need for some Christians—civil rights, peace, poverty, feminism, environmentalism, the so-called human potential movement, etc. Whatever the merits of each in its own terms, each has been responded to by some Christians (often in influential positions in the Church) almost messianically.

Not only are Christians often seduced into overlooking sinful and even anti-Christian aspects of the worldly movements they endorse. They are also drawn, sometimes unwittingly, into permitting the wholly secular use of Christian theology. There are now Christian spokesmen, for example, who never say anything except as it relates to some currently urgent worldly issue. They seem to regard faith as having validity only insofar as it can be applied to such issues. The meaning of religious belief comes to be taken as wholly secular, and there is a reluctance even to speak of supernatural reality lest it distract people from worldly tasks which are now defined as holy.

Modern Christians cannot even begin to confront the demonic aspects of contemporary civilization, except as these express themselves in ways which are condemned also by enlightened secular opinion. The possibility that Christianity might sometimes find itself standing in radical judgment over that opinion is implicitly denied. It would be instructive, for example, to take any given issue of *Commonweal*, or *The Christian Century*, or *Sojourners* and ask what in it would be seriously discomfiting to the average reader of *The New Republic*. In most cases the answer would probably be nothing.

Yet the demonic aspects of modern culture assert themselves with greater and greater force—in the "sexual revolution" which debases human sexuality and blights lives, in the alarming breakdown of the family and the kinds of human commitment on which it rests, in the proliferation of bizarre cults, in fanatical political movements, finally in a pervasive nihilism about moral and spiritual values which spreads everywhere in our culture. Many Christians, because of their misapplication of theological principles valid in themselves, have nothing compelling to say about this demonic condition. They cannot permit themselves to recognize the depth of the evil they confront, and they end up ignoring it, minimizing it, excusing it, even in some unhappy instances embracing it.

Many Christians, motivated by the desire to be open and optimistic toward the world, render themselves deliberately insensitive to what is happening around them. Although they wish to take the world seriously, they in fact do the opposite, since they studiously ignore both the long-run and short-run movements of historical change. Nothing could be clearer, for example, than that influential elements in Western society—in the media, in the educational system, in the government—

believe Christianity has outlived its day. They aim to hasten a demise which they regard as inevitable, and their efforts are bent toward the resuscitation of attitudes and values which can legitimately be called pagan and even pre-Christian.

Love of Enemies

Contemporary Christianity emphasizes the central importance of love and compassion with an insistence that is perhaps unique in the entire history of the Church. For although such attitudes were always recognized as binding on the Christian, in times past other Christian obligations like repentance were probably given at least equal weight. Contemporary Christianity has drawn out into its fullness the authentically biblical idea of the infinitely loving and merciful Father, whose children must imitate him in his abundance.

Christian love is astounding in its ability to see what is lovable in the person who appears wholly unlovable. Yet by the same token Christian love is not shallow or unrealistic. It claims that the sinner is lovable despite his sin; it does not deny the sin. When contemporary Christians seek to promote love, therefore, by overlooking what is unlovable, pretending it is not there, interpreting sin benignly, they are unwittingly admitting to a failure of love. For authentic Christian love cannot be based on illusion.

Christians can only manifest genuine love toward the world if they free themselves of all illusions about that world. They can only love their enemies if they recognize that they have enemies. When they persist in ignoring the fact that they have enemies, they do not thereby provoke a response of love equal to that which they seek to manifest. Rather they provoke a response of contempt, the perception of Christianity as soft-headed and wishful. They invite further acts of aggression against their beliefs.

The mass media are the obvious example of the contemporary situation. Religious values are rarely treated with respect and sympathy in the media. At best they are ignored, an enforcement of secularism just as extreme as the most extreme theory of the separation of church and state. Increasingly, religious values are subjected to attack and ridicule in the media, and a similar if somewhat less obvious pattern obtains elsewhere in society, including the educational system. Many Christians persist in believing that such things are not really occurring, or that they are the result merely of some kind of misunderstanding, or that Christians themselves are largely to blame because of their failings. However, nothing should dispel these fond illusions faster than to note that even Mother Teresa of Calcutta, despite the adulation which has been heaped on her, has not been immune from secularist criticism or condescending dismissal.

Secular society is far less tolerant than it presents itself to be, and its official ideology of "pluralism" is to a great extent an illusion. There are official or quasi-official opinions which are enforced on a whole range of controversial questions, and those who dissent from these do so at their peril. (An obvious example is Anita Bryant. Whatever one might think of her anti-homosexual crusade, her career was virtually destroyed because of it. The tolerance for dissenting opinion supposedly characteristic of our culture was not operative in her case.)

This pluralism is increasingly coming to be understood as meaning simply that religion is legally tolerated as a private, unobtrusive thing. But systematic efforts are being made to exclude it from all public institutions in whatever form. There, secular ideology will totally dominate. The blame for this situation lies less with the secularists who seek to bring it about than with the Christians who have shut their eyes to it and are correctly perceived as passively acquiescent in whatever is done to them. Many Christians make the fatal confusion between the forbearance appropriate to an individual who is subjected to persecution and the obligation to defend Christianity itself when it is attacked. It is also worth noting that many of those who believe it is wrong for Christians to fight for their rights do not make the same argument for passivity where economically or politically oppressed groups are concerned.

Love of Sinners

Love for the sinner obviously includes not only love for the enemies of the Church but also love for fellow Christians who may also seem unlovable. An image comes down to us of a Christianity of past ages that was stern, unforgiving, rigid, censorious, and vindictive. In many ways this image is unfair. Nonetheless it has helped to provoke a reaction which places love and forgiveness at the very center of the Christian's obligations to his fellow Christians and at the very center of the Church's mode of dealing with sinners.

Contemporary Christianity is unfortunately characterized by rampant kinds of intellectual confusion, and one of the most destructive of these is precisely over the meaning of words like "love" and "compassion." But the confusion is not primarily intellectual. Rather, the intellectual confusion is itself the result of more basic moral confusion. There is an old Catholic adage, "Hate the sin, love the sinner." Although, like all Christian principles, not easy to live up to, it nonetheless seems to embody the essence of the authentic Christian attitude.

Instead, however, the Christian notion of love has tended to degenerate into a kind of sentimentality which is often the exact opposite of real love. The root of this deterioration lies in the crisis of self-confidence alluded to earlier, in this instance both an ecclesiastical crisis and a personal one.

The ecclesiastical crisis is in the nagging suspicion that some Christians now seem to have that the history and traditions of the Church are embarrassing and even shameful. Thus they become very uneasy when the Church seems to speak with an authoritative moral voice, except when that voice has been confirmed by the right kind of secular opinion. There is a constant fear that, as it allegedly has so often in the past, the Church will prove itself rigid and unloving, will condemn instead of showing compassion. Much energy is therefore expended to prevent the Church from taking firm moral stands, and some theologians function primarily to keep most Christian moral teaching in a constant state of doubt.

On the personal level, many Christians have been seduced

into the false impression that not casting stones at other sinners means closing one's eyes to sin. Each of us is a sinner. Each of us ought, perhaps, to think of his or her own sins as the worst. Therefore, none of us is in the position of pointing the finger at others. But this is clearly to misunderstand the command of Christ. Especially within the Church, sin must be rebuked—lovingly and with compassion, but rebuked nonetheless. To wait until we are all saints will be of course to wait forever.

It seems possible that this attitude stems not only from a sentimental notion of Christian love (in fact, rebuking one's brethren is one of the obligations of that love) but also from a systematic flight from moral responsibility—we do not wish to rebuke the sins of others lest they in turn rebuke our sins. Furthermore, we do not wish to take responsibility for the moral well-being of others.

These attitudes tend to center, at present, on sexual morality—divorce, abortion, homosexuality, adultery, premarital sex. In each case reforming Christians decry what they see as excess rigidity and call for "compassion."

It would take more space than is available here to discuss the question of how important sexual morality is in the scale of Christian values, whether the Church's attitude in the past has indeed been excessivly rigid, and whether new pastoral strategies are called for at the present time. However, three important points about sexual morality can be made: that there is a very long and remarkably consistent Christian tradition on the subject, with few ambiguities; that it is precisely at this point that the contemporary pagan world has chosen to assault the Church; and that sexual morality, because of its intimate nature, is very close to the identity of each person.

When the question is asked, for example, "Is the Homosexual My Neighbor?" there can, of course, be only one possible answer. However, when the question is formulated, as it has been, as the title of a book, one begins to suspect that what is being urged is something more than compassionate concern, and this suspicion turns out to be correct. A certain kind of contemporary Christian apparently finds it impossible to extend compassion to homosexuals without also extending approval. Anything else is regarded as condescending, judgmental, or arrogant. However, to say this is to say that all moral judgments partake of these same qualities. Hence, logically, all moral judgments are invalid.

Authentic Christian love seeks to help the sinner to overcome his sin. A distorted kind of love now seeks to assuage consciences and to short-circuit the very possibility of repentance. In particular the sexual sins have been singled out for this treatment, because they possess a contemporary fashionableness and are the point at which contemporary secular opinion is most sharply at odds with the Church.

Freedom

The Christian Gospel sets men free, and from earliest times preachers have proclaimed this good news. Our age is especially sensitive to this fact, and deplores all religious faith which depends on coercion or manipulation. Ultimately, faith is not obedience to a set of rules but a loving and joyful following of Christ.

Also from earliest times, the Church has been plagued by recurring epidemics of antinomianism, the understanding of Christian freedom in which the believer conceives himself as being exempt from the law, possibly above the law, free in the Spirit to do whatever he pleases. Antinomianism is having one of its major recurrences at present.

As at every other point, the contemporary Christian's seeming embarrassment over the Church of the ages is a major operative factor, giving rise to a sometimes compulsive drive to be quit of every restraint from the past, along with an equal compulsion somehow to find the means to validate whatever departures from the moral law secular society itself sanctions.

The whole notion of freedom is now approached in a totally secular way. Worldly notions of personal rights dominate the thinking of some Christians, to the point where some denominations have practically been torn apart by groups in conflict with one another, each claiming its "rights" in the same litigious and confrontational way which characterizes secular politics.

It is extraordinary how the "needs" and the "rights" of individuals are now routinely equated with desires. It is sufficient to establish that an individual wants something, and feels oppressed at not receiving it, to establish likewise the legitimacy of the claim. The existence of a higher law by which individual desires are measured is not denied but is less and less honored in practice. Human feelings are given a kind of sacred character, and it becomes callousness not to accede to such feelings.

The working psychology of many Christians is now a popular notion of "self-fulfillment" which owes much more to fashionable secular schools of therapy than to Christian understandings of human nature. The very notion of self-denial, which has been central to almost all Christian schools of asceticism, has been discarded. The idea that God's will for the individual may be radically different from the individual's will for himself is now lost sight of.

Confronting religious traditions which may seem rigid, negative, outdated, dysfunctional, the contemporary Christian experiences a great sense of exhilaration, a kind of religious "high," at being able to break through the crusts of time and assert a new freedom. However, as T.S. Eliot pointed out years ago, liberal religion is much more adept at releasing energy than at refocusing it. Thus the liberal religious agenda soon becomes the sterile one of negating yet further traditions of the Church in each age, until there is finally little left.

Those who are at the beginning of this process—who confront a highly traditional and possibly rigid Church at just the point at which it is about to change—cannot imagine this possibility. To them the institution is so massively solid that it can safely absorb great amounts of flexibility. So also, its traditions are deeply ingrained in the reformers themselves, so that they can safely monitor the process of reform and mediate between innovation and tradition, flexibility and solidity. However, the history of the Roman Catholic Church over the past twenty years shows how vulnerable apparently solid institutions often are, and how quickly the most apparently cautious reformers can lose their moorings. (In this connection it is worth noting the inevitable process by which the torch of leadership quickly passes to a new generation of reformers whose interests may not be anything like those of their predecessors. Thus most of the influential Roman Catholic thinkers whose work prepared the way for the Second Vatican Council ended up saying that the Council was interpreted and applied in ways contrary to their intentions.)

In the end, freedom comes to be a goal in itself, so that some contemporary Christians give the impression that sin itself is somehow noble so long as it is the result of free choice. Likewise the antinomian Christian tends to cease believing in a genuine divine revelation and comes to think of religion as a splendid human creation, subject to endless experimentation, again as an exhilarating manifestation of human freedom.

Justice

Surely the heightened emphasis on social justice is one of the most positive developments in contemporary Christianity. Christians have been made to understand the demands of neighborliness much more comprehensively than ever before. It is in the area of social justice perhaps alone that avant-garde Christians seek to awaken the consciences of their contemporaries rather than lulling them and to preach a faith which is demanding rather than permissive.

It is, consequently, here in particular that the notion of heresy as a distortion of truth seems particularly applicable. The extreme cases are too familiar to require discussion—the Christians who are willing virtually to equate their faith with Marxist ideologies, those who become revolutionaries and engage in or justify terrorism.

However, the heresy deriving from a concern for justice also manifests itself in less obvious ways. One is a simple preoccupation with political and economic questions, as though these constituted the heart of the Gospel. (There are now Christians who have a passionate position on every contemporary social question but appear indifferent to matters of basic Christian doctrine.) Another is the assumption that the Church must first prove itself a progressive social force before its message can be taken seriously. A third is the assumption that in confronting the poor the Church must bring them primarily a message of worldly hope, often coupled with the patently false assertion that it is impossible to preach to those who have crying bodily needs. (If this were true, religion throughout history would indeed have been the preserve of the rich.)

While never losing sight of the legitimate Christian concern for social justice, it is necessary to remind some of our contemporaries that Christianity has never taught that bodily suffering is the greatest of all evils. Nor does the situation improve when the focus shifts from bodily suffering per se and toward one's social status or lack thereof. Christianity supports legitimate aspirations for greater social justice, but it does not make the mistake of thinking worldly progress defines the message of the Gospel.

It is crucial to recognize how a distorted concern for justice melds with the equally distorted concern for personal freedom, so that all sorts of people now define themselves as oppressed, develop an ideology, and a list of grievances, and then expect the Church to support them. Feminism is a case in point, and many Christians now seem to think the Church has an automatic duty to accept every one of these "liberation" groups at face value. Religious fervor is now commonly channelled into political paths and harnessed to secular purposes. Politics captures the Christian imagination, and a worldly utopia substitutes for the Kingdom of God.

Professionalism

Faith is no substitute for competence, and the Church has sometimes gotten a bad reputation when it attempted to act as though it were. In our time the personnel of the Church are professionalized as never before in history, not only in their own profession but also with respect to other professions which bear on their actions. We have a more highly educated, more professionally dedicated clergy and laity than ever before in our history.

Although professionalism may seem to be of a lower order of importance from other ideas I have been discussing, in the practical order its influence is immense. In part it is the means whereby other distorting ideas are transmitted to the Church.

All things being equal, professional competence is to be desired in any person working within the Church. However, just as faith is no substitute for competence, so the reverse is also true. Elsewhere Paul Vitz details the ways in which Christians have uncritically accepted certain theories of modern psychology, even when those theories are contrary to Christian values. Similar developments have happened in other disciplines. At few points does the contemporary Christian inferiority complex manifest itself more clearly than here. Many Christians allow themselves to be silenced when told that prevailing professional opinion contradicts a commonly held Christian belief. Many professionals who are personally people of faith cannot permit themselves even to think of going contrary to a professional consensus, even though this consensus (with respect to homosexuality, for example) might change overnight. Professionals are conceded an authority which the Church itself is denied.

The most obvious example is perhaps that of the psychological professions, of which Professor Vitz speaks. However, it is noteworthy that not a few devoutly Christian doctors, for example, have compromised and even capitulated where morally objectionable medical practices like abortion are concerned, once the medical profession had approved these practices. There are few recorded cases of judges bringing their Christian principles to bear on sensitive legal issues, even though secularists do so constantly. Many Christian lawyers, for example, seem to erect a high wall between their personal beliefs and their acceptance of an increasingly secularized legal system.

The same mystique of professionalism obtains within the Church, so that those who are designated experts in worship, in moral theology, in religious education, etc., often manage to silence all disagreement and to impose programs on their denominations about which people rightly have profound misgivings. An important instance of this is biblical scholarship, in which "demythologizing" theories have for several generations been retailed as scientifically proven facts. Despite the talk about "pluralism," professionalism tends toward the homogenization of opinion on most questions.

In summary, perhaps the greatest problem presently facing the Church in American society is intellectual confusion, a confusion which is the result of certain moral and spiritual uncertainties and which in turn spawns still more such uncertainties. Many Christians have unknowingly imbibed a secularistic way of looking at the world, and they unwittingly measure Christian doctrine itself by the standards of that secularity. That there is a distinctively Christian way of looking at the world is something which does not seem even to have occurred to many professed believers. Their piety may be intense, but it is personal only, and can often coexist with attitudes towards the world at large which have nothing discernibly Christian about them.

In this election year, this phenomenon can be most dramatically seen in the behavior of those political candidates who are most prominently identified in the public eye with particular forms of Christianity—the Irish Catholic Senator Edward Kennedy; the "born again" President Jimmy Carter; Congressman John Anderson, who once sponsored a constitutional amendment to declare America officially a Christian nation. Each of these men seemed to go out of his way in 1980 to demonstrate that personal religious convictions would not influence public political behavior. The expectations of an aggressively secular media have a lot to do with this, since any public figure who does manifest overt religious principles is likely to suffer for it. The mass media, unlike thirty years ago, are no longer interested in stories of religious conversion. Instead they prefer stories of deconversion. Public figures like Kennedy, Carter, and Anderson are presented as models of how Christians ought to behave in public life.

It is worth noting that none of the processes delineated here occur spontaneously, nor are they the result of irresistible impersonal forces. Generally what seems to happen is that a relatively few people in a given church, sometimes people with a rather marginal status, early imbibe an essentially secular viewpoint, usually without realizing it, and usually for motives which are consciously good. Because such people can frequently speak in what seems like a passionate, committed, even prophetic way, they often attract strategic support from other people who are respected and who are in positions of influence. Dubious ideas are promoted as at least being worth a try, and the freedom of expression which ought to characterize a Christian community is extolled.

A crucial point is passed once the criteria for judging new ideas change, which often occurs without notice. New ideas may originally be proposed as likely to deepen and strengthen the faith of the Church, make it more relevant to the world, purge it of outmoded and possibly un-Christian baggage from the past—in general improve it in every way. Soon, however, it becomes apparent that some of those who have promoted the new ideas, and others who have been influenced by them, are actually becoming less. Christian in a perceptible way. People are leaving the Church because they find a purely worldly calling more meaningful. Attempts are made to transform Christian doctrines or practices in such a way as to give them an essentially secular meaning (the Eucharist, for example, or the idea of Christian love). Once these facts become noticeable, rather than admitting that these are experiments that have failed, the advocates of change are likely to insist that a radically changed, essentially secular context is precisely what is needed. Those who defend traditional orthodoxy are put on the defensive. To an extent confusion is deliberately promoted in order to undermine past certainties.

It would be impossible to suggest, short of a paper at least as long as this one, how authentic reform or renewal can be carried out in the Churches. Obviously much prayer and a sincere reliance on God's guidance are indispensable and basic. On the human level it might be suggested that there is no substitute for clear thinking. Church leaders must have a very solid notion, first, of what their identity is and what in their tradition cannot be bargained away. They should cast a critical eye on all proposals for change and not allow gushes of euphoria to override calm analysis. New ideas should be made to prove themselves. Just as justice must not only be done but must be seen to be done, so fidelity must be seen to be honored even as necessary changes are made. Church leaders should be highly sensitive to the fact that changes which in the abstract may be perfectly justifiable on orthodox grounds may have a different kind of subjective effect on Church members (for example, in the Roman Catholic Church, certain kinds of liturgical change giving rise to the impression that the Mass was no longer a sacred action but rather a human creation solely). Much time and energy must be spent making people highly aware of the many ways in which their culture is in conflict with their faith. The sacrifices, possibly the heroism, which discipleship entails must be brought home. Examples of authentic renewal, either contemporary or historical, should be presented to people in dramatic ways.

Finally, the exercise of authority and discipline, which the modern mind tends to find unpalatable, cannot be ignored. There are times when love demands rebuke. It is not act of love toward the body of the Church to allow false teachers to abuse their positions in the name of freedom. It is the truth which makes man free, not the imbibing of fashionable opinion.

Response

Stephen Board

All of the characteristics Dr. Hitchcock mentions can be amply documented from the Protestant side.

Harry Blamires isolates one more symptom of the problem in the common modesty of church people toward speaking "as if we had all the answers."

> Why in God's name not? What is our Christian duty if not to make plain that in the Christian faith, the gravest doubts and worries of men are richly answered? What do those prevaricators mean? Have we not got the answers in their eyes? Is our Lord untrustworthy, the church founded upon an eternal question mark, the faith a fog? It will be time enough to put this slogan on our banner when we have heard a dying martyr proclaim it as the surety of his hope.
>
> The scene is worth picturing. The flames gather around the stake, but the martyr's eyes are ablaze only with faith. "I die gladly. I die at peace with God. My last message to you is this: We must not talk as if we've got all the answers."
>
> (from *The Tyranny of Time*)

This servility to modern culture is made explicit in Rudolf Bultmann's famous remark that, now that the electric light has been invented, we can never again ask people to accept a religion with miracles, a distinct revelation and a final judgment. Hence, revise accordingly.

In our more liberal Protestant seminaries, the social and behavioral sciences have almost completely taken over the normative positions, with the result that the seminarians incline toward either counseling or social action as the real work of the ministry. I recall a conversation with a young man, a couple of months before his graduation, in which he confided that he had never read the Epistle to the Romans. And this in one of our best-known seminaries.

But the distraction from revealed religion prevails even in conservative circles. Last Sunday I tuned to two Christian television broadcasts which feature "evangelical" preachers of some fame. One was given over to what you might call the Gospel of Optimism, in which people are invited to believe in themselves. The other was devoted to sounding alarms over our diminished national military defense. Both messages originated with men who would go to the stake saying they had, in fact, "the answers" in Christ.

In the summer of 1980, the Southern Baptist Christian Life Commission held a convention on "Ethical Issues of the Eighties." There the empirical dominated the normative, so that the distinctive Christian contribution to the ethical problems before us (which problems, on their reading, did not include abortion) was muted by secular heavyweights like Buckminster Fuller and Ramsey Clark.

Again, I note the periodical *Sojourners*, which I read with care, has allowed redemption to be almost entirely swallowed up in ethics, or perhaps equated with ethics, so that God's saving work seems to be accomplished best when people are most politically and socially in harmony. Law overcomes Gospel, and withal a view that sets church against culture loses its place to stand.

The point of my examples, and Dr. Hitchcock's as well, is that the distinction between Christian thinking and that of the reigning culture has become blurred. "I will make a distinction between my people and your people," Yahweh told Pharaoh (Ex 8:23), in the midst of the plagues. But how can the Lord's people maintain that distinction as well?

This distinction requires the awareness of Christianity as a body of knowledge with a truth claim in our thinking. Most of the unstable wavering Hitchcock describes comes from a weakened grasp of the truth of Christianity as a world-view. And if not truth, in the older universal or absolute sense, your faith comes to be regarded as an opinion, an emotion, or a matter of individual taste: "I'm into antiques, he's into opera, you're into religion."

Long ago I realized that 51 percent of the battle with secularism is won when you reach a confidence that Christianity, as a report of reality, is *true*. That may seem elemental, but numerous problems in the confrontation with secularism emerge from a neglect of the truth question, or from a shaky understanding that we have some true word from God out of which a world-view can be distilled.

The problem, then, appears to be a blurred distinction of Christ and culture, traced to a faulty grasp of Christianity as truth.[1]

We need a revelational standard to sift the new winds of doctrine blown in by the morning culture. But the standard must also sift the old winds of doctrine left over from the night before. Jesus himself cautioned against our traditions, which "make empty the Word of God." The old and familiar, as well as the modern and strange, bows to Christ; and the tendency, especially among High Churchmen, to prefer old to new out of temperamental dislike of modernity runs the risk of missing the truth of God for our day.

Thus submitting to the objective revealed standard, which Christians have known to be the scriptures as foundational, we have a place to stand in the sandy beach of contemporary culture.

The process by which people succumb to cultural pressures in the interests of religion needs more study. Dr. Hitchcock ventures into the psychology of it. Let me add an idea or two.

It appears we can begin with a normative body of truth, the Christian world-view of God, man, and the universe. We then can take a correct idea within that philosophy—say, the notion of the Kingdom of God, or the concept of natural revelation (God's revelation of himself to all people through nature), and, moving out from the idea, we stretch it to include some new attractive element. So, the Kingdom of God stretches to include wherever God's will is done; and from thence, to movements that may be explicitly hostile to God but which God is using in some way to achieve his purposes. Or with natural revelation, the biblically based (Rom 1) notion of the invisible God being known through the visible creation stretches, amoeba-like, to the creative suggestion that God has shown himself in all the religions of the world; and from there, it is a short step to something like *The Hidden Christ of Hinduism*, which finds the kernel of Christianity buried in a Christless system.

In such instances, the new proposal looks fresh and creative; it may even be applauded as a method of drawing new meaning out of old dogma. But eventually, following a temporary tension with the orthodox root idea, the new evicts the old and all that is left is the language—traditional words with culturally co-opted meaning.

To meet the new opportunities of the culture, we badly need good models. I recall an InterVarsity camp where we were trying to offer the students examples of Christians in every field. When we came to poetry, we rummaged around the choices and offered W.H. Auden, who is usually regarded as a poet who writes out of a "Christian" vision. But a shocked undergraduate from Agnes Scott College in Georgia blurted out, "Auden? When he came to our campus he was too drunk to finish his lecture." We did not elaborate on his other shortcomings as a model.

For many of us two twentieth-century figures have nourished our appetite for models: Dietrich Bonhoeffer and C.S. Lewis. Bonhoeffer may be criticized for his radical hospitality to the new age, so much that he stands almost as a symbol of too-eager embrace of the culture. Yet his sense of freedom to meet the culture of Germany and challenge it has a transcendent Christian root. Lewis more so. His awareness of how Christianity contradicted the fashionable cultural ideas coupled with his own poise and security as a man of that culture offers twentieth-century Christians a helpful model of sanctified relevance. Lewis, like Bonhoeffer, may weaken under closer scrutiny, though for different reasons. He disliked the new, and preferred the old, so much that he scorned daily newspapers. But C.S. Lewis will wear well for the generations to come.

In scripture, the passing reference in Acts 7 to David who

"served his generation according to the Will of God" offers us a model of two admirable qualities. This man after God's heart, as the Old Testament described him, lived in his own time, serving his generation, refusing the flight into irrelevance that tempts Christians of all generations . . . but he did it according to the revealed will of God. He took his cues from the Word of God, rather than the generation itself. He served—always imperfectly and as an unprofitable servant (Lk 17:10)—but according to the supra-cultural will of God.

Note

1. Two classics engage these problems: Richard Niebuhr's *Christ and Culture* discusses the various ways Christians relate to their world (Harper and Row, 1956). And the opening chapters of John Henry Newman's *Idea of a University*, especially "Theology As a Branch of Knowledge" (Doubleday Image Book, originally 1858).

Response

Edith Black

When I was asked to write a response to Dr. James Hitchcock's paper, I was at first hesitant, since I did not know how I could improve upon an analysis as penetrating as his. But after some reflection I realized that I could illustrate the points he makes by my own analysis of a theological position on divorce and remarriage which has developed in the Catholic Church during the last ten years and of an organization for civilly divorced Catholics which puts that position into practice. I have a familiarity with this theological perspective and its organizational outreach because of my attempts to inform a number of bishops on the issue.

The North American Conference of Separated and Divorced Catholics (NACSDC) exemplifies well the increasing professionalization of Church ministries in the last fifteen years to which Dr. James Hitchcock alludes—a phenomenon which is ironical because the Vatican II Fathers intended to reinforce existing lay ministries and to encourage the development of new ones. The priests and nuns who direct this organization do so under the guise of "democratizing" the Church so that the laity may have a greater voice. But it is they and not the laity who are in effective control. Moreover, their organization has gradually usurped the function of a genuinely lay-run ministry to the civilly divorced, the Judean Society, which was founded in the 1950s to minister to civilly divorced Catholic women and to encourage them to remain in harmony with the teaching of the Church on remarriage.

The method of argumentation of the advocacy theology which the NACSDC promotes and which now has the adherence of a number of "Catholic" moral theologians strongly exemplifies the antinomian tendency which Dr. Hitchcock cites as a distortion of the Gospel message of freedom.

First, these theologians effectively deny that God really legislates laws—that is, absolute norms of behavior which obligate us and which we cannot disobey without consequences. They argue instead that Jesus was not a lawgiver, that he taught only ideals—high standards of behavior which we should try to emulate but which we are not absolutely bound to obey. For them, Jesus' statement prohibiting divorce and remarriage quoted in all three synoptic Gospels (Lk 16:18; Mk 10:2-12; Mt 5:31-32; 19:3-9) constitutes an exhortation, not a simple declarative command as traditionally understood.

Secondly, these theologians deny the existence of objective spiritual bonds which endure even if subjective commitment falters—bonds such as those initiated by marital and baptismal vows. They therefore reject the traditional understanding of the passages cited above that marriage constitutes an objectively binding relationship that cannot be broken as long as both partners live. According to them, Jesus was not saying that remarriage *could not* occur because it constitutes in effect an adulterous union, but only that it *should not* occur.

By way of parenthesis I should say that I am putting aside the question of what Jesus meant by the exceptive clause which appears only in the Matthew version of Jesus' saying. The Catholic Church holds that it means that Jesus was excepting those liasons which were not valid marriages and was thereby providing the basis for annulment rulings. The Eastern Orthodox and Protestant Churches hold it means that a marriage can be dissolved when one of its parties is unfaithful, thereby freeing the injured party to remarry. The grammar of the statement allows either interpretation.

Thirdly, these theologians construe scripture as being itself permissive in its application of the sayings of Jesus to particular circumstances. In 1 Corinthians 7:10-16, Paul reiterates Jesus' prohibition of divorce and remarriage between believers but permits divorce of a believing spouse from an unbelieving spouse if the latter is an obstacle to faith and is unwilling to continue in the state of matrimony. But the theologians repudiate the traditional interpretation of this passage as one which refers to two distinct situations: (1) indissoluable marriages in which both partners are baptized Christians; and (2) dissoluable marriages in which only one partner is a baptized Christian. Instead they argue that Paul "accomodated" or "modified" Jesus' original saying to fit difficult circumstances—that is, he made an "exception" to the principle of indissoluability. If Paul could make an exception to the principle of indissoluability laid down by Jesus, these theologians argue, surely then the modern Church can do so also.

Fourthly, these theologians redefine traditional words in such a way that activity which was formerly prohibited now becomes permissible. For instance, they interpret the "til death do us part" of the traditional marriage vow to mean not only physical death but also "mental death," that is, the breakdown of a relationship. Marriage is no longer indissoluable until the physical death of one of the partners but may dissolve if the relationship "dies." As Fr. Young puts it: "the sacramental union dies when the love relationship dies." When such occurs the partners have a "natural right to remarry."

These theologians also aptly manifest what Dr. Hitchcock calls the "flight from moral responsibility"—that is, the refusal to confront another in his sin, a refusal which passes for Christian love. They locate the authority to judge acts of serious sin in the individual conscience only and deny the official representatives of the Church any right of rebuke and disciplinary jurisdiction. This is in contradistinction to the clear scriptural mandate to the Church to exclude from the sacraments those who persist in public violations of its moral laws (see 1 Cor 5, etc.).

The Catholic Church does not presume to judge the subjective culpability or motives of those who make a decision in conscience contrary to her own moral law. But she does hold that her priests in the privacy of the confessional have the obligation to judge objective acts of serious sin and to refuse absolution to those who persist in committing them. She therefore holds that remarried Catholics whose prior marital unions have not been judged invalid by annulment tribunals and who are not willing to live in a brother-sister relationship may not receive the sacraments because they are, objectively speaking, living in adultery. They may, however, attend mass and other Church functions.

The theologians under discussion argue, however, that reception of the sacraments is entirely a matter of individual conscience and that any attempt of the Church to withhold the sacraments from someone is "judgmental." Accordingly, they promote a pastoral practice called the "in conscience" or "good faith" solution which, contrary to the Church's official discipline explained above, admits remarried couples to the sacraments if they are willing to continue in a stable relationship and attend church regularly.

A favorite sermon of Fr. Young emphasizes Jesus' compassion in approaching the woman at the well who, as he aptly points out, was despised not only because she was a Samaritan and a woman but also because she was a divorcee. He loses the balance of the Gospel, however, when he fails to mention that Jesus lovingly rebuked her in her sin. His message, and that of the moral theologians who support him, is not the Gospel of "Christ and him crucified" which St. Paul preached but rather a false gospel which lulls Christians into a false sense of complacency. Their theology is one of "cheap grace" which takes the Cross out of discipleship and which repudiates the central insight of the saints through the ages—that God gives us the grace to bear whatever burdens he permits us to suffer in this life.

CHAPTER FOUR

From a Secular to a Christian Psychology

Paul C. Vitz

In this paper I will focus on major anti-Christian aspects of those types of psychology which are both popular today and especially influential in Christian settings. The purpose of such an analysis is to alert Christians to the serious dangers posed by the widespread acceptance of these psychologies and to facilitate the construction of a framework for a genuine Christian psychology. However, before the nature of a Christian psychology can be discussed, even briefly, secular psychology's challenge to the faith needs our attention.

Contemporary secular psychology is a complex, varied, sprawling field. Rather than consider particular theories in detail, my approach here will be to identify major assumptions which are common to most of these psychological theories. Taken together, these assumptions represent in a loose way the essential foundations of modern secular psychology. These foundational assumptions are rarely understood or acknowledged either by psychologists or Christians, but since they constitute the ground rules or underlying intellectual control mechanism, they heavily determine, in advance, how human nature will be seen and valued. It is therefore necessary for Christians to become aware of these assumptions and of their expression in psychology.

121

Assumption 1: Atheism or Agnosticism.

It is unfortunate but true that all the major theories of personality and counseling are either explicitly or implicitly based on atheism. Freud, of course, is well known for his attacks on religious belief as an illusion, but all the other major theories are implicitly anti-religious as well, since genuine religious motivation is ignored or treated negatively when it occasionally comes up. In none does spiritual life figure as essential or even as important. The only partial exception to this is Jung's psychology. Even Jung, however, is far from reliable on this issue, and my own experience with Jungian Christians is that Jungian categories have powerfully overshadowed their Christianity.

What is little known is that such psychologists as Fromm, Rogers, and Skinner were or are personally hostile to religion, especially Christianity, and are on record as being so, sometimes officially but usually in their informal comments. Other theory, such as Transactional Analysis, etc., is simply functionally atheistic in that it completely ignores God, religious motivation, and spiritual life. Christians should always keep this what I will call "functional atheism" in mind and should do everything possible to correct for it. Otherwise, involvement in these theories shifts one from a primary concern with God to a primary concern for man—almost always the self. The pattern of priests and ministers going *into* psychology and *out of* the faith is extremely common. It is caused in large part by extensive exposure to psychological theory and practice which functions without any reference to God.

Assumption 2: Naturalism

Closely related to atheism is Assumption 2: Naturalism. In psychology this assumption means that all mental events are assumed to be either ultimately physical or that the mind considered on its own is a purely natural thing—and that it can be completely understood by reason and observation. Most especially the assumption of naturalism means that nothing "supernatural" actually exists. For example, Abraham Maslow, sometimes thought a friend of religion, is rather well known for a concept he described as the "peak" experience. Christians might think Maslow has therefore accepted religious experience. This is not the case, for Maslow writes:

> It is quite important to dissociate this [peak] experience from any theological or supernatural reference, even though for thousands of years they have been linked. . . . this experience is a natural experience, well within the jurisdiction of science. . . ."[1]

For these bald assertions, he offers no reasoned explanation.

To my knowledge no one has challenged or even seemed to be especially concerned with Maslow's assumption that religious experience is a strictly natural phenomenon.

Assumption 3: Reductionism

The secular modernist assumes that all so-called "higher" things, especially religious experience and related ideals, are to be understood as really caused by underlying lower phenomena. Examples: Love is reduced to sex and sex is reduced to physiology, as in Kinsey, and in Masters and Johnson. Spiritual life is reduced to sublimated sex, as in Freud. Even the ego is reduced to underlying ego states, as in Transactional Analysis. In contrast the Christian is a constructionist who sees higher meaning and divine significance in psychological experiences. Sex is seen as love, love as sacred, marriage as a sacrament.

As an example of reductionism I would like to look briefly at the psychological treatment of sex as represented by Masters and Johnson—and the kind of sex therapy which they have "spawned," as it were. In this summary of what might be called the "Masters and Johnson understanding," I will draw heavily on the work of Hogan and Schroeder, two secular psychologists who are part of a recent critical stance toward modern social science which is growing in the secular world, at the time many Christians are still trying to catch up with secular sexology. Somehow the Christian world is always buying into secular ideas at the top of their influence, and selling out Christian ideas just when they have no place to go but up! This is the classic "buy high and sell low" behavior of the stock market victim. (As an example, secular psychologists have just discovered such ideas as character, virtue, chastity and celibacy, and even virginity. Soon these will be hot topics in the secular marketplace—just as these ideas and values have almost totally dropped out of Christian use.) To return to Masters and Johnson: in general, they deal almost entirely with anatomy and physiology. Masters and Johnson do not purport to cover the emotional and social aspects of sex, much less religious aspects. Nonetheless, they explicitly criticize traditional cultural teachings:

> The omnipresent religious orthodoxies, social intolerances and ignorance of sexual matters by health-care professionals, contributed immeasurably to our culture's lack of comprehension of sexual response as a natural physiological process, a process comparable to other natural functions such as respiratory, bowel or bladder function.[2]

Thus, they reject the cultural teaching of the past and view sex in a purely biological light. The effect of the volume has been to amplify Kinsey's implied message: sex can be regarded perfectly objectively; one need not feel the socially bestowed compunctions about sexual activity. Although Masters and Johnson did not intend to encourage sex without responsibility, they contributed significantly to that effect.[3]

In *Human Sexual Inadequacy*, Masters and Johnson discuss clinical difficulties in sexual functioning. They use a concrete, reductionistic approach emphasizing overt behavior, anatomy, and physiology. They explicitly do not view sexual functioning as symptomatic of deeper or broader psychological factors. Hogan and Schroeder describe this attitude very lucidly:

> A major theme [in Masters and Johnson's *The Pleasure Bond*] is how individuals have been overburdened with the responsibility to meet their partner's needs. For Masters and

Johnson, individuals are responsible primarly for their own gratification.[4]

Of course this is a complete reversal of the Christian injunction that the body of the husband is for his wife and vice versa. Hogan and Schroeder come to a similar conclusion when they comment that the Masters and Johnson position "would seem to turn the entire sexual process back on itself. What is generally construed as an expression of affection for another becomes an expression of interest for one's self."[5]

Somehow the reductionist strategy of focusing first on the individual, and then only on the physiology of sex, has resulted not only in losing sight of the many higher meanings of sex. It has led to an active rejection of such meanings.

Thus at the end we see how interwound and mutually supportive are the reductionist and the individualist assumptions. We turn next to this latter assumption—individualism.

Assumption 4: Individualism

Secular psychology assumes that the isolated, autonomous self-preoccupied individual is the only significant social and psychological reality. Specifically, the modernist is devoted to what he considers to be independence, while the Christian is aware of and cultivates interdependence, and indeed dependence on God and obedience to him. Modern psychology emphasizes the isolated individual, while the Christian is focused on family and community. Secular psychology emphasizes self-will and its decisions in a life of calculated self-advancement, unconcerned with others, while the Christian is concerned with following God's will and living a life of Christian love and holiness. It is most revealing that there is not one major psychological theory of personality which does not assume the isolated individual as the central unit and primary concern of its theory. Nor is there a single influential psychological theory which has any major positive theoretical terms for the important fact of human interdependence, even less of course for the concept of obedience.

This reduction of the person to the isolated individual ex-
presses itself in many ways. It begins with the simple physical
fact that the person who seeks counseling leaves whatever
group he or she is in and as an isolated unit goes to the
psychologist's office for counseling. A Christian procedure
would normally reverse this: the psychologist would counsel
the couple or family as a unit and would try to become
knowledgeable about the person's community as well. (This
latter procedure is showing signs of acceptance in certain
areas of psychology.)

Here are some examples of the concern with individualism
expression taken from a recent expression of self-help popularized by Dr. Wayne Dyer in his book *Your Erroneous Zones*
(1976). First he announces, "Declare your independence," and
that "Psychological independence means total freedom from all
obligatory relationships, and an absence of other-directed behavior." "[In] any relationship in which two people become
one, the end result is two half people."[6] Dyer goes on to assume that the ideal marriage or any other relationship is based
on the complete interchangeable equality of roles and total independence of each person. His book is filled with examples of
the breaking up of traditional relationships between husband
and wife, parent and child, etc. For example, he constantly
attacks guilt as a useless emotion, is always talking about
breaking free, taking charge of yourself, and escaping from the
past. A recurrent theme is tolerance for adultery, sexual exploration, and getting out of unfortunate marriages. Also, not
being open and fearing the unknown are favorite negative
themes. Dyer gives a long list—and in many ways a preposter-
ous list—of fears of the unknown in our culture.

Examples are: eating the same kinds of food out of fear of
exotic cuisine, wearing the same kind of clothes all the time,
reading the same magazines, living in the same place, seeing
the same movies, staying in a marriage that doesn't work,
going to the same place for your vacation all the time, fear of
new activities like yoga, meditation, astrology, etc. This list of
great American fears needing to be overcome reads like an
advertising excutive's delight. But more about the economic

significance of this kind of psychology later.

The ideal continually upheld by Dyer and the other self-help psychologists is the perfectly independent person who has broken all ties to family, heritage—and of course to God. Dyer, in *Your Erroneous Zones*, is often explicit in his rejection of God and of religion, but the same message is at the core of all the other secular self-helpers. For example, turning to Transactional Analysis (TA) we find the goal of its approach is the completely autonomous individual described as follows:

> Parents, deliberately or unaware, teach their children from birth how to behave, think, feel and perceive. Liberation from these influences is no easy matter. . . . Indeed, such liberation is only possible at all because the individual starts off in an autonomous state, that is capable of awareness, spontaneity and intimacy. . . . The attainment of autonomy consists of the overthrow of all irrelevancies. . . . First, . . . the weight of a whole tribal or family historical tradition has to be lifted; . . . then the influence of the individual parental, social and cultural background has to be thrown off.[7]

And finally after all this one arrives at *autonomy* from which one can now build a new personality based on only one's choices.

First, even if this kind of autonomy were possible or desirable, the desired state of autonomy, which according to TA requires constant vigilance to be maintained, sounds very like "Freedom's just another word for nothing left to lose." Perhaps this kind of psychology should be called "liberation psychology," and in that light it probably has many anti-Christian aspects analogous to the political form of liberation theology. In any case, this kind of psychology is a secular form of preaching—a kind of secular evangelizing which is deeply anti-Christian and which has no even modest claim to scientific respectability. Throughout all these books there is almost no relevant evidence of an impartial kind used to support the many extreme claims. (For a detailed critique of self-help psychology regarding its theoretical origins in Carl Rogers and others. (See Vitz, *Psychol-*

ogy as Religion: The Cult of Self Worship, 1977.)

The curious thing about the selfish goal of autonomy is that it is almost unanimously made throughout popular psychology and yet I have not found one writer who has attempted to defend the goal as morally worthwhile or even to demonstrate that this "autonomy" is possible. It is incredible to me that the very idea of the "secular, autonomous individual" has not been seen as the illusion that it is. First of all, the typical exhortation to break free, to live only on the basis of your choices, to forget about others, your past heritage, etc., is itself an ideology, a hopelessly American cliche. To follow such an exhortation is to be other-directed, to be following in one of America's oldest traditions.

Second, it is not possible to *do* it. Instead what we end up with is an illustration of freedom in which autonomous choices are made exclusively from a pitiful array put before us by the media, by corporate America, by big business and big government, etc. This incredible notion that if you only break free you can be the boss, you are in the driver's seat, "Can have it your way," I have elsewhere characterized as "the Burger King theory of personality." Unfortunately it is true. The alternative to the influences of our parents, our family, our community, and, above all, of our faith is not to be free of influences but to be controlled by the social environment of mass society. Indeed, the big New York publishers, and TV talk shows and lecture circuits which provide the outlet for Drs. Berne, Harris, Dyer, and the rest of the pop psychology and self-help writers is simply an expression of the modernist mass technological society and its organs of social control. These modernist economic forces attack what Ellul (as in Kinzer) calls "natural groupings." The whole argument is so patently false and perhaps even consciously deceptive that it is a wonder that Americans haven't seen through it. Today's individualistic psychology repetitively implies that the enemy is the past created by natural groupings, but not the past and present, dominated by modernist isolated egos separated from all that is natural, with each ego being told that it is free. In addition the entire process feeds the consumer society's economic needs so directly that one wonders again that Americans so skeptical of advertisements haven't seen the illusion of autonomous choice as the fraud that it is. Dyer's list of fears of change is, as I said, an advertising executive's dream; each new move to supposed autonomy is a move toward indulgence in more and more types of consumer activity. We are free to choose among twenty brands of beer, or among thirty brands of birth control, among fifty brands of designer jeans, but we are not free to choose more basic material needs, much less free to search or to find a Christian—or even "noble pagan"—environment in which to bring up our children. The self-help psychology is the psychology of the perfect consumer. It is a theory for improving the balance sheets of gourmet restaurants, fancy hotels and casinos, Club Mediterraneé, and the manufacturers of hot tubs.

Assumption 5: Relativism

The secular modernist assumes that all values are relative to the individual or to the culture. In spite of this assumption, secularists take an absolute position toward relativism and, in flat contradiction to their philosophy, they take an absolute position on certain modern, secular values, e.g., egalitarianism. In contrast, the Christian assumption is one of absolute values across all cultures and times—values revealed in scripture, expressed in the church's tradition and values always mediated through the absolute of absolutes, namely the love of God and of neighbor.

As examples, consider briefly models of the secular moral education known as Values Clarification.

> Very generally VC is a set of related procedures designed to engage students and teachers in the active formulation and examination of values. It does not teach a particular set of values. There is no sermonizing or moralizing. The goal is to involve students in practical experiences, making them aware of *their own* feelings, *their own* ideas, *their own* beliefs, so that the choices and decisions they make are conscious and deliberate, based on their own value systems.[8] (Emphasis in original.)

As this passage indicates, the VC approach is contrasted with the direct teaching of morality or ethics ("sermonizing"), which Simon and Raths reject as a hopelessly outdated form of "inculcation of the adults' values upon the young" (sic). This position is outdated, they say, because today's complex society presents to the young so many inconsistent sources of values. In the context of the "confusing contemporary scene" the developers of VC reject moralizing; they also reject indifference to the problem of values, since a *laissez-faire* position just ignores the problem and leaves students vulnerable to unexamined influences from the popular culture. Instead it is argued that what students need is a process which will enable them to select the best and reject the worst in terms of their own values and special circumstances.

In order to enable young people to "build their own value system," Raths' system focuses on what is conceived as the "valuing process." Valuing according to these theorists is composed of PRIZING one's beliefs and behaviors; CHOOSING one's beliefs and behaviors; ACTING on one's beliefs. Now it is significant that the three major processes of valuing are in this order: prizing, choosing, and acting. That is, the first emphasis is on the prizing of already existing values. (The theorists use the term pride as a synonym for prizing; they see proud and prideful students as desirable.) There is no concern with whether these values are *worth* prizing. That would obviously raise the *bête noire* of absolute values. In the second stage of the model, the student is encouraged to choose from alternatives, and after considering consequences; in the third stage the student is urged to act on his values. These two stages, coming only *after* prizing, scarcely constitute an adequate evaluation of or reflection upon what the authors assume are the student's initially confused values—prized nonetheless. The difficulty created by this order of consideration is particularly acute since the main thrust of Values Clarification is only on consequences for the "autonomous self." Thus, like all forms of moral relativism, this process does not encourage serious rational reflection on moral issues. Instead, it begins with the irrational, emotional prizing of whatever the student already happens to have as values or goals, and the secondary purpose of evaluation of consequences is overshadowed by the initial prizing and by the emphasis of self-acceptance rather than on the needs of others or of society.

The actual moral position of Raths, Simon, *et. al.* is personal relativism. What is good and bad is so only for a given person *or* it is antinomian. That is, values don't actually exist—there are only things which one likes or dislikes. In both cases, it follows that blaming and praising others—and even oneself—are to be avoided. The relativist and antinomian positions involve Values Clarification in a number of very basic contradictions. These contradictions, combined with other weaknesses to which I will return, completely undermine the coherence of the system. The first basic contradiction is that in spite of the relativity of all values, the theorists clearly believe that Values Clarification is *good*; that is, that students *should* engage in their VC program, they *should* prize their program of how to clarify values, etc. Raths, *et. al* attack values inculcation by teachers and yet they urge teachers to inculcate the value of clarifying values by using their system. Indeed when they argue for *their* system they begin moralizing and sermonizing like anyone else. They criticize values inculcation as "selling," "pushing," "forcing one's own pet values" on children at the price of free inquiry, and reason, etc. But when it comes to the value of *their* position, relativism has conveniently disappeared.

A typical passage revealing this incoherence of the system—of how while arguing against values in general, they constantly slip into their own social and political ideology—is worth quoting:

> If a child says that he likes something, *it does not seem appropriate* for an older person to say, "You shouldn't like that." Or, if a child should say, "I am interested in that," *it does not seem quite right* for an older person to say to him, "You shouldn't be interested in things like that." If these things have grown out of a child's experience, they are consistent with his life. *When we ask him to deny his own life, we are in effect asking him to be a hypocrite.* . . . As a matter of fact, in a

society like ours, governed by our Constitution, teachers *might well see themselves as obliged to support the idea* that every *individual is entitled* to the views that he has and to the values that he holds, especially where these have been examined and affirmed. Is this not the cornerstone of what we mean by a free society?[9]

The sermonizing of this passage is altogether striking. In spite of the original claim of a neutral relativist position and the continued argument against judging anyone's values at all, they themselves judge other educators, other political and social values, while aggressively pushing their own special set of values.

The second major contradiction in Values Clarification derives from the anti-value or antinomian assumption found in the system. The antinomian position ends up—oddly but perhaps predictably enough—in authoritarianism. This conclusion is beautifully identified by Nicholas Wolterstorff, whose analysis I will follow here.[10] When Raths, *et. al.* bring up the question of whether the child should be allowed to choose anything he wishes, they answer: no. Parents and teachers have the right (sic) to set some "choices" as off-limits. But they don't have this right because those choices are wrong. Instead, they say that they have this right because certain choices would be *intolerable* to the parent or teacher. As Wolterstorff cogently concludes, "Thus does antinomianism turn into arbitrary authority." The only rationale for the forbidding of a particular choice is that the teacher or parents finds the choice personally offensive or inconvenient. And, of course, teachers and parents (usually!) also have the power to enforce their will. This most disturbing "logic" is instructively portrayed by the VC theorists in the following remarkable example:

Teacher: So some of you think it is best to be honest on tests, is that right? (Some heads nod affirmatively.) And some of you think dishonesty is all right? (A few hesitant and slight nods.) And I guess some of you are not certain. (Heads nod.) Well, are there any other choices or is it just a matter of dishonesty vs. honesty?

Sam: You could be honest some of the time and dishonest some of the time.

Teacher: Does that sound like a possible choice, class? (Heads nod.) Any other alternatives to choose from?

Tracy: You could be honest in some situations and not in others. For example, I am not honest when a friend asks about a dress, at least sometimes. (Laughter.)

Teacher: Is that a possible choice, class? (Heads nod again.) Any other alternatives?

Sam: It seems to me that you have to be all one way or all the other.

Teacher: Just a minute Sam. As usual we are first looking for the alternatives that there are in the issue. Later we'll try to look at any choice that you may have selected. Any other alternatives, class? (No response.) Well, then, let's list the four possibilities that we have on the board and I'm going to ask that each of you do two things for yourself: (1) see if you can identify any other choices in this issue of honesty and dishonesty, and (2) consider the consequences of each alternative and see which ones you prefer. Later, we will have buzz groups in which you can discuss this and see if you are able to make a choice and if you want to make your choice part of your actual behavior. That is something you must do for yourself.

Ginger: Does that mean that we can decide for ourselves whether we should be honest on tests here?

Teacher: No, that means that you can decide on the value. I personally value honesty; and although you may choose to be dishonest, I shall insist that we be honest on our tests here. In other areas of your life, you may have more freedom to be dishonest, but one can't do anything any time, and in this class I shall expect honesty on tests.

Ginger: But then how can we decide for ourselves? Aren't you telling us what to value?

Sam: Sure, you're telling us what we should do and believe in.

Teacher: Not exactly. I don't mean to tell you what you should value. That's up to you. But I do mean that in this class, not elsewhere necessarily, you have to be honest on tests or suffer certain consequences. I merely mean that I cannot give tests without the rule of honesty. All of you who choose dishonesty as a value may not practice it here, that's all I'm saying. Futher questions anyone?"[11]

From this example we might suggest as analogies: "You are not to be a racist in my class, but elsewhere—that is up to you." Or: "You are not to assault me in my class. I insist that you be peaceful here (after all I'm stronger than you), but if you choose to beat up your other teachers—that's up to you."

A major part of Values Clarification is the set of classroom exercises which exemplify the system in action. These procedures, called "strategies," are easily used vehicles for discussing and clarifying values within the framework of the Values Clarification philosophy. They have been a major reason for the popularity of the approach and even those Christian educators aware of the anti-Christian philosophy of Values Clarification have often used the exercises, under the assumption that they are neutral tools with which to approach the topic of moral education.

Although I have not carefully evaluated each of the seventy-nine strategies in the latest handbook, it is possible to make some useful generalizations about them. The emphasis in all the strategies is on the isolated individual with no reference to anything or anyone outside; the emphasis is on the feelings and desires of the person. There is no real concern with thought, or with external truth, and therefore the assumption is established that values are emotional and intrinsically subjective in nature. There is never any hint throughout the strategies that values, like other forms of reality, exist outside of one's self. Always the message is to look to the self and to feelings. This very general and—it must be said—anti-Christian assumption characterizes all the strategies and makes all of them unacceptable as they stand.

Almost always the strategies focus on the child's self—what does he like, want, feel, what would he *vote for*. This kind of "opinion poll" questioning has become a cultural reflex to Americans today. In contrast, an absolute system of knowledge and values would focus attention on the objective truth, on the external reality which the student attempts to come to know. Thus, a Christian teacher might ask not "What do you love?"; "What do you presently value?"; but "What are those things which are to be loved?"; "What are the things or actions of *greatest* value?" This would be a very different approach, and one which shows how the apparently straightforward VC strategies are far from neutral.

There are many other important and little-noticed expressions of relativism in the strategies of Values Clarification—though we have probably spent enough time on this assumption. One last comment, however. The other major secular approach to moral education which is popular today is Kohlberg's model of the stages of moral development. I have criticized it extensively elsewhere[12]; for the present it will suffice to note that Kohlberg's theory upon careful consideration also can clearly be shown to be a form of relativism and to be based on a variety of ideological assumptions which derive from anti-Christian secular philosophy and which have nothing whatever to do with science or empirical findings.

Assumption 6: Subjectivism

Much of modern psychology is based on the assumption that all we really know are states of the mind or the kind of knowledge found in the physical sciences. As a result it assumes that psychological, moral, and spiritual truth is intrinsically non-objective and non-rational. Closely related to this assumption is the idea that the important thing is to express, understand, and communicate your thoughts and feelings, and to be open to this same thing in others. Again we find a kind of emphasis on the self and on feelings, rather than on others, on God—and on religious, moral, and social truths which exist independently of and outside of ourselves. One of the reasons for the popularity of psychotherapy is undoubtedly its ability to focus on and cultivate the subjective world of the patient and to attribute great worth to the person's feelings and opinions. One symptom of this is the frequent use of the word "feel" where formerly the word "think" would have been used. As in "How do you feel about Iran," or "How do you feel about so-and-so's interpretation of Hamlet," etc. A common expression of this in psychology is found in encounter groups and related therapies where the emphasis is on getting in touch with your feelings, for example primal therapy, or the vogue for touchie-feelie groups in the early 70s which had an extreme emphasis on catharsis. Now, no doubt there is a place for catharsis in psychotherapy—at least up to a point. But, persistently delving into your personal emotions in private or expressing your feelings in extreme ways in public has no basis in scripture or in Church tradition. In particular, public, i.e., group expression can often lead to deep divisions between the person "catharting" and the person being catharted about! The Christian emphasis is always on the outside reality, of God and others—there is no basis for today's almost blatantly narcissistic preoccupation with getting in touch with feelings at the expense of getting in touch with God through prayer, or getting in touch with others through charity.

Assumption 7: Gnosticism (Knowledgism)

This assumption, which is very closely related to subjectivism, is commonly made by contemporary psychology; it involves the belief that if there is any truly better state, i.e., if there is any kind of "salvation," then it comes by knowing, by knowledge. In the older, rational atheism, the better state could come through science and reason. Today, however, the gnostic way is primarily psychological, with an emphasis on self-knowledge. As an example of this category, consider

Jung's psychology, which is described as follows by one of his foremost students, Jolande Jacobi:

> Jungian psychotherapy is . . . a Heilsweg, in the twofold sense of the German word: a way of healing and a way of salvation. It has the power to cure . . . in addition it knows the way and has the means to lead the individual to his "salvation," to the knowledge and fulfillment of his personality, which have always been the aim of spiritual striving. Jung's system of thought can be explained theoretically only up to a certain point; to understand it fully one must have experienced or better still, "suffered" its living action in oneself.
> Apart from its medical aspect, Jungian psychotherapy is thus a system of education and spiritual guidance.[13]

The process of Jungian movement on this path is, Jacobi continues, "Both ethically and intellectually an extremely difficult task, which can be successfully performed only by the fortunate few, those elected and favored by grace."[14] The last stage on the Jungian path, the goal stage of individuation—the salvation—is called by Jung *self-realization*.

I suppose this says it all in a nutshell. But, the gnostic goal is widely found throughout all the psychology which places the achievement of self-realization or actualization as the highest aim of life. In every case the command "seek to know thyself" replaces "seek to love God and others." Many years ago it was noted with approval by the liberal Protestant Harry Emerson Fosdick that psychological integration had replaced salvation.[15] Today integration is called wholeness. In general wherever you find a preoccupation with wholeness and self-actualization, God and Jesus have been put aside for the fundamentally ego goal of self-enhancement. I believe this is often true in the writing of John A. Sanford, whose emphasis is on the Self within three contexts: the Jungian, the ancient mythic, and the Christian—in order of decreasing importance. For example, Sanford writes, "the Self, which is our greatest friend . . ."[16]

Returning to psychological gnosticism for one more example: A recent article by Jack Trux in *Faith at Work* contains the following statements: "The pilgrimage I've been on since that day four years ago has been more of trying to find out who I am than of trying to learn theology or scripture. . . . People who know scripture but who do not know themselves are not useful to me. . . . Jung, as I have come to know him through the writings of John Sanford and Morton Kelsey, have helped me to understand my complexity and my incompleteness and some of what I need for wholeness."[17]

These are most remarkable statements for a supposed Christian. The entire focus is on the problems and feelings of the author—a classic case of the prima-donna complex of self-love and its preoccupation with wholeness. Jesus did not come to make us whole, nor did he come to give us self-knowledge. The ancient world was well aware of the proposal that self-knowledge was the road to salvation. This was the road taken by the Greek philosophers with their concern with "Know thyself" and the assumption that "The unexamined life is not worth living." The Greek way is the way of gnosis and a great deal of the early heresies in the Church were attempts to fuse the gnostic way with the Christian way.

As Christians, we know many reasons why gnosticism cannot work. One is that salvation comes from putting down the very self—the old man—that the gnostics think can be repaired and made whole. The very will which drives people to find wholeness of self is the same self-will that is at the center of our sin—it is this will which must be laid aside in order to do God's will. Furthermore, the way of knowledge is a terribly elitist way since it is restricted to the small number of people with the ability, time, and education to take up the gnostic disciplines. The gnostic way is not open to the poor of the world or to many many others. We may become whole by putting down our old self and putting on Jesus, but this is not certain; what *is* certain is that we must accept Jesus to be saved. And even if we do become whole (whatever that means) we know we are not to *search* for wholeness. We are to search for God and then many other good things, perhaps including wholeness, will also be added as well.

The Common Operator of
Secular Psychological Assumptions:
Two Examples

It will be instructive, I believe, to observe how the preceding seven assumptions operate in the case of two particular contemporary challenges to Christianity. Take abortion as an example. Although it is possible to be an atheist and philosophical naturalist and still be against abortion, the odds are very small. Without a doubt, one of the major bulwarks against abortion and for the value of life is belief in a transcendent God, and the related beliefs of a revealed morality and of judgment after death. Take these away and abortion almost always becomes an acceptable act with no deeply spiritual significance. All the great theistic religions in their orthodox forms reject abortion. The assumption of reductionism also aids the pro-abortion position by allowing a human to be reduced to a strictly natural phenomenon and the fetus to just biological tissue. Individualism favors abortion by assuming that only the autonomous individual counts in a moral decision and that neither the unborn baby, nor society, much less the father have any acceptable moral basis for affecting the decision to abort. Relativism has much the same effect by making all claims to an absolute moral law no longer acceptable—indeed they are made intolerable. In the case of a decision to abort, subjectivism has much the same effect as individualism. The last assumption—gnosticism—makes all moral knowledge and private discovery for the few, and further rejects the authoritative status of scripture and tradition. All this, of course, favors abortion.

As another example, I take a recent article in *Review for Religious* titled "Maximizing Human Potential," by Sheila Murphy, a school psychologist. I suppose the title is a giveaway, but let's look at some of the author's comments, all of which are directed to Catholic sisters in religious communities. Her remarks, however, could just as well be directed toward any religious community, or for that matter to anyone in a Christian family. She begins with a most unchristian comment, but one few seem to reject—namely, that "healthy personality development" is the center of all religious life. The theory of personality which she comes out for is that developed by Abraham Maslow, with its emphasis on self-actualization. In this article, responsible personality growth is understood as self-growth. We will overlook the fact that Maslow's theory was first published in 1954, and that in the intervening twenty-five years it has received many severe criticisms from psychologists of many persuasions—not one of which is even noted by the author. Instead, in loosest vague, optimistic phrases, she sees nothing but good in Maslow. She also appears to think that his ideas are also somehow new and the latest thing. Instead, the author is just another example of Christians getting on a bandwagon that has been going for years and is beginning to grind to a halt. There is nothing, absolutely nothing, more absurd, than to see Christians abandoning their critical capacity and running after secular ideas which are being severely criticized and abandoned by the secularists themselves. The Christians who are doing this, and the disease seems to be especially common these days, are of course neither Christian nor competent.

Near the end of the article the writer declares, "Each sister has the personal responsibility to become the most complete, mature, integrated person that she can become. If this growth cannot be facilitated totally within community, then the sister has an obligation to work this out with her community, or to look elsewhere." Here we see many of the preceding secular assumptions in action. First, the preceding statement and the article are what I call "functionally atheistic," since no mention is even made of God or Jesus, much less of our obligations to God or to religious vows! This neglect of the transcendent and this interpretation of psychological growth as the center of life is also an example of reductionism. Perhaps the major assumption behind all of this is individualism. The entire focus is on the isolated sister; she is urged to get her growth or to leave the community to find it. Relativism is also implicit since the article only speaks of needs with respect to each individual and of *her* judgment of what her needs are. There is an explicit denial that human needs are to be defined by the community, and an implicit denial that God or scripture is relevant by the glaring ommision to any reference to these sources. Subjectivism is present in the entire focus on the individual, on feelings of wholeness. Gnosticism is apparent in such comments as this: "Development through the hierarchy of needs (which culminates according to Maslow in self-actualization) is precipitated by knowledge, especially self-knowledge, and it is for this reason that the development is difficult." This self-knowledge is presumably to arise primarily from reading psychologists, from self-reflection, and from talking to psychologists. In short, all systems emphasizing self-actualization are classic examples of modernity, in which salvation is placed in this life—is made imminent instead of transcendent.

As a third example take gay liberation and with it the strong contemporary emphasis on the androgynous or unisex life style with its criticism of traditional sex roles. Here again atheism comes in to support homosexuality. A good atheist certainly doesn't have to worry about Church tradition here or about what scripture says. Reductionism helps, since love is reduced primarily to sex and such an obviously simple biological activity does not need to be considered in the light of its religious, spiritual, or even much of a social context. Individualism helps greatly, since the isolated person is the sole center of legitimate moral choice. Relativism also provides strong support, since if morality is relative, what's there to fret about? Subjectivism and gnosticism both add further support, if any were needed, since they both lead to the supposed discovery of and the valuing of the androgynous nature in every one. This wonderful androgynous you is to be warmly cherished. And if, after all, you are psychologically speaking both hetero- and homosexual, then why not explore the *full* you: why not make all the contradictory yous an integrated *whole* by living in such a way as to express all your potential? Thus bisexuality receives considerable support from these last two assumptions.

The push toward the androgynous personality is often very directly advocated by secular psychology. For example, while I was preparing this paper an advertising flyer came across my desk from a major publisher which has branched out into films for use in psychology courses. These films, which replace lectures, are typically presented as the latest in scientific psychology. One of this company's films is called "Sex Role Development," and it is clearly hostile to traditional sex roles, which are described as stereotypes instilled in Americans. The advertising copy says that this film presents "the ways in which some people are currently trying to find better models for human behavior." The film ends with a positive portrayal of children raised in androgynous or sex-role reversal environments. Such material is not at all atypical, for I have found introductory psychology texts which actively push the unisex model of personality as an ideal—while describing the evidence as the newest frontier of scientific research.

In concluding, I should point out that the use of unisex vocabulary is almost unanimous today in psychology with respect to the roles of mother and father. These two powerful traditional roles, deeply rooted in the language and theology of scripture are rarely distinguished but instead are collapsed into the term "parent." But, enough of all this!

All these examples show how modern secular psychology has through its assumptions created an interpretive framework of human nature which has profound anti-Christian consequences. In short, one of the best ways to lose your faith is to uncritically accept modern psychology.

Toward a Christian Psychology

Now with respect to psychology all is not bleak: there is on the intellectual horizon a new kind of psychology which is just emerging. I believe it can be best described as "Christian" psychology. It is the work of several Christian psychologists, and it offers the possibility of a real challenge to the secular stuff. Indeed, in the long run, I believe it will be possible to baptize large portions of secular psychology so as to permanently remove its anti-Christian thrust. After all, if the threat of Aristotle to the faith could be dealt with by St. Thomas Aquinas, then there is hope that this newest expression of the Greek mentality can also be defused. In any case, something like this is absolutely needed, since psychology is here to stay. Unless a

Christian model of psychology is found, Christianity will continue to lose millions of souls to the message of secular psychology. It is not enough to diagnose the modernist ailment: we need to work on the cure.

Very briefly, I would like to outline Christian psychology.

Point One: Christian psychology is based on the assumption of the existence of God, specifically of a Trinitarian God. This point, however obvious perhaps, must be boldly stated, not only to expose and challenge the hidden assumption of atheism existing in most contemporary psychology, but also to make clear that this assumption has major positive consequences for psychology as a whole. The acceptance of God enlarges and enriches psychology by making religious life relevant and interpretable. The relationship of God and man, and in particular the nature of spiritual life, now become topics of discussion, topics in great need of understanding. The existing secular and materialist psychology, to the extent it is in fact valid, is not a threat to a Christian psychology any more than mathmatics, physics, or biology are threats. Indeed, a sound Christian psychology will have to be built on a solid understanding of natural man—most especially of sinful or fallen man. So the first point to make is that a Christian psychology would be both a bigger and a better psychology—that is, a broader, deeper, and truer psychology.

Point Two: A Christian psychology (at least an orthodox one!) comes with a clear and well worked out morality and value system. Now every psychology, most especially any form of psychotherapy, always has a value system and a morality. This issue cannot be avoided. The great problem with the present secular humanist psychologists is that although they do acknowledge the inevitability of a value system, they have not clearly said what theirs *is*. Further, if they *did* explicate their value system, it would become clear that it is often *ad hoc*, extremely inconsistent, and frequently at odds with the values of their patients. The commonest value system seems to be of a permissive relativist type. Now whatever can be said in favor of relativism, I don't think it has ever been a successful ethical system in any society for more than a few decades at most.

Relativism is simply based on so much sand that its incoherence soon destroys those who live by it. But Christian values and morality, which are similar to many other traditional moral systems, are clear, familiar to many, and generally held in high esteem. This moral system thus gives a Christian psychology an enormous advantage over the innumerable competing, secular value systems.

A summary of how theistic psychotherapy would differ in its values from today's secular humanist approach is shown in Table 1. This table with a few very small changes is taken from an important article by Professor Allen Bergin.[19] Bergin is a devout Mormon with a deep commitment to Jesus who is also a prominent clinical psychologist. (He recently has publicly acknowledged his faith and its relevance for psychotherapy, as he understands it.)

Point Three: A Christian psychology introduces fundamental new concepts and practices into psychology and counseling. For example, both prayer and fasting have been used by various Christian psychologists. In addition, whatever healing takes place is understood to occur as the result of the Holy Spirit and not due to the gifts or qualities of the therapist. Indeed the invoking of the power of the Holy Spirit is an enormous factor, unique to Christian counseling, and its effects are so evident that the dramatic changes reported often make traditional psychotherapy look quite inadequate.

Of perhaps even greater interest are specifically Christian psychological concepts which can greatly enrich an understanding of psychological change. For example take the notion of forgiveness, an idea central to the Christian life. Forgiveness is a powerful force for healing. Yet no secular theory of psychology mentions, much less uses, forgiveness. After all, in the secular world of the ego, to forgive is a sign of weakness, or perhaps it is just irrelevant. In secular therapy one can *only forget, not forgive*. In any case, forgiveness with its many benefits is not part of any secular approach to psychotherapy or counseling.

Closely related to forgiveness is the notion of responsibility for our actions, and above all being responsible for our harmful

Table 1
Theistic vs. Clinical and Humanistic Values

Theistic

1. God is supreme. Humility, acceptance of (divine) authority and obedience (to the will of God) are virtues.

2. Personal identity is eternal and derived from the divine. Relationship with God defines self-worth.

3. Self-control, in terms of absolute values. Strict morality. Universal ethics.

4. Love of God and of others, affection and self-transcendence primary. Service and self-sacrifice central to personal growth.

5. Committed marriage, fidelity and loyalty. Emphasis on procreation and family life as integrative factors.

6. Personal responsibility for own harmful actions and changes in them. Accept guilt, suffering and contrition as keys to change. Restitution for harmful effects.

7. Forgiveness of others who cause distress (including parents) completes the therapeutic restoration of self.

8. Knowledge by faith and self-effort. Meaning and purpose derived from spiritual insight. Intellectual knowledge inseparable from the emotional and spiritual. Ecology of knowledge.

Clinical-Humanistic

1. Man is supreme. The self is aggrandized. Autonomy and rejection of external authority are virtues.

2. Identity is ephemeral and mortal. Relationships with self and others define self-worth.

3. Self-expression, in terms of relative values. Flexible morality. Situation ethics.

4. Personal needs and self-actualization primary. Self-satisfaction central to personal growth.

5. Open marriage or no marriage. Emphasis on self-gratification or recreational sex without long-term responsibilities.

6. Others responsible for our problems and changes. Minimize guilt and relieve suffering before experiencing its meaning. Apology for harmful effects.

7. Acceptance and expression of accusatory feelings is sufficient.

8. Knowledge by self-effort alone. Meaning and purpose derived from reason and intellect. Intellectual knowledge for itself. Isolation of the mind from the rest of life.

*Adapted from Bergin, *Journal of Consulting Clinical Psychology* 1980, 48, p. 100.

actions, even though we felt justified in hurting, hating, or striking back at another. This important idea has been especially well discussed by the Christian psychologist Stanley Strong. I will summarize and quote from his astute analysis.

> The concept that people are responsible for their own acts is under heavy attack today and has been badly damaged by psychology. Recent research on how people account causally for their behavior shows a wide endorsement of the philosophy that people are responsible for their acts only if other causes in the environment or in their past cannot be found (Strong 1976). For example, if I yell at my wife, hit her, and, in general, plot to make her life miserable, I will not hold myself personally responsible for my actions if I perceive that she is doing the same things to me. Her actions justify my actions. Similarly, if I believe my actions arise from my mother's shoddy treatment of me in the past or represent "uncontrollable" impulses, I will not hold myself personally responsible but will feel that my acts are justified and I myself am the victim of these unfortunate events.

Strong continues:

> The "justified commission" theory of responsibility is directly counter to the teachings of scripture. Both Old and New Testaments rebuke the idea of justified commission and repeatedly assert that we are responsible to God for what we do. The oldest story in the Bible proclaims the principle. When Adam and Eve ate the forbidden fruit and God confronted them, Adam responded by pointing out that Eve gave him the fruit and God gave him Eve. He was not personally responsible (Gn 3:12). God cut through Adam's justified commission theory and condemned him to work and death. He held Adam responsible for his actions, and He holds us responsible for our actions today. A first task for the Christian counselor is to counteract the client's theories of justified commission. . . .
> In Christian counseling the conviction of sin means free-

ing behavior from having to justify it by current pressures, historical causes, and unintentionality. By fully owning their actions and the consequences of their actions, clients are led to the need for forgiveness and change. Focusing on sin (attitudes of pride and selfishness) as the cause of problems provides the client with causes that can be changed. Repentance mobilizes the will to change. New nonsinful actions are richly rewarded by a new self-respect, positive values, and the joy of doing God's will. The child of God has been equipped to assume his place as a responsible being.[20]

Strong's analysis of the Christian basis for the need to accept responsibility for our actions and to reject our justification is more thorough and significant than these quotes can convey. However, enough has been given to show that a Christian rationale for responsibility provides a relevant and powerful concept for a theory of counseling.

Point Four: A Christian psychology is Christ-centered. Because God was made man and dwelt among us, Christian psychology has available a model of how to live. Now the Incarnation may be a scandal, particularly to philosophers and to others who prefer a distant or abstract God. But for psychology this fact is of enormous positive significance. Jesus, as the perfect expression of God's will in human form, provides the model with whom we can identify.

However brief this treatment of Christian psychology has been, it should be clear that much of Christian theology has direct and powerful and at present very distinctive, indeed novel, psychological significance. And the preceding psychology is only a small part of what appears to be applicable to psychotherapy—and to the large realm of spiritual psychology. (For example, the psychological barriers to prayer, etc., remain largely unexplored.)

In conclusion, I think that the immense harm that contemporary psychology has done to many Christians can in part be offset by making them critically aware of the dangers. But, as always, the best defense is a good offense. In this instance that means the development of a powerful Christian alternative which can absorb and baptize the legitimate secular psychological material by providing a sound new framework and many new concepts and useful techniques. In short, such a Christian psychology would provide both the best conceptualized and most easily understood criticism of secular anti-Christian psychology, and would also offer a positive alternative with which to repell and replace the secular gospel.

Notes

1. Abraham Maslow, ed., *Motivation and Personality* (New York: Harper and Row, 1970), p. 164.

2. William H. Masters, et al., *The Pleasure Bond* (Boston: Little, Brown and Co., 1975), pp. 4-5.

3. Robert Hogan and David Schroeder, "The Joy of Sex for Children and Other Modern Fables," *Character* 1, no. 10 (1980), p. 3.

4. *Ibid.*, p. 4.

5. *Ibid.*

6. Wayne Dyer, *Your Erroneous Zones* (Scranton: Funk and Wagnalls Co., 1976), p. 198.

7. Eric Berne, *Games People Play: The Psychology of Human Relationships* (New York: Grove Press, 1964), p. 182.

8. Sidney B. Simon, Leland W. Howe, and Howard Kirschenbaum, *Values Clarification: A Handbook of Practical Strategies for Teachers and Students*, 2nd ed. (New York: Hart Publishing Co., 1978), p. 18.

9. Louis E. Raths, Merill Harmin, and Sydney B. Simon, *Values and Teaching* (Columbus, Ohio: Charles E. Merrill Publishing Co., 1966), pp. 143-49.

10. Nicholas Wolterstorff, *Educating for Responsible Action* (Grand Rapids: Eerdmans, 1980).

11. Raths, et al., *op. cit.*, pp. 114-15.

12. Paul C. Vitz, "A Critique of Kohlberg," *New Oxford Review*, 1980.

13. Jolande Jacobi, *The Psychology of C.G. Jung* (New Haven: Yale University Press, 1973), p. 60.

14. *Ibid.*, p. 127.

15. Paul C. Vitz, *Psychology As Religion: The Cult of Self Worship* (Grand Rapids: Wm. B. Eerdmans Publishing Co., (1977), p. 70.

16. John A. Sanford, *Healing and Wholeness* New York: Paulist Press, 1977), p. 94.

17. Jack Trux, "Profile of a Pilgrimage," *Faith At Work* 43, no. 1 (1980), p. 13.

18. Sheila Murphy, "Maximizing Human Potential," *Review for Religious* 38, no. 1 (1979), p. 91-104.

19. Allen Bergin, *Journal of Consulting Clinical Psychology* 48 (1980), p. 100.

20. Stanley R. Strong, *Counseling and Values* 21 (February 1977), pp. 89-128.

Response

Russell P. Spittler

I am very grateful to Professor Paul Vitz for his presentation. Here are a few responses mainly augmenting the points he has made.

I mention first two perspectives found in two authors whom I find helpful in understanding the invasion of secular humanism into the culture of which we are a part. These two are very different books, but I think they are very helpful in understanding where we are at this point in the twentieth century.

The first is Carl F.H. Henry's book titled *Remaking the Modern Mind*. That book, published by Eerdmans in 1946, was an early benchmark in the post-war evangelical renaissance; the work deserves to be better known and more widely used. No doubt playing upon J. Herman Randall's classic survey *The Making of the Modern Mind* (Houghton Mifflin, 1926), Carl Henry in this volume itemizes four theses of secular humanism that describe the *content* of humanism just as Paul Vitz' paper has given to us its *assumptions*.

Henry critiques these humanist doctrines mainly from the standpoint of a philosopher of religion.

The first of the four doctrines of humanism is *the inevitability of human progress*. Human progress, it is thought, is inevitable. It's just a question of which way or how fast or how soon or what best facilitates it. Progress in any case is inevitable. Such thinking spread broadly over the sciences, fueled by nineteenth-century evolutionary thought.

The second point is *the inherent goodness of man*. Not the sinfulness of mankind, as the Christian tradition would affirm. Not evil at heart, man is viewed as essentially and inherently good. The human person is worthwhile and innately good. On such assumptions, progress is assured.

The third plank is *the uniformity of nature*. The continuity of scientific law in the universe is unbroken; hence miracles are impossible. There can be no such thing as a miracle, for nature is uniform and natural law is unbroken. The task of science is to discover and utilize those laws.

The fourth point is *the ultimate animality of man*. The human person is merely the highest form of animal life, and the form and style of human behavior only tops off the zoological scale.

Henry's critique of this foursquare humanist plank points to the invidious centripetalization of technological advances appar--ent in the serialization—within a generation—of global war. Like no other episode in history, the Nazi experience disclosed a moral accompaniment to the alleged "animality of man": moral progress was clearly not so inevitable as technological growth. The Cross could be offered as justification for the ovens.

A second perspective, from a very different viewpoint, converges on the critiques offered by Carl Henry and Paul Vitz. I refer to Donald Gelpi's work *Experiencing God* (Paulist Press, 1978), subtitled "A Theology of Human Experience." The volume is a very hefty paperback, written (as was Henry's book) by a philosopher of religion.

Fr. Gelpi's work is the most thoroughgoing statement of charismatic theology in print. Heribert Mühlen's works, once they are translated from German, may require eventual modification of that assessment. But at the moment it is fair to speak of Donald Gelpi as the leading published American charismatic theologian. (His theology of the Holy Spirit is forthcoming.)

What strikes me about Fr. Gelpi's work is his line of approach. Very much interested in the American intellectual tradition, Fr. Gelpi came to believe that if he were to produce a theology which at once is American, Catholic, and charismatic, he would have to address himself to the particular shape of American thought. To do so, he read through the American literary and philosophical tradition. As a result, he found the notion of "experience" to be the controlling motif in American thought.

Here is a quote that catches the flavor of Gelpi's approach:

As I pondered the result of the research I had done in the history of American religious philosophy, certain themes began to assume greater speculative importance than others. It seemed to me, for example, that the Augustinian cast of Calvinist theology had shaped American religious attitudes profoundly. It had found a philosophical echo in a succession of Platonic or quasi-Platonic approaches to human religious experience: Edwards, Emerson, Brownson, Abbot, Santayana, Whitehead. And Platonic preoccupations had in turn endowed American religious experience with a penchant for individualism, subjectivism, personal mysticism.

I also realized, however, that Platonism was only one way of philosophizing in the American mode. Indeed, the more I pondered the development of American speculation, the more convinced I became that it had been given to Jonathan Edwards to strike the dominant chord in American religious philosophy: that of preoccupation with the structure of experience. From Edwards on, almost every major American thinker has wrestled with the question: What does it mean to experience anything? What does it mean to undergo a religious experience? Platonic solutions to both questions had, of course, been offered. But there were other solutions as well, solutions that provided important correctives to the inadequacies of Platonic theory. If my insight into the genius of the American speculative tradition was correct, any attempt to construct a systematic philosophy or theology in the American mode, would have to adopt experience as its central category.

I propose that the selfist psychologies described by Paul Vitz emerge predictably from the mix of secular humanism (notably its insistence on inherent human goodness) with the American penchant for "experience." What is selfism but the experiential pursuit of personal progress thought inevitable on the one hand and unaided by miraculous forces outside the self on the other?

We do not write off the psychotherapeutic enterprise, but we are cautious about some of the styles and methods which are used in the process. As I have learned mainly from my associations with the Catholic charismatic community, we need to preserve a sense of mystery about personhood. We cannot fully fathom the depths of human personality. And there is always something we will never know about human beings. Mystery persists. . . .

What Paul Vitz has suggested should yield caution about the invasion of these same humanistic assumptions into certain sectors of the evangelical and the charismatic movements— even within my own classical Pentecostal tradition. Certainly dangers abound for self-centered individualism, for thinking that religion is only between God and me—as if there were no responsibilities to others who are members of the community. A restored sense of community will correct that.

Similarly, the integrity of external religious authority is corrupted by the invasion of subjectivism into charismatic traditions, as if there were not an objective revelation of God which gives adequate saving knowledge.

There is further the threat of modified varieties of gnosticism, a prideful sense of possession of insight that lets one be above all others somehow in the style of knowing and experiencing God. Against such experiential gnosticism is the supremacy of love—a message which is the essence of First Corinthians.

A final threat to charismatics lies in the corruption of sudden wealth. How odd that some who grew up in the storefront churches of the depression, now successful in business, forget their past—which is the present of many—in proclaiming the gospel of affluence currently in vogue.

I make a plea. Will somebody please help in distinguishing for us the role of the self in Christian growth? I came to Ann Arbor with great interest in part to hear and meet Mark Kinzer and to get a copy of his book, *The Self-Image of a Christian: Humility and Self-Esteem* (Servant Books, 1980). On the other hand, I am told that there is something wrong with an interest in self.

There is a self which is to be denied and crucified. There is, on the other hand, a self which is the measure by which we are to love the neighbor. There is a self that is good, there is some self that is bad. There is an introspective navel-gazing that is not right in the Christian tradition, but there is a healthy self-examination as well.

Would somebody who knows more about it than I, please nuance the idea of the self for us and help us to know which self is good and which self is bad? Maybe in Paul Vitz's development of a Christian psychology that distinction will emerge.

Finally, I reflect on a few biblical texts brought to mind by Paul Vitz's address.

First, John 5: I am unwilling to surrender to the humanists the beautiful concept of wholeness. If they've got a hold on it, I want it back; it belongs to the New Testament. I hear Jesus saying to the man at the side of the pool, "Wilt thou be made whole?" Beautiful term. And the man crippled for decades says, in effect, "I have no man to help me, but when I am moving towards the pool someone else is there ahead of me."

According to my sense of understanding what salvation is, wholeness is a good biblical way to describe it: wholeness of body and soul and spirit, wholeness in community, wholeness in personal relations, even wholeness in history—which implies the necessary eschatological dimension of Christianity. By that I mean, any wholeness not achieved within human time looks for fulfillment at the appearance of the Lord at what we've come to call the Second Coming. So I for one cannot do without the Christian doctrine of the future. Wholeness is a concept I will fight for as a biblical person; I will not give it up to the humanists. Healing, health, wholeness are linguistic cognates, but they are theological bedfellows as well.

Second, Matthew 16: "Whom do men say that I, the Son of Man, am?" Oh, they responded, Jeremiah, or Elijah, or John the Baptist, or one of the prophets. Then Jesus asks, "Whom say ye that I am?" "You are the Messiah, the Son of the Living God." "And I say unto you, you are Peter. . . ." The beautiful thing about that is that we come to know ourselves by first knowing who he is. This point is often made by Robert Frost (the charismatic teacher—not the poet). That is the best way to self-knowledge and to understanding ourselves.

Finally, 1 Corinthians 8: Here is a passage that turns all gnosticisms upside down on their heads: "If anyone imagines that he knows something, he does not yet know as he ought to know. But if one loves God . . ."—how would you complete it? I would have said, "one is loved by God." The text, however, runs this way: "But if one loves God, one is known by him."

It is far more important to be known by God than to know any kind of thing that we can know. To be loved by God, to be the object of the love of God, is one of the most insurmountable experiences of the Christian reality that I can imagine. According to Christian theology, there is only one true human being who ever existed, and that is the Man Jesus Christ. So speaks the book of Hebrews as I hear it. We humans are persons who rise out of sin and by God's grace will eschatologically move into God's design for humanity. Our forebears, Adam and Eve, were people who started with that ideal humanity but who fell and lost by sin the ideal humanity God had given in the beginning. Only One was truly human.

The challenge Professor Paul Vitz has given is to fashion an unprecedented psychological model which will fully utilize the resources of theistic presuppositions. I pray God that he will give Professor Vitz the courage and the insight to develop a fully Christian psychology.

Response

Daniel Sinisi

First of all, I loved Dr. Vitz's paper. That is the most refreshing psychological teaching that I have heard, and it gives me great hope that God can take this science of psychology and use it as a valuable service within the Christian churches. As Paul Vitz went through the assumptions of secular psychology—aetheism, naturalism, reductionism, individualism, relativism, subjectivism, gnosticism—I recognized many assumptions I have seen in church life, especially among priests, seminarians, and religious.

I want to first make a note about relativism. In teaching moral theology, and in reading book after book in the field, I see the disintegration of objective moral values. In the Catholic Church, the clearest example in this century is the Catholic Theological Society's document of a few years ago, *Human Sexuality*. I think the authors ruled out rape and incest. They thought that just about every other type of sexual behavior is permissible in certain circumstances. In another recent book, one entitled *Sexual Morality*, the author distinguishes between what he calls "ontic" evil and "moral" evil. He suggests many areas of sexual behavior are "ontically" wrong, but are not morally wrong because of circumstances. This is the same kind of reasoning that is leading to the disintegration of moral values among people who should be upholding them.

One theory abroad today which greatly contributes to this disintegration of moral values is the idea of "consequentialism," the notion that an act is moral if it doesn't hurt somebody else. But this view ignores the first commandment—our duty to love God. It also ignores the fact that *all* sin has social effects. Sin affects not only me but my neighbor as well.

Another theory very much connected with the assumption of relativism is the idea that if you are open about something, sincere about something—if you have come out of the closet about it—then somehow it's alright. But sincere and open adultery is still wrong. Adolf Hitler was open and sincere, but he did great evil.

I'd like to turn now to the second part of my response: my particular experiences with religious and seminarians. I was dean of students in a major seminary nine years. I've done much retreat work and counseling with religious. When I was a graduate student in theology, the book that had the greatest impact one year was *The Secular City* by Harvey Cox. The next year, the prominent book on campus was *Honest to God* by Bishop Robinson. The following year, everyone was reading the "death of God" theologies. Every one of those books in its own way attacked the supernatural dimension of Christianity. . . .

I want to mention some incidents with seminarians and religious. Some of the popular songs in liturgy in those days were secular. One of the songs we sang frequently at communion was "Bridge Over Troubled Waters." It's hard to see how that song has any transcendent dimension to it. Seminarians would say to me, "Father, I don't understand the place that confession or the sacrament of penance could have in my life because the confession of sins gives you a bad self-image." . . . One seminarian came to me several years ago and said, "What do you think about this? I got a letter from a seminarian friend in the Midwest. He's working in a social ministry with a young woman, and he believes they need to have sexual intercourse so that they can have unity in their social ministry." It's subjectivism, relativism at its highest.

In the sixties, social concerns were paramount. As the seventies went on, emotions got the most attention. Seminarians were constantly depressed, discouraged, self-pitying. Introspection was a major thing. There was constant analysis of feelings, constant analysis of what I'm like, am I growing, does somebody like me? This was accompanied by an overemphasis in individual spiritual direction. Individual spiritual direction is not a bad thing, but at the seminary it became very tied in with what Dr. Vitz was saying about individual-ism. The attitude became "nobody can understand me except my spiritual director." . . .

I was at a workshop recently which purported to help leaders of religious communities become more effective Chris-tian leaders. The primary sources used were transactional analysis, Maslow, various psychological theories of personal-ity, and Kohlberg. One of the major points of the workshop was that modern theories of leadership have dismissed the characteristics approach, that is, the idea that personal charac-teristics or qualities are important for determining what makes good leaders. This is in complete contradiction to what Paul says to Timothy. The workshop concentrated on various psy-chological and management theories, and yet that very week, in the Liturgical Office, we were reading St. Augustine's teach-ing about pastors, which stresses personal qualities. There was no mention of that, no mention of Gregory the Great's teaching on pastoral care, or *The Character of a Christian Leader*, by St. Bonaventure.

I mention these "horror stories" to show that the kind of individualism, subjectivism, relativism that Dr. Vitz talked about has gotten like a cancer into the Church. It has gotten into many of the people who by vows are committed to dedi-cating themselves to the church.

Why did this happen to so many priests, religious, and semi-narians? I want to very briefly suggest nine things that must be present in Christian life, and which to a large extent weren't present in the lives of a generation of religious. I believe that their absence has led to the psychological errors that we have been discussing. This is not a complete list, but I believe that these nine things are essential to correct the problems we have. . . .

The first point is the need for religious truth. In many reli-gious communities, truth has become unclear. There has not been constant pastoral teaching of Christian truth, gospel teaching, and, in the case of religious, teaching about the val-ues of religious community. However, teaching about religious truth in itself is not sufficient. Many priests, religious, and seminarians have received good teaching, and yet are still vulnerable to errors. Thus, while proclamation of religious truth is essential, other areas are just as crucial.

The second area is the experience of God. I am not speaking about a momentary kind of experience, but a constant experience of a personal relationship with God, the power of God, and the power of the gospel. When we don't have that personal relationship with the living God, religion becomes impersonal or legalistic, and we become prone to error. A sense of God is needed for a sense of sin. As Pope Pius XII observed years ago, the modern world has lost a sense of sin. The reason is that the world has lost the sense of God.

Third, we need basic ongoing conversion—daily repentance. A lot of us in religious life forgot that. The fact that we have taken vows does not free us from the need to repent for sin in our lives. Also, since there is a need for basic ongoing conversion, there is a constant need for inspired preaching.

Fourth, we need to be clear about what is the true source of evil. I'm a Roman Catholic theologian and I've just rediscovered Adolph Tanquerey's *The Spiritual Life*, the great American Catholic classic on the spiritual life published more than fifty years ago. Tanquerey shows that the source of evil is sin. Evil does not come from people being unable to understand one another, or from this or that issue. The realities behind sin are the three classic enemies—the world, the flesh, and the devil. I was recently reading Aelied Squire's very fine book *Asking the Fathers*. In it is an excellent chapter on spiritual warfare where he reminds us that spiritual warfare is a constant part of the Christian life, and that we have to aggressively fight sin and the world, the flesh, and the devil.

These last three areas—the experience of God, basic ongoing conversion, and clarity about the source of evil—are all supernatural realities. The secularization in theology, the kinds of things that *The Secular City* and *Honest to God* represent, moves completely against these ideas.

My fifth point is taken from the last chapter of Harry Blamires' *The Christian Mind*. The title of the chapter is "The Sacramental Cast"; in it he talks about a healthy kind of Christian romanticism. In some sense, what God has done with the gift of sexuality is to open us up to the greater things of life, basically the fact that only God can satisfy us. It is tragic that the good purposes of sex have been so distorted in our culture. What sexuality should show us is that there is a need for a passion for God, a vision of God and his plan.

The sixth point is a suggestion for combatting the introspection that is so common today. We combat it by living in the presence of God, a traditional, spiritual teaching. Self-examination is not done by oneself, but in the presence of God as well as in the context of Christian community living.

My seventh point is the importance of building solid Christian communities, for it is impossible to live the gospel as an isolated individual. I will mention only one example of the strength of community life. On St. Francis Day at our monastery, one of the things we did was to take time to honor each person there. Our purpose was to affirm how God has worked in a few areas of each man's life. A priest was present who was visiting us from another house in the community; he had been a Franciscan for over forty years. When we finished honoring each other, he got up and said, "You know, I can't tell you how much I have been affected by this. If we can have this kind of support and respect and love in the houses in our province, many of our problems wouldn't be there."

The eighth area is the need for directive authority. Harry Blamires points out that many of us have difficulty seeing how love and power can be combined. I saw the truth of this at the workshop for leaders of religious communities. When someone mentioned directive authority, the response was that you can't stress it because authority is often oppressive and domineering. And yet, such directive authority is needed to guide God's people.

Finally, we need to accept the whole gospel. I plead that we come to see that it isn't a matter of sexual morality *or* social morality, a matter of personal righteousness *or* social righteousness. We leave ourselves prone to many errors when we leave out part of the gospel. One of the reasons we are having so many problems with sexual morality today is because people pick and choose among the social encylicals of the church. If you can pick and choose that, then why can't you pick and choose in the whole area of sexual morality? We must see that the virtues are interrelated.

In conclusion, I hope that Christian teaching and formation will return to the true nature of religious teaching as found in Sirach 39:1-11, a passage about teaching the Word of God. If Christian teachers will do that, if they will teach the Word of God and avoid pop psychology and leave to people like Paul Vitz the development of Christian psychology, we will not have a lot of the mess we have today.

CHAPTER FIVE

Modern Approaches to Scriptural Authority

Stephen B. Clark

In the course of this conference, a picture has emerged of the Christian people maintaining their way of life but under constant challenge, and even attack. Some of the challenge arises simply from the undermining effects of the great change in human life produced by technological society. Much of the attack, however, is consciously directed by proponents of modern ideologies who would like to replace the Christian way of life with another approach. Many of these proponents of modern ideologies do not identify themselves as Christians, but much of the attack is consciously or semi-consciously carried on by theological secularists, members of the Christian churches, who advocate these ideologies and who see the refashioning of Christianity by eliminating much of its orthodox content as its only hope for survival. Those Christians who are still orthodox in belief and practice face the task of maintaining a distinctive way of life.

This paper treats the question of modern scripture scholarship in the context sketched by the colloquy. It will begin with a brief discussion of the strategic importance of scripture for both Catholics and Evangelicals for the maintenance of the

Christian way of life. Then it will analyze three common modern approaches to biblical exegesis, and will focus on the way in which one of these approaches, the secular historical one, undermines the ability of Christians to maintain their way of life in the modern world. It will conclude with some pastoral recommendations for the area.

The Strategic Importance of Scripture

A common way of life has to be based on something authoritative. For a way of life to be common, there have to be norms accepted by everyone. If there is no common authority accepted by a group of people as standing behind the common norms, their way of life will not survive much challenge. The authority behind the Christian way of life is God, the one who has revealed it and enjoined it. Insofar as it can be found expressed in a way which people can read and discuss, the will of God is written in scripture. Scripture, therefore, is the authority behind the Christian way of life. Scripture contains norms which all Christians must accept and be bound by, and the authoritative account of the events or facts behind those norms. In this respect, Christians are different from Communists, for instance. Communists have a common way of life and an authority behind it, but the authority is more the party than it is the writings of Marx and Lenin (and Mao). Even the Catholic church, which gives the most authority among Christian churches to church leadership to make judgments about how Christian doctrine is to be understood and applied, would hold firmly that that authority is bound by what is in the scripture and is not permitted to add anything or subtract anything from the deposit of faith which was completed by the time of the death of the last apostle. Since scripture is the preeminent written authority, the approach to scripture becomes even more crucial now as the Christian way of life is under attack. Unless Christians can find authority in scripture their way of life will not stand. An attack on the authority of scripture cannot but be an attack on the Christian way of life.

Let me add here a personal observation. Expounding on the

place of scripture in the Christian life can sound very theoretical, but it is a practical pastoral matter. Perhaps there was a time when the role of scripture might have been less immediately of practical concern than now, because in the Catholic church and in many Protestant churches the normal churchgoer would have been inclined to trust what their priest or minister had to say about moral matters. But when one discusses with Christians nowadays whether to engage in homosexual relations or not, or whether to fornicate with their boyfriends or not, or whether or not to commit adultery with someone else's wife, who no longer loves her husband, of course, one often discovers that they have heard almost every opinion on the subject from the collection of priests or ministers that they have discussed it with. In such a time, the matter of how one approaches scripture is very practical. It is also very practical when groups of Christians come together to begin something new, like a Christian community, and have to determine on what basis to make decisions about what they should do together in every area of human life.

As has been observed throughout this colloquy, the Christian way of life has been undermined very seriously by theological secularists, people who profess to be Christians but who reinterpret Christianity in a way that empties it of its core content—the supernatural intervention of God in the world in Christ—and that undercuts its authority by denying and ignoring the authoritative revelation of God as expressed in the teachings of Christ and his apostles. As has also been observed, theological secularism has seriously affected not only the major Protestant churches throughout the world, but also Catholics and Evangelicals, descendants of people who in the nineteenth and first half of the twentieth centuries strongly opposed it. Among both groups, one of the first channels of penetration has been in biblical scholarship. Biblical scholarship is perhaps the quickest place to begin undermining the Christian way of life for Protestants, but it is likewise a good place to begin with to work on Catholics. In fact, in recent years it has been an increasingly effective place to affect Catholicism because of the biblical and liturgical renewals and their work to restore the place of scripture in Catholic life.

Many Evangelicals believe that since the Bible has held a different place in Catholicism than in Protestantism, Catholics should not be affected the same way in this area as Protestants. The differences between the Catholics and Evangelicals in their view of scripture do not, however, affect the role of the authority of scripture in establishing a common way of life. Catholics and Evangelicals differ in the way in which they regard tradition and church authority as authorities in addition to scripture. Catholics would consider the consensus of the Fathers or of tradition as a whole as well as the dogmatic definitions of the pastoral authorities of the universal church (the popes and ecumenical councils) as having binding authority in the interpretation of Christian teaching. But they do not think that those authorities are permitted to contradict scripture. Some Catholic theologians do not believe that they can even contain anything of divine revelation that is not also contained in scripture. Certainly they do not believe that they can replace it. And both the Vatican Council in the sixth chapter of the *Constitution on Revelation* and the liturgical movement as approved in the 24th section of the Vatican Council's *Constitution on the Liturgy* have stressed that Christian teaching should normally be based on the explanation of scripture (and not, for instance, on an explanation of the encyclicals of popes). For a Catholic, church authority and tradition are important for the proper interpretation of scripture, but they are not a replacement for scripture. The teaching of Christian doctrine and the Christian way of life is primarily based on the scripture.

There are other differences between Catholics and Evangelicals. Catholics would be much more inclined to stress the authority of the pastoral leaders of the early church in establishing the canonicity of the books that are now contained in our scripture, although the Catholic teaching is by no means that the authority of the church establishes the authority of the scriptures. God establishes the authority of the scriptures. As the Vatican Council says, "Holy Mother Church, relying on the belief of the apostles, holds that the books of both the Old and New Testaments in their entirety, with all their parts, are sacred and canonical because, having been written under the inspiration of the Holy Spirit, they have God as their author and have been handed on as such to the Church herself." There likewise is a certain difference in the area of inerrancy. The Vatican Council taught that "since everything asserted by the inspired authors or sacred writers must be held to be asserted by the Holy Spirit, it follows that the books of scripture must be acknowledged as teaching firmly, faithfully, and without error that truth which God wanted put into the sacred writings for the sake of our salvation." It did not teach the absolute inerrancy that many Evangelicals nowadays would hold out for, although many other Evangelicals would find themselves in agreement with the Vatican Council here, and many Catholics a hundred years ago would have held to absolute inerrancy.

Nonetheless, as the above quotes make clear, there is no difference between Catholics and Evangelicals in their basic view of scripture. Both hold to the traditional Christian view of inspiration and consequently both hold that the scripture comes from God through the Holy Spirit and is the Word of God. Both hold that the New Testament was written under apostolic authority and therefore is to be accepted as foundational to Christian life and teaching. Both hold to the canonicity of scripture and therefore to its position as being of highest authority. Both hold that nothing can contradict scripture and be true. Therefore both are confronted by the same problem in the area of biblical scholarship due to the impact of the theological secularists. To undermine the authority of the Bible is, for both Catholics and Evangelicals, to undermine the Christian life.

Biblical scholarship has certainly provided one of the chief challenges to orthodox Christians, Evangelical and Catholic alike, who have sought to maintain themselves as a Christian people with a distinctive way of life faithful to the teachings in scripture. Its effect has been undermining, as C.S. Lewis put it in his essay "Modern Theology and Biblical Criticism," where he said, "The undermining of the old orthodoxy has been mainly the work of divines engaged in New Testament criticism. The authority of experts in that discipline is the authority in deference to whom we are asked to give up a huge mass of beliefs shared in common by the early Church, the Fathers, the Middle Ages, the Reformers, and even the nineteenth century." He was speaking of the Church of England in the postwar period, but his comments apply in good part to the Roman Catholic Church since 1964 and, surprisingly, to Evangelicals increasingly in recent years. Many of us would be reluctant to say that the cause of the problem is biblical scholarship in itself. Lewis, however, was careful. He attributed the problem to "the *work of the divines* engaged in New Testament criticism." That poses the question: what is it about the dominant group of New Testament scholars or about their methods or about their work in general that might produce such a result?

Before beginning the discussion, I would like to indicate the perspective I intend to take. My perspective throughout will be a pastoral analysis. This is not a paper on methods of studying the New Testament, but on the pastoral results of certain methods of studying the New Testament. Nor do I intend to give a defense of orthodox Christianity. I intend here simply to assume orthodox Christianity as it has been believed by the mainstream of Christian churches prior to the influence of theological secularism and as it is summarized in the Apostle's Creed and the Ten Commandments. I intend to raise the question of how orthodox Christianity should cope with the de facto results of the predominant form of contemporary biblical scholarship. I do not intend to raise questions about how one deals with perceived discrepancies or inconsistencies in scripture, how one deals with apparent historical facts that do not seem to fit in with what one would expect if Christian orthodoxy were true, or with any other sort of argument that might challenge us from the direction of biblical scholarship. It is only fair to observe that I am skipping a very important matter. Many orthodox Christians have joined the theological secularists because they lacked an ability to handle such questions, and hence judged Christian orthodoxy to be indefensible. I am passing over these questions because my concern is pastoral rather than apologetic. I am simply asking what effect some kinds of scholarship have on the life of the Christian people.

Three Types of Biblical Exegesis

There are three different approaches to biblical exegesis that have existed among Christian scholars and that still can be found today. The first is the traditional method, which I would like to term the theological method. It is the method found in New Testament exegesis of the Old Testament, in the Christian Fathers—Irenaeus, Chrysostom, Augustine, and the rest—and in much of Christian tradition, for example, Aquinas, Luther, Calvin, Wesley, and Newman, and can still be found alive and well in a variety of Christian groupings, both Eastern and Western, usually those described somewhat disparagingly as "conservative" or "traditionalist." Central to this approach is the idea of authority. Scripture, and often other writings, are seen as an assemblage of authorities or of authoritative utterances, ranked in order of importance. The New Testament, for instance, ranks ahead of the Old Testament or over the Fathers or church confessions. When one wants to interpret the meaning of a particular text in the New Testament, one reads other texts in the scripture on the same point, and one interprets the first text in the light of those others and in a way which does not contradict them. Or if one wants to know what the New Testament teaches on a subject, one surveys all the texts on that subject, combines them into a unified result, and states that as the New Testament teaching. One would then go on to compare one's results with other accepted authorities and their views of the text or the subject in question—the Fathers, the church creeds or confessions, a theological position one is committed to, to see if one has adequately understood the matter.

In the theological method, authority determines the result. The scholar submits to the recognized authority of a text and its author. The basis of that authority is the degree to which the text is seen to be a writing which can convey God's mind. The more authorization or reliability it has, the more it should determine the result when it has significant input to give. By means of the process, scholars or teachers believe that they are discovering truth given by revelation. They submit to it and teach it and proclaim it, confident that they are not just passing on their own thoughts but God's word. Furthermore, in such a method it is the subject matter, the Incarnation or sexual morality, for instance, which on the whole controls the process rather than the literary or historical character and antecedents of the text. A text is primarily related to other texts on the same subject or to anything else known about that subject. To be sure, such a method can easily be distorting and can lead to people reading into the text the content of later theological positions. But on the other hand, it is not rare for teachers who use the theological method of exegesis to observe that a particular text does not seem to teach or to clearly teach something that is known from another source. To summarize, the theological method is one in which the authority of the text as a medium of transmission of revelation determines the outcome and in which the truth known about the subject matter shapes the proceedings.

The second approach is one which can be called the secular-historical approach. Here I am thinking of the approach used by people like Bultmann, Käsemann, Marxsen, Nineham, Perrin, and many others like them. I am also, however, thinking of people like Stendhal, Vawter, Brown, Vogtle, Jewett, and others, who seem much more devout as Christians. In addition, I am thinking of many Christian writers who are not professional scripture scholars, but who use similar methods in their writings. Most Catholic and Evangelical feminists would be in this category. The term "historical secular approach" designates the way many who identify themselves as Christians do biblical exegesis. The term could certainly cover the way in which non-Christian scholars study the New Testament, but the focus of concern here is on exegesis done by people identified as Christians. It is the dominant approach in academic theology today, both in departments of theology in secular universities in the English-speaking world and in the faculties of theology in seminaries and theological schools controlled by the older Protestant denominations. It likewise now dominates among Catholics, and my observation leads me to surmise that within five years it will be accepted among many Evangelicals. In this matter I would guess that the Evangelicals are at the same place that Catholics in the United States were in 1962. It might be possible to speak of a variety of secular-historical methods, the historical-critical method, the history of religions method, etc., just as it might be possible to speak of a variety of theological methods, but for our purposes, to describe it as one method or approach will be accurate.

The secular-historical method begins by categorizing exegesis as a branch of history, not theology. Theologians may, and should, find the results of interest, especially if they want to base their views on what the scripture really says, but the method, in theory, is the historical method of any historical study and not a theological method. This implies that the exegete cannot guarantee ahead of time that he will produce results that will support what the theologian (or what the church that the exegete belongs to) believes. He simply has to study things objectively and to see what results he gets. This also implies that historical method and historical study shape the proceedings and the matters of interest. Attention is paid primarily to historical similarities and differences, to sequence in time and to influences. The goal is to construct a history of religious thought (and perhaps practice), and the concern is therefore to be able to use the materials the New Testament provides to write a history. Since we know that later ages always misread earlier ages (until, perhaps, the discovery of the historical method), the Fathers, church authorities, even texts from other parts of the New Testament, will probably be of only limited help in establishing the meaning of a New Testament text and quite likely will be positively misleading.

There is another characteristic of the secular-historical method of scriptural exegesis which is not in my experience characteristic of most historians, at least not in the English-speaking world, but which does seem to prevail among many biblical scholars, especially those who use the historical-critical method. That is the tendency to try to get behind the text, to analyze it and to reconstruct it so that we can have access to a saying or an event which the text does not give us, for which it is often the only evidence, but which, in this view, it undoubtedly distorts. Those who use the historical-critical form of the secular-historical method believe that they have tools to remove the distortion and provide us with the original saying or event or at least a closer approximation to it. Possibly this approach originated in a nineteenth-century German approach to historiography and perhaps in Hegelian philosophy of history.

The term secular-historical approach or method, then, refers to an approach which Christians use as an approach to Christian exegesis. It rests on the claim either that the historical method is a sufficient means to explicate scripture or at least that the results of historical method should be given preference over any other consideration. The scripture is only or primarily to be treated like any secular text. The secular-historical approach, in other words, is more than just the use of historical method in exegesis. It is an overall approach to exegesis.

The third approach to exegesis is one which I am going to call here the historical-biblical approach. This term is borrowed from Gerhard Maier and is used in the absence of a better one. Maier advocates an approach similar to that which many others have used. It is currently the official Roman Catholic approach, as represented by the documents of the Vatican Council and of the Pontifical Biblical Commission, and it is the one used by many Evangelical scholars, like Bruce, Morris, Ladd, and others, who neither want to abandon the scriptures as the Word of God nor all of modern biblical scholarship. The historical-biblical approach accepts the use of all modern historical methods and tools and affirms them as being helpful for the study of the scripture, but it also maintains the canonicity and authority of the whole of scripture. In fact, it lets the authority of the scripture as a whole, and not just the historical method, determine the results of the exegesis. This approach can be seen as a mixture of the first two, giving the preference, at least in theory, to the theological approach. It often issues in biblical theologies, written on the premise that the teaching of the scripture can be synthesized into a whole without distorting any of the texts, and that biblical theology can provide material for more complete theologies using other materials. I do not intend to spend a great deal of time discussing this approach to exegesis, because while it is the official Roman Catholic approach and dominates in many sectors of Evangelical exegesis, it is in fact not the dominant Roman Catholic approach, and my prediction is that it's losing some of its hold on the evangelical world where it has one.

The Problem

This paper has presented three types of biblical exegesis in order to situate the current major source of the undermining of the Christian way of life. It is among those who take the secular-historical approach, in the sense described above, that most problems develop regarding the scriptures as authoritative for the Christian way of life. Many of the divines who work according to such methods end up undermining the authority of the scriptures for Christian living. Normally they do not directly contest the authority of scripture except perhaps in discussion on the nature and authority of scripture. Rather, the difficulties generally come in various assertions and approaches in the course of their exegetical writings.

Perhaps the most obvious sort of underming caused by those who use such methods involves straightforward denial of the creed and the commandments. It would not be difficult, for instance, to find many Christian writers nowadays who would deny the Incarnation. Many of them would be scripture scholars or theolgians using the secular-historical method in their exegetical work and claiming their exegetical results as support. *The Myth of the God Incarnate* provides examples of a number of them. Nor would it be all that difficult to find theologians and scripture scholars allowing fornication among the unmarried or homosexual relations, only under certain conditions of course, and basing their views on exegetical conclusions. This might not be as overt among Roman Catholics and Evangelicals as it is among Episcopalians and Presbyterians, but it is by no means absent. Letha Scanzoni's and Virginia Mollenkott's book, *Is the Homosexual My Neighbor?* would provide an Evangelical example, as the Catholic Theological Society's book, *Human Sexuality*, provides a clear Catholic example. Moreover, where it is not going on in the most overt ways, it is often present in a disguised form. It is not rare to find scholars, for instance, who no longer can find scriptural support for the "traditional" ban on premarital sex.

It is not, however, with direct denials that I am mainly concerned. More serious, in my opinion, are the indirect ways of using exegesis to undermine the authority of scripture, especially in its support of a distinctively Christian way of life. There are many conclusions that do not constitute direct denial, but which undermine the scriptural support that either allows people to have confidence in the Christian way of life or undermines their ability to have faith in the facts that support that way of life and make it possible. Consider the following opinions:

—Jesus was mistaken in his understanding of the prophecy in Daniel when he quoted it to the high priest at his trial, misunderstanding it to be a support for his view of himself as the eschatological judge who would come to judge the world.

—Jesus only gradually discovered his mission, and like the rest of mankind he was forced to live with the ambiguity of human existence and confront opposition to his desires to do good to humans; the early church suppressed this uncertainty in the light of their later conviction of his divinity.

—Paul asserted a difference of social role between men and women only because he was unable to overcome his rabbinic training and draw the full implications of faith in Christ.

—the Christian prohibition of premarital sex was based on the late Jewish view of sexuality rather than on the pagan one or on the earlier Jewish one.

—the early Christian community invented the story of Jesus' confrontation with the Pharisees over divorce to back up their position in their conflicts with later rabbis.

Many more such opinions could be cited, but these will do for examples. Let us observe that none of these are direct denials of any doctrine. They do not assert that Jesus is not the coming judge, that Jesus was not God, that one should not maintain a role difference between men and women, that premarital sex is acceptable, that divorce is acceptable. But while they do not deny these views outright, they do not leave us with much support in the scripture for holding these views. To be more precise, they eliminate a particular support we get in scripture for those views. And they do so despite the fact that a first reading, a so-called "uncritical" reading of the scripture, would lead one to believe that there is scriptural support. They do so by undermining the authority of scripture in its support of various positions by adducing certain historical-critical considerations.

The Sources of the Problem

The next question is how such secular-historical exegetes arrive at either direct denials or indirect underminings. I see three main ways. The first has to do with the historical method itself and is not in principle specific to the secular-historical approach. The historical method tends to create a certain perspective which is itself easily relativizing, because it tends to see all views of the past as representative of a historical situation rather than as true or false. The method's perspective poses certain problems and tends to produce certain difficulties with orthodox views. This was observed earlier. However, there is another aspect which needs to be pointed out. Many of the historical difficulties are there in the exegetical conclusions of secular-historical scholars only because they have been created by secular-historical theories. Often it is not the *facts* which cause the difficulties, but the exegetical *theories* which cause the difficulties. These theories may be more or less well-substantiated, but they are not the same thing as facts. When we read in *The Myth of the God Incarnate* that Hellenistic thinking of a proto-gnostic sort influenced the early Christians to come up with the view of the Incarnation that is now propounded as Christian orthodoxy, it is only fair to observe that that is only one theory or way of accounting for the facts, and while it may have something to recommend it, it is not a fact that one automatically observes by studying the historical data.

Moreover, some of the theories and positions taken by exegetes using the secular-historical approach can be attributed to a lack of good historical method rather than to historical method itself. For instance, critics of the critics have picked out the following approaches and criteria as being common among exegetes using the secular-historical approach which are in fact faulty historical method:

—ruling out supernatural intervention a priori so that all passages in which anything supernatural occurs must be historically unreliable, later invention, etc.

—adopting the view that since the scriptures are faith documents (or even propaganda pieces) they cannot provide us reliable access to the events they are referring to, despite the fact that historians normally use faith documents and propaganda pieces as useful and often reliable historical sources. Such documents in fact represent a high percentage of the available sources in many areas.

—taking as a methodological presupposition the Kantian perspective that the text tells us more about the author or the community of origin than it does about Jesus or his teaching or the practice of the early church.

—using the criterion that the only way to be sure that we have an authentic saying of Jesus is if we can show it to be distinctive of him, that is, dissimilar to known tendencies in Judaism before him or the church after him—thus insuring that it will never be established that the authentic Jesus learned anything from Judaism or that the church faithfully learned anything from him.

—showing lack of discipline in scholarly speculation by a readiness to produce plausible theories and reconstructions that can never be controlled by the available evidence that we have and using them for accounts of early Christianity.

—often using bad judgment in handling questions of literary form and historical evidence, not recognizing when a source is good or when a piece of writing is historical rather than mythical.

The point is not that these elements are intrinsic to the secular-historical approach or that all practitioners of the art fall prey to them. It is rather simply that these faults are common among those who are engaged in using it. Moreover, these faults cause a fair amount of the trouble that at first sight seems to be a problem caused by historical data. As one historian put it, history is not the problem. Historians are the problem.

The second way in which exegetes who use the secular-historical approach arrive at their undermining results concerns the non-factual elements of their theory and method. A certain amount of their theory and method is based upon historical facts (that they are dealing with twenty-seven books of a certain description, for instance) and also historical method (e.g. one begins with primary sources, one confirms with archaeological evidence when available, etc.). But, like most history writing and other kinds of scholarly writing, some of the result is produced by the non-factual elements of their approach. The following is a brief list of some commonly recognized non-factual elements in the method which exegetes (and many other kinds of scholars) use. Let me note for clarity that this is not a list of elements that are in themselves automatically problematic.

—categories for analysis not given in the data; for instance, the category "early Catholicism" or "Hellenistic Christianity."

—models; for instance, the dialectical model of development or a particular model of unity and diversity.

—ethical evaluations; for instance, the judgment that such-and-such a teaching leads toward or supports equality or freedom.

—constructs; for instance, reconstructing the original text and then arguing from it, or positing Q and then analyzing the theology of its author.

—assumptions; for instance, that it would take at least seventy years for a Christology like that in the gospel of John to develop; or views derived from sources other than the data, for instance that Jesus' teaching *must* reflect some class perspective.

—the amount of evidence one requires to substantiate a particular view; for instance, for many exegetes it would take a huge amount of evidence to establish the authenticity of a miracle story, but it would require only an indication of plausibility to establish that a particular story was invented by the early church for purposes of its own. Related to this are decisions about the burden of proof.

Other non-factual components of historical theories could be listed. I am not saying that there is something wrong with using non-factual components. They can be used well or badly. There is some evidence that many exegetes are using them badly at the moment because of a certain disarray in the field. Peter Stuhlmacher, himself an advocate of the historical-critical version of the secular-historical method, in his evaluation of the recent state of the art in *Historical Criticism and Theological Interpretation of Scripture* (Phila: Fortress, 1977, p. 86) called for new developments in regard to method because "only by scientific and theoretical apprehension of the way in which we handle the tradition can we master the continually astonishing and at times even horrifying experience that a historical exposition of texts seldom leads to really commonly recognized results, but as a rule yields quite disparate data." He goes on to express the point being made here, namely that the methods require non-factual elements, when he says, "The reasons for this are that historical study always contains an element of subjectivity and that the complex combination of methods which comprises historical study (text- and literary-criticism, form- and redaction-criticism, lexicography and the history of religions) can be quite variously used and accented."

Nonetheless, even were the non-factual elements of theories used well as evaluated by the criteria of secular historiography, they might not be acceptable as evaluated from the point of view of results for Christian life and for the authority of scripture. It may be perfectly acceptable for a nonbelieving historian to decide, and on personal grounds derive from sources other than the data, that the teaching in the pastoral epistles on order and subordination in the Christian community is an example of oppression. But it surely is a different matter for a Christian scholar to say that the canonical Word of God teaches oppression. It may be acceptable for a nonbelieving historian to take the differences in approach that can easily be noted between the epistle of James and the epistle to the Romans, to impose a model of dialectical development which is derived from a philosophy of history and is not obvious in this particular situation in the early church, and then to decide that here we have an example of two antithetical movements in contradiction to one another. It is another thing for a Christian scholar to see the canonical Word of God as a collection of contradictions produced by different early Christian movements in conflict with one another.

In other words, it is legitimate to use non-factual elements to form historical theories. Nonetheless, it is crucial to realize that the particular selection of non-factual elements is not forced on the exegete by the data. The fact that they can be made to square with the data does not mean that they are derived from the data. Their legitimation often rests, in fact, upon something other than historical study. They are not necessary to hold in order to be a good historian responsibly using the data. When they are drawn from sources that are at variance with Christian orthodoxy or lead to results at variance with Christian orthodoxy, Christian exegetes can reject them or replace them without feeling that they are doing something unscholarly or dishonest. Those Christians who use the secular-historical approach, however, often simply adopt (and sometimes construct) theories and views which are at variance with an orthodox Christian view or which take away some of the support for it, simply on the basis that the theory or view is a legitimate historical position or that it is the currently prevailing one among scripture scholars. When they do so, they frequently undermine the authority of the scripture and its support for Christian life.

The third way in which exegetes who use the secular-historical approach produce their undermining results arises from the criteria they use to determine questions of normativeness, that is, ways in which the scripture can determine belief or practice. In principle they should not have to face issues of normativeness, except off-hours, because secular-historical exegesis is simply history writing and hence does not deal with normativeness. The documents do not provide normativeness, because they are simply examples of first-century religious thought. The writings of the biblical scholar do not contain normative statements because the business of history is not to say what ought to happen in the future. It only describes what has happened in the past. In this approach they differ from both the theological method and the historical-biblical method, which begin with the canon and with a view of the scripture as a book that speaks with authority rather than as simply a first-century writing.

Yet, exegetes who use the secular-historical method always seem to get involved in questions of normativeness for doctrine and life. Perhaps that is due to the fact that the New Testament is the kind of book whose normative claims cannot be ignored. The book itself does not let you alone, so to speak, and it does not seem to have let biblical scholars alone, no matter how dedicated to scholarly historical objectivity. Perhaps it is due to the fact that most biblical scholars start out as theological students and have many theological interests.

For a variety of reasons, then, people who use the secular-historical approach do come up with normative statements based on their exegesis of scripture. Since they do not accept canonicity as an adequate criterion for the truth of the teaching of scripture, and since they are relying on a method that is basically a historical method, they naturally tend to come up with historical criteria for making normative judgments. However, since they do not accept all of the positions in scripture, and do not feel that they have to accept all the positions of scripture because of their view of scripture, their criteria are often criteria that accept some scriptural positions but reject others. The historical criteria, in short, become criteria for sorting out scripture, and the very fact of using these criteria itself undermines scriptural authority.

One of the most common criteria for normativeness used by exegetes is that of origins. We can read in feminist books that since directives for the roles of men and women originate with Paul and cannot be traced to Jesus, they must not be authoritative for us. Influences is another criterion. For instance, feminists also tell us that since Paul's teaching on the roles of men and women can be traced to rabbinic influences (usually on the grounds that similar positions can be found in one or more rabbis) it lacks authority, unlike elements he derived from his grasp of the meaning of the gospel, such as justification by faith. Issues of unity and diversity often provide criteria for authority. For instance, something which can adequately claim to represent the unified teaching of the scripture has authority. Other things are merely allowed but not essential. Many feminists tell us that since the specific New Testament teachings on the roles of men and women can only be found in Paul's writings, they are at best a permissible Christian approach. Commonly, scholars assert contradictions in the New Testament and on that basis hold that one has to choose between New Testament traditions. Popular nowadays, for instance, is the discovery of the contradiction between Galations 3:28 and the rest of Paul's teachings on women, so that one is forced to choose between them. Good Evangelicals have been known to take this view under the pressure of feminism. Evolution also provides a criterion. It is increasingly common, nowadays, to look for the trajectory of development in scriptural teaching. It is, of course, a criterion that can cut both ways, some preferring the earlier positions on the trajectory, some the later ones. While Brown seems to find the growing emphasis on Mary in the New Testament a positive trajectory, Leipoldt finds the growing emphasis on the subordination of women in the New Testament a negative trajectory (although he does not use that specific term). Perhaps the most popular criterion of all is the cultural criterion. Anything that can be attributed to first-century culture can be dismissed as only of authority within that culture. Perhaps this criterion is so popular because of the general popularity of cultural relativism. It turns out to be a versatile criterion, because there is very little that cannot be seen as culturally relative. The New Testament teaching on the roles of men and women, on homosexuality, on sexual ethics in general, on the redemption, on the Incarnation, all have been eliminated with a treatment of their cultural relativity. Related to all these criteria is the search for a canon within the canon. Those who are looking for a canon within the canon are seeking some part of the New Testament that will be more authoritative and will allow them to eliminate the rest of the New Testament and some of its opinions.

At this point, two observations on the various criteria for normativeness that we have been discussing will suffice. First, there is no consensus among those who use the secular-historical approach as to which criteria are true, successful, helping, life-enriching, self-actualizing, or whatever one might use for determining criteria of authority. There is, in short, a crisis of authority produced by such methods which itself reduces the authority of scripture and induces people to look elsewhere than the scripture for authority. Second, all these criteria automatically reduce the authority of the scripture because they say in various ways that it is not the scripture itself as scripture which is normative, but something else. Moreover, potentially, used individually or in combination, they allow all of scripture to be undermined.

To sum up what has been said of the problems in the secular-historical approach, the approach undermines the authority of scripture as a basis of Christian teaching and life by: (1) problems caused by the historical method itself or faulty historical methods; (2) non-factual elements of theories; and (3) approaches to issues of normativeness. In addition, secular-historical exegetical results regularly seem to find the positions of nineteenth- and twentieth-century ideologies in first-century writings. In principle this should not happen. A scholarly historical method should produce objectivity, at least as far as it goes. In fact, however, the secular-historical approach has seemed to open the way for all sorts of modern ideologies to be read into the New Testament and reappear as exegetical results. Most modern exegetes would readily admit that this happened with the nineteenth-century Liberals who saw Jesus and many of the apostles as nineteenth-century Liberals upholding the ethical theories of the fatherhood of God, the brotherhood of man, and the categorical imperative of disinterested love. In writing on the subject of men's and women's roles in the scripture I have, however, recently examined many pages of the best biblical journals in which I discovered degreed and tenured exegetes assuring us that Jesus, and even Paul, were twentieth-century feminists millenia before their times. Similar results can be seen in the writings of liberationist exegetes, who assure us that Jesus was a precocious Marxist. Many would say that this is simply an abuse of the method which shows the great hold one's own culture and opinions have on one and which prevents us from reading texts with objectivity. We can certainly allow for that, though not without pointing out that our concern is not with the method as much as with "the work of divines" engaged in using the method, and that such divines do seem to fall prey to this error fairly commonly. There is, however, another cause of their falling prey to it which is closely connected with the method itself; and that is the ease with which the method allows one to define anything in the New Testament as historically conditioned. Since everything in the New Testament is found in a first-century writing, it can be seen as some sort of first-century view (and hence, by implication, can easily be seen, when so desired, as only having validity for its time). This allows twentieth-century people to claim the aspects of New Testament teaching which coincide with their own ideological position without having to be too concerned with the rest.

Here is the point: The first type of approach to scripture—the approach I termed the theological approach—seems on the face of it to involve reading presuppositions into the New Testament and then producing them as exegesis. However, the work of the divines engaged in the secular-historical approach in fact shows much the same result. I would say in fact that they do it even more, because they do not have the protection of a theological tradition against the influences of modern ideologies.

Some Pastoral Conclusions

A few pastoral conclusions can be drawn from all this. First, letting exegesis be classified as a branch of history rather than as theology or Christian teaching is a perilous step, possibly a fatal one. It leads to making paramount criteria which for a Christian should not be paramount. History should be illuminative for exegesis, but it should not control exegesis. Christian truth should control exegesis. In fact, throughout much of Christian history, Christian doctrine was taught by exegesis, and if we really do believe that Christian doctrine can be found in scripture (as both Catholics and Evangelicals do in theory), we should be able to do our teaching as a commentary on scripture.

Second, our theology should in fact color exegesis. Very often one hears the view stated that our theological views should not color our exegesis. In my experience, that opinion has always been stated as a cloak for letting something else color our exegesis, usually a secular ideology. If it is true that there are always non-factual elements that shape our exegetical results, then we ought to take great care in determining which non-factual elements they are. All too often for contemporary exegetes they are contemporary philosophies and ideologies. If we believe in Christian truth, we should let it shape the way in which we develop our exegetical views. We do not have to be untrue to the facts by doing so. In fact, if we genuinely believe that God gives us light, we should be able to see better what is there. After all, "The unspiritual man does not receive the gifts of the Spirit of God, for they are folly to him, and he is not able to understand them, because they are spiritually discerned" (1 Cor 2:14). How can we think that a pagan who happens to be learned in the scripture will be as reliable a judge as the Christian who understands the subject matter and has some insight into the real mind of the Author? In all the places where his views are not strictly determined by the facts, but depend on his concepts, evaluative judgments, choice of models, good judgment, etc., the pagan scholar will commonly be guided by something which distorts or fails to capture the truth of the text.

Third, we should not allow among us the view that the results of exegesis do not line up with the creed and the commandments. Scripture scholars who do not find scripture supporting basic Christian teaching should not be allowed to say, "Well, that is just the result of exegesis. It is up to the theologians to figure out what to do with it."

Fourth, Christian scripture scholars should not look to the world of secular academic scholarship as their peer group or their judges. If they primarily associate with them in professional meetings, get their main formation in their schools, read their journals and try to get articles accepted into them, and look to their works as their primary source of new understanding, sooner or later they will accept their criteria and become more and more paganized in their thinking. I do not mean by this that Christian scholars should avoid all contact with the secular (and theological secularist) world of scripture scholarship. But I do mean that they have to make their prime environment and their prime college the body of believing scripture scholars who are more concerned to be faithful to the Lord than primarily seeking acceptance among secular academicians. I believe the scripture would term this latter course "love of the world." Perhaps this is the time for orthodox scripture scholars to band together across the old divisions of Catholic and Evangelical so that they can support one another.

Finally, we should not teach scripture the way exegetes who are mainly historical scholars talk about it. When we, for instance, speak of "Paul's thought here" or of "the theology of the Gospel of Mark," we are already introducing a perspective into our teaching which undermines its authority and its power in our lives, because it treats it primarily as a human book produced by human authors. We do not always have to say, "God says here," but when we speak of Paul's teaching, we should speak about him as a man speaking with God's authority because he is speaking under God's inspiration. It is only when we have the power and wisdom of God behind us that we will be able to withstand the pressures of the modern world and live a faithful Christian life in its midst. And our teaching ought to create faith in those who hear us that we do have the power and wisdom of God with us and that his word is a reliable channel to receive both.

Response

J.I. Packer

My basic response to Mr. Clark's paper is one of gratitude. He offers an analysis of what goes on. I recognize this analysis as true, and nothing in it seems to me to require radical challenge. The academic community in which technical Bible study takes place is one and international these days, and embraces both Roman Catholic and Protestant scholars, and it looks to me from my side of the fence just as it does to Mr. Clark from his. I wholly share his concern that scripture should function as the decisive authority for the faith and life of God's people, and also his conviction that "secular-historical" methods make this impossible. What follows is essentially a buttressing of his arguments, offered from the standpoint of an Anglican evangelical (that is, as I would like you to understand the word, a Bible-and-gospel man) who theologizes for the most part within the Reformed tradition.

I start with a comment on Mr. Clark's typology of the three approaches to exegesis, the "theological," the "secular-historical," and the "historical-biblical." I think it is important to see the third as the necessary twentieth-century form of the first, and to lay it down that theologically determined exegesis which will not pass muster as a product of *a posteriori* historical study of the text will not do. It is never enough to cite the opinions of, say, Chrysostom or Augustine or Luther or Calvin; you need to be able to show that what you find in the text is being read out of it and not read into it, and that necessitates inductive analysis of the flow of thought of which it is part—in other words, it requires historical study. A fully historical approach to exegesis is demanded by traditional Christian theology, which claims that God's saving revelation of himself to men took the historically particular form of a sequence of space-time events from the Protevangelium onward, climaxing in the life, death, resurrection, and ascension of Jesus Christ, God's incarnate Son, our Savior and Lord. This has in fact been clear to exegetes since the sixteenth century, and only ignorance will suggest otherwise.

I know it is often said, and truly, that there was a great deepening in the historical sensibility of the Western mind at the start of the nineteenth century, making subsequent Christian scholarship much more deeply aware than before of the cultural difference between eras and so between the outlooks of those who lived in them, particularly in the shapes and limits of their presuppositional horizons. I recognize that this deepening of historical sensibility has brought exegetical enrichment in both Old and New Testament study, as scholars have focused on the historical question with which theological exegesis must always start—"what did the passage means as communication from the human writer to his own first intended readers, those contemporaries to whom and for whom he wrote?" But the allegation, often made, that there was no historically responsible exegesis of this kind before the nineteenth century should be dismissed as merely ill-informed. Let anyone who doubts that examine Calvin's commentaries and Matthew Pool's *Synopsis Criticorum* (5000 folio pages, 1669-76), and he will doubt no longer. At least since the start of the sixteenth century the best scholars, Protestant and Catholic, have known perfectly well that their exegesis must vindicate itself historically as well as theologically. The names Mr. Clark gives to illustrate methods one and three (no one after Newman for method one, no one before the Pontifical Biblical Commission and the evangelical trio, F.F. Bruce, Leon Morris, and George Ladd for method three) surely point to the fact that the difference here is essentially between the same method as practiced before and after the technical and imaginative deepening of historical study of which I spoke. If we allowed ourselves to treat the three methods as distinct to the point of supposing that it belongs to the first not to take historical exegesis as seriously as the second and third do, we should be wrong historically; and if we embraced the first method, so misunderstood, in preference to the second or third we should lay ourselves open to a charge of vicious obscurantism to which there could be no answer. I do not think this is what Mr. Clark intends, but his way of spelling out the three types might have this effect.

The truer formula surely is that there are in principle two basic approaches to exegesis rather than three, and that each handles scripture differently because of a decisive difference in the exegete's doctrine of God: whether (to put it crudely, for clarity's sake) he believes that our Maker uses his own gift to us of language in order to tell us things, or not; whether, therefore, it is proper exegetical procedure to treat God's recorded utterances and the doctrinal and ethical instruction given by biblical writers as revealed truth, or to decline so to treat it. Both methods of exegesis are historical from one standpoint and theological from another, but the theology underlying and controlling the second is a doctrine of God from which the prophetic and incarnational reality of divine speech, a reality which is in fact the paradigm for all scripture, has been systematically excluded. It should be noted that wherever this doctrine of God is consistently maintained it excludes the incarnation itself; for once it was allowed that in the teaching of the Galilean rabbi-prophet-wiseman named Jesus, God incarnate was telling men things, then the theological Maginot Line built to keep the notion of revealed truth from getting through would be breached, and the currently fashionable concept of a verbally uncommunicative God would have to be given up. So the decisive difference is not whether modern historical techniques of enquiry are used, but what is done with them; whether use of them is governed by belief in revealed absolutes of truth and duty, and in the Christ of the New Testament, or not. With Mr. Clark, I must resist the temptation to argue for the orthodoxy to which these beliefs are central; I would simply endorse his point that unlimited cultural and historical relativism in our handling of all the contents of scripture is inescapable once we commit ourselves to locate the results of our exegetical work outside the revealed-truth frame of reference which was demonstrably part of the mind-set of the authors being studied. The arbitrariness which this procedure involves makes it bad scholarship, and its unbelief makes it bad Christianity into the bargain. Its claim to be scientific and objective because free from dogmatic *a priori* prejudice in the Bible's favor is a bluff that has to be called, for what it exhibits is in fact *a priori* prejudice against the Bible, as dogmatic as anything on the other side. As Mr. Clark says, the problem is not history, but historians; not the data, but the presuppositional sausage-machine through which it is fed.

This being so, I repeat my plea that Mr. Clark's third method be seen as the first brought up to date, and that none of us excuse ourselves from the discipline of vindicating theological interpretations of scripture by showing their naturalness historically. Good historical exegesis is in any case the only effective counter to the bad historical exegesis which the arbitrarinesses of method two tend to produce. . . .

My second comment concerns the hostage which I think Mr. Clark gives to fortune when, having noted that Catholic theologians understand Vatican II's statement about inerrancy as implying the full truth only of that in scripture which Protestants once called "saving knowledge," he observes that this differs from the insistence of "many Evangelicals" on the total inerrancy of scripture as such and then moves on as if the matter were tangential and did not bear on his main argument. Four remarks are, I think, in order.

1. For the sake of the record, it should be said that belief in the trustworthiness of all biblical affirmations (i.e., inerrancy) belonged, *pace* some few scholars whose arguments fail to convince, to the whole mainstream of Lutheran and Reformed theology till the end of the last century, and to the whole mainstream of Catholic theology up to the middle of this century. The accepted understanding of the matter was that inspiration, God's work of enlightenment and providential control in the composing of scripture which produced human witness to him that was also and equally his own witness to himself, entailed the inerrancy of all that was written, inasmuch as God does not err nor mislead.

2. Vatican II states that "since everything asserted by the inspired authors or sacred writers must be held to be asserted by the Holy Spirit, it follows that the books of scripture must be acknowledged as teaching firmly, faithfully and without error that truth which God wanted put into the sacred writings for the sake of our salvation." That certainly does follow, but it also follows that every biblical statement of fact should be received as truth taught by God; and it must be judged arbitrary and unnatural to gloss the Council's statement, as some do, with the explanation that what the Church identifies as saving truth is all that scripture is really asserting. (Nor in any case would this explanation entitle you to call anything in scripture erroneous; for error is a quality of assertions as such, not of the speech-forms and literary devices used in making them. But surely the explanation is nonsense. Is it "saving knowledge," truth taught "for the sake of our salvation," that Jesus has brothers? Yet exegesis of Mark 6:3, John 7:3, Acts 1:14 shows three New Testament authors asserting it was so—etc., etc.) Were I a Roman Catholic, I should think it important to challenge the murky and muddle-headed way in which this conciliar statement is nowadays being used to legitimize the Protestant type of biblical skepticism, which so freely accuses scripture of error on nonessentials.

3. While we may hesitate to go all the way with the domino thinking of writers like Harold Lindsell, who claim that if biblical inerrancy falls at any point then the certainty and authority of scripture fall at every point, yet there is no denying that to the extent that one queries the truth of any biblical assertions, to that extent one abandons the "incarnational" identity of God's given word with man's, which is the theological essence of the inspiredness of scripture as traditionally understood; and this must lead a consistent thinker to redefine inspiration in lower and lesser terms across the board; and that procedure at once raises a Christological problem to which Evangelicals have been calling attention (without much effect, alas) for over a century, namely that the identity of God's and man's word in Holy Scripture was an avowed presupposition of our Lord's own thought and teaching—not about peripheral things, but

about discipleship and his own Messianic vocation. What are we to say? That on these points, in one respect at least, our Lord did not know what he was talking about? Then at what points, and in what respects, dare we say that he did know what he was talking about? To part company with him on something so fundamental as his claim to be fulfilling the God-given scriptures is really like pulling out the foundation-stone in such a way that the whole house falls down, as happens in one of Graham Greene's more macabre short stories. I do not believe that one cannot be a conservative Christian, Roman Catholic or Evangelical, nor believe in the Incarnation, without holding to biblical inerrancy, for as Mr. Clark notes many exponents of such positions exist. But I contend that the position itself is inconsistent, and that some arbitrariness in handling scripture is bound to appear sooner or later in the teaching of anyone who urges us to take our faith and lifestyle from the Bible but not to believe quite all that exegesis shows its writers to be asserting, and that this arbitrariness, once admitted into one's thought at any point, is likely to grow greater in the manner of a hole in a dike.

4. Inasmuch as (i) nearly 300 representative Evangelical leaders, including scholars, and young men as well as old, subscribed the elaborate Chicago Declaration on Biblical Inerrancy in 1978, and (ii) the Declaration has won general acceptance in subsequent Evangelical discussion all over North America, and (iii) Evangelical feeling against the views of Jewett, Mollenkott, and Scanzoni, mentioned by Mr. Clark, has been notably solid and strong, I think it is incorrect to imagine that Evangelicals generally are about to lapse into a practicing commitment to the "secular-historical" method of handling scripture. Some few may, but most will not; and I for one am glad this is likely to be so.

So I come to Mr. Clark's admirable conclusions: that biblical exegesis should be practiced in a way that recognizes scripture to be the Word of God and is informed by historic Christian theology; that exegetes must be careful lest preoccupation with their secular peer groups in the academic world make them forget their churchly identity and lose sight of the fact that the judgment to which their work must finally be submitted is that of the fellowship of believers; and that "perhaps this is the time for orthodox scripture scholars to band together across the old divisions of Catholic and Evangelical so that they can support one another." I want to say Amen to all that, and to put on record my conviction that if, first, we think of tradition—*traditio tradita*, I mean—as essentially a venture in biblical exposition by believers who went before us (and to Roman Catholics it is surely not less than that, just as to Protestants it is certainly as much as that); if, second, we understand our dialogue with tradition as essentially an extending of the fellowship in biblical study which we enjoy with other believers today; and if, third, we agree that countering the onrush of "secular-historical" exposition with believing proclamation, apologetic and polemic is the prime task to which our situation calls us; then Mr. Clark's suggestion of Evangelical-Catholic partnership is undoubtedly practical politics. The job to be done may be defined in positive terms as getting Biblical Theology back on the road. I use the name Biblical Theology as it has been used for the past half-century, to denote that faith-full exegetical procedure that reads the Bible "from within," in terms of its authors' own convictions and commitment as reflected in the text, and finds there both unity of witness and God-given norms of faith and life. Biblical Theology flourished both sides of the Atlantic for more than a generation in such writers as Cullmann, Hoskyns, Hebert, Alan Richardson, Michael Ramsey, H.H. Rowley, F.F. Bruce, G.E. Wright, John Bright, and J.D. Smart among Protestants, and Bouyer and Charlier among Roman Catholics, but in recent years it has been derailed through technical weaknesses (Brevard Childs' *Biblical Theology in Crisis* tells the story) and replaced by "secular-historical" procedures which imply ultimate plurality (not just of form, but of content) in scriptural teaching. Truth and need both require reversal of this fashionable trend, which, like most matters of fashion, was never necessary (for Biblical Theology's technical weaknesses were superficial only), and I hope that together we can very soon roll up our sleeves and get down to the task.

Response

Michael Wrenn

The implications of some of the observations in Stephen Clark's thorough, excellent, and thought-provoking paper might be spelled out further in the following case history of a recent theory of ongoing revelation, which, to some extent, continues to receive a hearing in certain Roman Catholic religious education and pastoral circles in our country.

Between the years 1973 and 1977, the Roman Catholic Church in the United States was involved in a consultation process aimed at the preparation of a *National Catechetical Directory*. This document contains guidelines for the handing on of the faith in religious education programs on all levels in both school and non-school programs. One of the chief problems in successive drafts of this document was that of the concept of ongoing revelation. In the final draft of the *Directory* it seemed as though a compromise had been struck by the use of a capital *R* to signify Revelation completed with the death of the Apostles, and a lower case "r" to signify continuing revelation.

Nevertheless, in a letter from the Holy See's Congregation for the Clergy (10/30/78), which finally approved these guidelines, it was stated: "The employment of capital and small letters (Revelation, revelation) to distinguish various meanings of the notion of revelation tends to engender confusion. It would seem to be less open to misunderstanding, if the word 'revelation' standing alone, without modifiers, quotation marks, or italics, were to signify public divine revelation in the strict sense, and that other expressions be chosen to indicate other modes by which God manifests Himself to men."[1] The section on revelation in the *Document* was accordingly revised and published.

This theory of ongoing revelation, as it found its way into Roman Catholic educational efforts, and continues to find acceptance in certain quarters under the alleged rubric of theological pluralism, was due to the effort of one man, and it might be worthwhile to mention briefly how this theory started and what it ultimately led to.

For Brother Gabriel Moran in 1966, "the only thing which can save the catechetical movement from self-strangulation is to prepare teachers who have a theological understanding of Christian revelation."[2] In numerous publications, Moran attempted to set forth his view, "at times obscurely and later on in a plainer and almost informal fashion." Revelation can be viewed as "present in the life of every individual."[3] For Moran, revelation is treated as a continuous, presently occurring process, not merely a collection of events from the remotest past. Revelation is "neither doctrine nor message, but is a real, personal intercommunion,"[4] and knowledge arises out of encounter and experience rather than words and concepts. By 1970, Moran would write that if religious education is to be a genuine field of study, and not a cover for indoctrination, it must be born from a combination of sound religion and good education, and for Moran, this did not necessarily afford Christianity a normative position.

Brother Moran's continued insistence, over the years, not that revelation isn't mediated in particular communities, but that first of all "it" (revelation) is not the possession of any particular community found its most recent expression in an article written for the January 19, 1979 issue of the *National Catholic Reporter*. The article was a reaction to the already mentioned clarification regarding the meaning of revelation in the *National Catechetical Directory*, which was sought by the Congregation for the Clergy. Moran wrote as follows:

> Revelation is a central category for Christian, Jewish, and Muslim religions. The Roman Catholic Church has no right to insist that its official documents constitute the sum total of public divine revelation . . . to admit the Catholic Church does not have exclusive rights to "public, divine revelation"

is threatening but the only possible route after Vatican II. . . . What neither the Catholic Church nor other religions can claim is their documents are *the* "public, divine revelation." Religion teachers daily face this issue with any student capable of turning on a T.V. series like the Long Search.[5]

One could analyze even further what lay behind such an approach: the tension between an inductive and deductive approach in education or between the transcendent and the immanent, the sacred and the secular. Suffice it to say that the very suitable reflections on the major biblical themes of the history of salvation, the so-called kerygmatic approach, were soon replaced in certain religious education programs by the exegesis of articles and editorials in the *New York Times* and Kahil Gibran's *The Prophet*. . . .

Interestingly enough, in the *Syllabus Condemning the Errors of the Modernists, Lamentabili Sane*, of July 3, 1907, proposition 21 proscribed the notion that "Revelation, constituting the object of the Catholic faith, was not completed with the Apostles."[6] The constant concern of the Magisterium regarding a number of the issues mentioned in "Modern Approaches to Scriptural Authority" was evident even back then, especially in the following propositions which were proscribed by this document:

12. If he wishes to apply himself usefully to Biblical studies, the exegete must first put aside all preconceived opinions about the supernatural origin of Sacred Scripture and interpret it the same as any other merely human document.[7]

14. In many narrations the Evangelists recorded, not so much things that are true, as things which, even though false, they judged to be more profitable for their readers.

15. Until the time the canon was defined and constituted, the Gospels were increased by additions and corrections. Therefore there remained in them only a faint and uncertain trace of the doctrine of Christ.[8]

33. Everyone who is not led by preconceived opinion can readily see that either Jesus professed an error concerning

the immediate Messianic coming or the greater part of His doctrine as contained in the Gospels is destitute of authenticity.[9]

35. Christ did not always possess the consciousness of His Messianic dignity.[10]

36. The Resurrection of the Savior is not properly a fact of the historical order. It is a fact of merely the supernatural order (neither demonstrated nor demonstrable) which the Christian conscience gradually derived from other facts.[11]

It is encouraging to note that the need for caution and the importance of establishing proper parameters for historical criticism is beginning to be expressed in some scholarly circles.

In the preface to his work *Acts and the History of Earliest Christianity*, which makes a bold departure from some radical New Testament scholarship by supporting the historical integrity of the Acts of the Apostles, the prominent Tübingen scholar, Martin Hengel, observes:

> Two things, above all, concern me. First, to question the radical historical scepticism which is so widespread in a number of areas within German scholarship; this scepticism is often coupled with flights of imagination which suggest a retreat from any historical research worth taking seriously. Secondly, however, I am no less vigorously opposed to the primitive ostracism of historical—and that always means critical—methods, without which neither historical nor theological understanding of the New Testament is possible.[12]

In an appendix, Hengel supplements this present work with a number of propositions concerning the problem of historical methods and the theological interpretation of the New Testament. I submit that several of these reflect a number of concerns expressed in Stephen Clark's paper and quite possibly, in the propositioned forms in which they are set forth, are preparing the way, in scholarly circles, for that type of balanced dialogue called for in this session. Regarding criticism of the historical-critical method, Hengel observes:

1.2.3 There has not been enough critical reflection on the limits and consequences of this "historical-critical method", which has been reduced to a "dogmatic" positivism.[13]

1.2.7 In the sphere of "biblical history" in particular, we keep coming up against the question of the possibility of "unparalleled events". With its dogmatic fixation, the "historical-critical method" must rule out this possibility *a priori*.[14]

As for the multiplicity and complexity of historical knowledge and the consequences for "historical" and "theological understanding," Hengel states:

2.2.3 Knowledge of historical facts does not in itself amount to understanding. Rather, the latter is primarily identical with grasping the intention of the author of a text.[15]

2.2.4 On the other hand, the claim that we might be able to understand the intention of the author of a text better than he does himself (W. Dilthey) is often questionable.[16]

2.3.6 The acknowledgment of theological truth in a statement made by a text can be prepared for, but not produced, by the use of historical method. Conversely, an inappropriate application of historical methods can distort the truth-claim inherent in a text both for me and for others.[17]

2.4 When it comes to the question of certainty, there is a difference between historical and theological judgments. Theological judgments give unique saving significance to particular events of the past.[18]

2.4.3 Thus theological judgment will assign some degree of certainty to the "fact" of God's free communication of himself at a specific point in history, which historical research either cannot or will not achieve, for all its methods.[19]

2.4.4 However, it cannot provide a basis for the truth-claim of theology. This basis lies in the certainty of the divine promise in Jesus Christ, behind which we cannot investigate, a promise which comes to us in the unity of the message of the Old and New, Testaments and to which new witness is constantly borne in the history of the Church.[20]

On the question of the necessity of historical discovery of truth and its limitation, Hengel observes:

3.3.4 For the individual as for mankind as a whole, the question of meaning is resolved in connection with God as Creator and Lord of history and with the kingdom of God as the consummation of creation and history.[21]

3.3.5 There are christological reasons for a reference of this kind: i.e., as Creator and Lord of history and thus also of the future, God discloses himself to man through the revelation of his love in Christ Jesus as the "one Word of God that we have to hear, that we have to trust and to obey in both life and death" (First thesis of Barmen).[22]

As for the New Testament as a historical source and witness of faith and the appropriate application of historical methods, he reflects as follows:

4.3.4. Thus the truth of the New Testament message does not need any additional methodological "guarantees." The faith of the Church and the efficacy of Holy Scripture are expressed in this freedom.[23]

4.4.4. In all this we can never escape the appropriate application of historical methods. We cannot avoid the question of historical truth and are always in danger of engaging in speculative constructions which take us a long way from the text. It is exegesis which begins from a prior understanding based on faith that will make use of the historical methods at its disposal with particular care and accuracy.[24]

In conclusion, I would like to quote from an address given only a month ago at the Catholic University of America on the occasion of the reception of an honorary doctorate by Father

Hans Urs von Balthasar, one of Roman Catholicism's most revered theologians, scholars, and spiritual writers. I believe his words, in a fittingly meditative fashion, powerfully reinforce the well-founded pastoral concerns masterfully detailed in Stephen Clark's presentation.

This perfect being (Jesus) becomes manifest only from the testimonials of faith: those of Paul which are as important as the ones in the Acts of the Apostles; John is as authoritative as that of the synoptics. They, all together, form a magnificent polyphony—not a pluralism in the contemporary sense. They can be compared to views of a freestanding statue that has to be observed from all directions to understand its self-expression. The more facets we can view, the better we can grasp the unity of the inspiration. The possessor of this inspiration is the Church, the early charisma of which was to compose the New Testament and establish its canon. Only her eye of faith, guided by the Holy Spirit, could see the whole phenomenon of Jesus Christ.

Hence the fundamental principle that exegesis—which is indeed a legitimate theological science—can be practiced meaningfully only within the comprehensive view of the Church. If one stands outside, one will—unavoidably—begin to break up the indivisible unity of the figure [of Christ] by changing words to more fashionable ones which most likely do not mean the same, or to words that can be found also in other religions so that while one hears familiar expressions, these are merely generically religious and not uniquely individual (to Christianity). Such manipulations are just as destructive as if, for example, someone would omit every fifth or tenth beat from a phrase of a Mozart symphony or every second verse from Edgar Allan Poe's "The Raven."

Please believe me that in stating this I do not defend some kind of fundamentalism or biblical literalism, but the inspired spiritual phenomenon, the active, unified comprehension that is gained from the New Testament. The issue is not the letter but the content. To give an example: Already in pre-

Pauline tradition, and then, even more, by him and by John, but also in some of the words of the synoptics, the meaning of the Passion is understood as Christ's representative suffering for us (*qui propeter nos homines* and *propter nostram salutem*). If you relativize and flatten these statements, the entire Catholic faith collapses; the Eucharist loses its meaning; the flesh given for us and the blood shed for us make no sense. Neither is Christ's divinity necessary because only by this can he carry the sins of the world in his incarnation. Consequently, the Holy Trinity is also eliminated, as well as the central postulate of the New Testament—that God is Love—because the proof of this, according to John, is that the Father gave his Son in a superabundance of love to this world.

If we deny the *pro nobis* of the Cross, then we regress into being one of the general religions of history where God is either mythological in his involvement with the fate of the world (e.g. in process theology), or he hovers like a platonic sun of goodness above all the suffering of the world.

Moreover, if the integrity of the figure of Christ is lost from view, it cannot be demanded that the faithful identify their lives with him and, under certain circumstances, even endure martyrdom. Everything that deserves the name of ecclesial sanctity originates from this unified view. Regardless of what particular facet of Christ's figure was reflected in an individual saint, he or she always points to the whole. Teresa of Avila demonstrates not only love of God but also love of neighbor. Teresa of Calcutta derives all her love of neighbor from the love of God.[25]

Notes

1. Sacred Congregation for the Clergy, Second Office, *Prot. No.* 158897/11, Letter of October 30, 1978 to Archbishop John Quinn, President of the National Conference of Catholic Bishops," *Origins* 8, p. 374 (cf. left-hand margin).

2. Gabriel Moran, F.S.C., *Catechesis of Revelation* (New York: Herder and Herder, 1966), p. 151.

3. Gabriel Moran, F.S.C., *The Present Revelation: The Search for Religious Foundations* (New York: Herder and Herder, 1972), p. 19.

4. Gabriel Moran, F.S.C., *Catechesis of Revelation*, p. 33.

5. Gabriel Moran, F.S.C., "Bishops Preempt 'Revelation' for Themselves," *National Catholic Reporter* 15 (19 January 1978), p. 16.

6. Holy Office, *Syllabus Condemning the Errors of the Modernists, Lamentabili Sane* (3 July 1907), Boston: St. Paul Edition, p. 72.

7. *Ibid.*

8. *Ibid.*

9. *Ibid.*, p. 73.

10. *Ibid.*, p. 74.

11. *Ibid.*

12. Martin Hengel, *Acts and the History of Earliest Christianity* (Philadelphia: Fortress Press, 1980), p. vii-viii.

13. *Ibid.*, p. 129

14. *Ibid.*

15. *Ibid.*, p. 131

16. *Ibid.*

17. *Ibid.*

18. *Ibid.*

19. *Ibid.*, p. 132

20. *Ibid.*

21. *Ibid.*, p. 133-34

22. *Ibid.*, p. 134

23. *Ibid.*, p. 135

24. *Ibid.*, p. 136

25. Hans Urs von Balthasar, Acceptance Address to the Faculty of the Catholic University of America at a Convocation conferring the Doctorate of Humane Letters, 5 September 1980. Unpublished manuscript in files of the responder.

CHAPTER SIX

The Challenge Facing the Churches

Donald G. Bloesch

The Church in Crisis

The crisis of the modern church has its roots in the Enlightenment of the eighteenth century when the autonomy of human reason was emphasized over the authority of divine revelation. Horizontal concerns, those that deal with man's relationship to the world, came to preempt vertical concerns, those that deal with man's relationship to the transcendent. God came to be seen as a means to the realization of purely human goals, such as life, liberty, and the pursuit of happiness.

The alliance of the modern church with ideology is a sign of the capitulation of the church to the spirit of the times (*Zeitgeist*). Ideology in this context signifies a complex of ideas designed to reorganize society in such a way as to serve or protect the vested interests of a particular group in society. We see ideologies on the right: fascism, patriarchalism, monarchism. On the left we can mention feminism, socialism, and welfare liberalism. Such groups as Moral Majority and Christian Voice betray an accommodation of a section of the church to right-wing ideology.

Other organizations such as Abortion Rights Mobilization and Clergy and Laity Concerned signify an attempt to ally the faith with socially progressive or radical ideology.

It would be a mistake, of course, to detach ourselves from the political turmoils of our time on the grounds that we need to keep ourselves pure from ideological contamination. It is sometimes said that there is no "Christian" position on social issues; there are only Christians who hold positions. But such an attitude simply indicates that secularism has triumphed in a new way, because the world of politics and economics is then abandoned to the principalities and powers arrayed against the kingdom of Christ. Religion is not a private matter but embraces the whole of life. It is important to become involved in the social conflicts around us even at the risk of succumbing to the ideological temptation, for only in this way is our faith made relevant and credible to people today. At the same time, we need to maintain the focus on the transcendent goal of our faith, since in our social work we endeavor to turn people's attention away from the satisfaction of temporal and physical needs to Him who can satisfy the deeper spiritual needs of humanity (cf. John 6).

The modern church is challenged by an aggressive paganism from without and by apostasy and heresy from within. The principal adversary is what Jacques Ellul calls "technological humanism," the super-ideology of the technological society. This ideology corresponds roughly to what Charles Reich in his book, *The Greening of America*, terms "Consciousness II."[1] The two virtues of the technological society are utility and efficiency, and those individuals and groups that are deemed no longer useful are often unobtrusively and sometimes blatantly pushed to one side. Statistics is the measure of success in a society under the spell of technocratic humanism. In the technological milieu, conformity is stressed over individuality, docility over personal initiative, peer loyalty over personal independence. Such a mentality leads invariably and directly to collectivism, which fosters a servile dependence on the ruling organization, whether this be the union, the corporation, or the state.

Unable to withstand the appeal of technological values, modern religion is characterized by the loss of the supernatural or transcendent. A religion that rests upon faith in an authoritative revelation is supplanted by rationalism, which seeks to resolve mystery into a rational formula. The miracles in the Bible are explained away according to the canons of scientific rationality.

But rationalism is not the only adversary of biblical Christianity today. There is a new fascination with mysticism and occultism in which reason abdicates before mystery. In contrast to rationalism, biblical faith strives to preserve the mystery inherent in revelation. In opposition to mysticism, where reason is overwhelmed by mystery, biblical faith sees meaning within mystery.

New forms of the sacred appearing on the horizon seek to fill the spiritual vacuum created by the technological society, but they prove upon close examination to be in the service of technology. The new myths are valued for their utility and efficiency in making humanity safe or secure in a technological world. Technology itself is becoming sacralized: technique is elevated into a magical means of gaining control over one's destiny. According to Ellul, sex and politics are the new axes of the sacred.[2] Secular religions are emerging that enthrone social programs and promise utopia through social engineering.

The old language is still used, but it is given a radically new content. "God" becomes a creative force or energy rather than a living, personal, supreme being. "Salvation" generally signifies the realization of human potential as opposed to deliverance from sin and death. "Sin" indicates instability and alienation rather than revolt against God. "Faith" increasingly means trust in the creative potential within, not absolute dependence on the Wholly Other.

The spell of the technolgical society is evident in Evangelicalism and Catholicism as well as in Liberalism. Even in religiously conservative circles we witness a capitulation to the magic of technology. A preoccupation with size and numbers characterizes the new secular religiosity. Prayer is reduced to a technique or consciousness-raising experience. Regeneration comes to mean something that can be empirically measured. Salvation is reduced to a method of finding God or oneself. God becomes a means to the fulfillment of self or the welfare of humanity.

Erosion of Biblical Authority

There is nothing that highlights the crisis of the church in our time as much as the erosion of biblical authority. Whereas once the Bible was seen to be a book containing the very oracles of God, it is now reduced to a record of the religious experiences of an ancient people.

Biblical authority has been undermined by the rise of spiritualism, where the appeal is to the inner light or the voice of the Spirit rather than to the written Word of God. In these circles it is assumed that there is a discontinuity between what the Spirit said in biblical times and what he says today. It is also contended that the Spirit is speaking through the social sciences and politics, and this means that the Bible is therefore interpreted in the new light that comes to us from the social sciences.

Biblical authority has also been eroded by the prevalence of a narrow biblicism. Here there is an appeal to the Bible without focusing attention on its center and divine content—Jesus Christ. The Bible becomes grounded in itself and is thereby divorced from the interior witness of the Spirit. The Bible is considered primarily or even exclusively as a divine book; its humanity is said to be an aspect of its divinity. It is regarded as authoritative in everything that it touches upon. There is a one-to-one identity between the Bible and divine revelation. Correspondingly, the revelation of God is held to be directly accessible to human reason.

The same defensive mentality is evident in Roman Catholicism where we see the rise of a narrow ecclesiasticism, which also serves to bind the Spirit or the living Word of God. In this context, the church is exempted from criticism by the gospel, just as in a narrow biblicism the Bible is exempted from criticism by the transcendent criterion of the gospel or by what

Paul calls "the mind of Christ" (1 Cor 2:16).

We need today to recover a sacramental understanding of biblical authority. The Bible is not just great religious literature which points to revelation (the liberal-modernist view). Nor is it a collection of direct divine utterances, revelation in and of itself (the fundamentalist view). Instead, it is a divinely appointed channel and sign of revelation, an effectual sign by the action of the Spirit (the historic Reformation and original evangelical view). The ultimate standard of authority is neither historical scholarship nor the inspired original manuscripts but the cross of Christ shining through the Bible; it is the Bible illumined for the community of faith by the action of the Spirit.

The Bible is over the church, but it comes alive within the womb of the church. Its message is the judge and standard for the church, but it is communicated to the world by the proclamation of the church. The Bible might be likened to the light bulb and the church to the lamp. Jesus Christ, the living Word, is the light, and the Holy Spirit is the electricity. Unless the light shines forth from the lamp, both the Bible and the church are empty vessels.

The infallible criterion is neither the Bible nor the church, but the Word and the Spirit. The church shares in this infallibility when it proclaims the Word in the power of the Spirit. The Bible, too, partakes in this infallibility when the letter is united with the Spirit, when it functions as the sword of the Spirit (cf. Eph 6:17).

The God Problem

If there is anything that characterizes modern theology, it is the loss of the supernatural, living God of the scriptures. Instead of the personal-infinite God of biblical faith, we have a God that is impersonal and even finite or limited.

A cursory examination of current movements in theology reveals how drastically the doctrine of God is being reinterpreted. In liberation theology, it is fashionable to describe God as "the power of the future" or "the event of self-liberating love." In process theology, God becomes the creative process within nature, the directive of history, or the principle of integration. In Neo-Catholic theology, God is sometimes described as "the infinite in the finite" or "the absolute in the relative." In the Neoplatonic mysticism of scholars like Paul Tillich, God becomes the ground or depth of being, the infinite abyss beyond personality. In neo-mysticism, which tends to align itself with naturalism as opposed to idealism, God is reconceived as the creative surge within nature.

What is occurring in Western technological society is the democratization of God. In line with technocratic values, God becomes the facilitator or director of the world process rather than the Lord of the Universe. No longer the Creator, he is now the power of creativity or simply "the force."

As biblically faithful Christians today, we must affirm in unequivocal terms that God exists as Lord and Creator of the world. Furthermore, we need to stress the fact that this living, personal God has revealed himself decisively and definitively in the person of Jesus Christ. His self-revelation in Christ is not exhaustive, but it is final as far as human history is concerned. The Bible speaks of a general knowledge of God (Rom 1, 2), but this is not adequate for salvation. Nor does it give us a true picture of who God really is and what his plan is for us. It is a knowledge that renders us inexcusable, since we know something of the good but do not do it (Rom 1:20-21).

In a time when God has become a mystical blur, it is well to emphasize that human language can convey the knowledge of God through the power of the Spirit. God is supra-rational, but he is not irrational. Because God as the seat and ground of wisdom contains authentic rationality within himself and because we are created in his image, we can understand something of what he reveals about himself, including his will and purpose for humankind. We can truly speak of God by analogy, the analogy that only faith can discern in the encounter with Holy Scripture.

God is, indeed, the embodiment of rationality, but he is more than rationality. He is dynamic will and energy. It is misleading to define God as "absolute rationality" (Van Til), because this means that God is exhaustively rational. Nor should we refer to God as the "ultimate irrationality" (Whitehead), because this denies that God is a rational, personal being. Instead, we should conceive of God as the unity of wisdom, holiness, and love. He is the all-wise, all-holy supreme being who loves in freedom.

Reinterpreting Salvation

Once God is reinterpreted by avant-garde theology, the meaning of salvation is obviously drastically altered. The word "salvation" has too rich a history to be simply dismissed or abandoned. Instead, it is reconceived to signify something other than its biblical and historical intent.

Modern theologies reveal the extent of their divergence from the traditional view in the way they understand salvation and related terms, such as justification, redemption, and sanctification. In liberation theology, salvation is equated with liberation from economic and political oppression. In process theology, salvation has come to signify the realization of creative potential or the creative advance into novelty. In existentialist theology, salvation denotes the breakthrough into meaning and freedom. Or it is reconceived to mean liberation from the anxiety of meaninglessness. In neo-mysticism, salvation means entering into the depth dimension of existence. In the Gnostic strand of the new mysticism, salvation is equivalent to inner enlightenment.

To counter these grave misunderstandings, we need to reaffirm the objective, historical focus of salvation without minimizing its subjective pole. The death and resurrection of Jesus Christ are pivotal for the salvation of humankind. Jesus was not just the supreme example of self-giving love but the sin-bearer and mediator. His death was a vicarious, substitutionary sacrifice. The deliverance he achieved was not from political powers but from the spiritual powers of darkness, from what Luther called "the tyrants"—sin, death, and the devil.

Salvation, in the biblical view, is not conditional on man's moral status; on the contrary, it is to be understood as unconditional election, grace that goes out to the undeserving sinner.

It signifies not the justification of those who are already righteous or who are on the way to righteousness but instead the justification of the ungodly (cf. Rom 4:5; 5:6). The complementary truth, however, is that those whom God justifies he also begins to sanctify, for he does not leave us in our sins.

The Bible attests that salvation has a future as well as a past and present dimension. While our salvation has been decisively accomplished in God's act of reconciliation in Jesus Christ and while it has been efficaciously transmitted to us by the Holy Spirit in the decision of faith, it still needs to be revealed and fulfilled in that climactic act that signifies the culmination of the salvific process—the resurrection into glory. Justification and sanctification need to be completed in glorification if the salvific process is to achieve its aim. In our day, it is important to recover this eschatological dimension of salvation. Calvary and Pentecost need to be related to the second Advent if we are to see the plan of salvation in its total biblical perspective.

In opposition to liberation theology, we insist that our hope should be focused not on utopia, a new social order that humanity can achieve on its own, but instead on the eschaton, which signifies the inbreaking of the kingdom of God into worldly history. Our hope is not in what man can do through social engineering but in what God will do through his irresistible grace. The kingdom of God is not a product of human effort but a gift that God will bestow in his own way and time. This does not excuse us from working for a greater degree of justice within worldly history, for this is the divine commandment. We should realize, however, that the justice we can achieve even with the aid of grace is not the same as the perfect righteousness of the kingdom that can be anticipated now in fellowships of sacrificial love but that will eventually characterize the whole of human existence in the eschatological fulfillment of time.

Reappraising the Mission of the Church

Under the impact of the new theologies, the mission of the church, too, has undergone drastic revision. It is understood no longer as the conversion of the heathen but as the self-development of oppressed peoples. At the Ecumenical World Mission Conference in Bangkok (1973) the German theologian Jurgen Moltmann advocated salvation in and through "economic justice, political freedom and cultural change."[3] Frederick Herzog gives voice to this same mood:

> It [Christian missions] is not an attempt to impose strange dogmas upon other men not Christian, but the radical risk of sharing corporate selfhood with the wretched of the earth. . . . It is not at all conversion of . . . heathen to the Christian religion, but the surrender of the private middle class self.[4]

Behind the reconceptualization of mission is the heresy of universalism, which has increasingly taken a hold in both Roman Catholicism and mainline Protestantism. In the universalist perspective, God's grace is so all-encompassing that the reality of being spiritually lost is thereby denied. For Karl Barth, all are in the order of redemption, whether they believe or not. The Catholic theologian Karl Rahner envisages every person as "surrounded by grace," and those who live up to the light within them, even though they be Buddhist or atheist, are to be considered "anonymous Christians." According to the liberation theologian Gutiérrez, "not only is the Christian a temple of God; every man is."[5] Robert McAfee Brown insists that the mission of the church is not to bring Christ to the peoples of the world but instead to find Christ already among them.

While it is held that missions in the old sense still have a place among backward tribes who have not profited from the benefits of civilization, missions to the established world religions should take the form of dialogue rather than proselytization. It is said in some circles that while Christianity is the extraordinary way of salvation, the world religions are the ordinary way (Hans Küng). Particularly in avant-garde theology today, there is opposition to missions to Jews, since they supposedly represent one of the two religions of the covenant of

grace. This stance was already evident in Karl Barth and Rein-
hold Niebuhr. The German Christians, that party within the
German church that sought to come to terms with National
Socialism, also opposed missions to the Jews, but this was
because of their belief that religious and racial purity belong
together. The messianic Jew, Martin Meyer Rosen, suggests
that opposition to missions to the Jews has its basis in sub-
Christian motives:

> The subtlest form of anti-Semitism is to believe that Jesus is
> the way, that heaven and hell are realities, and then to de-
> cline to preach the gospel to the Jews. Any Christian who
> takes this path does so because he either regards his gospel
> as being unworthy of the Jews or the Jews as unworthy of
> his gospel.[6]

In the new perspective, the aim of missions is mutual enlightenment rather than conversion. We here see the pro-
nounced influence of the German philosopher-theologian
Ernst Troeltsch, who roundly attacked the idea of the abso-
luteness of Christianity. In his view, there can only be agreement and understanding but not conversion and transformation between the great religions. In the position that I
uphold, we should seek the conversion of both parties in the
dialogue to Jesus Christ, since he represents the negation as
well as the fulfillment of all religions, including the Christian
religion. Even the Christian partner in the dialogue needs to
have his faith renewed and deepened; he needs to be converted from a broken understanding to a fuller understanding of his Lord and Savior. If we see that Jesus Christ stands
over and against all purely human philosophies and religions, we as Christians can enter the inter-religious dialogue
in a spirit of humility and love and still entertain conversion
as the aim of the dialogue.

Against the new theology, we are called to recover Forsyth's
great insight that "the great motive for missions of every high
kind is not sentiment, but salvation."[7] The rapid decline in the
missionary force of both mainline Protestantism and Roman

Catholicism shows that missions have generally come to be regarded no longer as a matter of life and death but instead as a matter of mutual enrichment.[8] In place of a religious eclecticism that seeks to draw upon all the world religions in order to attain a more inclusive or global vision, I propose an evangelical catholicism that seeks to bring all peoples under the lordship and mastery of Jesus Christ. The holy catholic faith is both inclusive and exclusive. While it upholds the uniqueness of the biblical claims concerning Jesus Christ as God incarnate and as the only way to salvation, its goal is to include all peoples in the kingdom of Christ. It does not regard the world religions as wholly devoid of truth concerning God and his moral law, since all peoples are in contact with God's preserving or common grace. At the same time, it insists that the partially true insights in those religions need to be corrected and fulfilled by the perfect truth embodied in Jesus Christ.

An Emerging Confessional Situation

With the rise of theologies that substitute secular panaceas for the biblical gospel, a confessional situation looms on the horizon. The church needs to confess its faith anew when it is threatened by heresy from within. The time is fast approaching when the church will have to define itself as the true church as over against the false church. A confessional situation exists where the church is called to recover its identity in the midst of confusion and compromise. A confessing church will confess the true faith against misunderstandings and perversions of this faith. It will seek to rediscover and reaffirm orthodoxy in the midst of heresies that claim to speak in the name of the true church.

Can there be a confessing church without a confession of faith? This is certainly a possibility, but such a church cannot remain a confessing church without the theological ferment that eventually gives rise to a confession of faith. On the other hand, a confession of faith can become the basis for a confessing church as was the case in pre-Second World War Germany where the Barmen Confession created the resisting church movement against Hitler.[9]

Confessions must be seen as broken symbols. They do not embody the whole truth, yet they give a partial but potent testimony to the real truth. Because they are human formulations, though based on the illumination of the Spirit, they are constantly open to revision. Confessions should never be placed alongside the Bible but should always stand under the Bible. They express the will of God and the word of God for a particular situation. Authentic confessions of faith are addressed to the whole church, not just to one faction within the church. Their purpose is to reform and purify the church.

Our age has witnessed many new confessional and creedal statements, but for the most part they lack what constitutes an authentic confession of faith. The purpose of some of these statements of faith (for example, the Presbyterian Confession of 1967) is simply to express in words and deeds the meaning of the gospel for contemporary life. Or they signify attempts to protect particular traditions or the party line of the denomination. A true confession will speak a new word from God that stands in continuity with his past words but that calls the whole church to a fresh doctrinal stance and also to a style of life in keeping with the gospel. A true confession is born out of "absolute, dire need in which the very life of the Church" is at stake.[10] It arises in a situation where the church is devastated by heresy and error. When the church is in bondage to ideology, this is a sign of a confessional situation. Arthur Cochrane believes that with the rise of technocratic secularism on the left and nationalism on the right, we in America are on the verge of a church struggle (*Kirchenkampf*) that might parallel the struggle in Germany in the early 1930s.

A true confession will speak on ethics as well as dogmatics. It will address itself not only to misunderstandings in doctrine but also to immoralities in life. Grave social evils that currently pose a real challenge to the church are abortion on demand, the breakup of the family, increasing reliance on weapons of mass extermination in waging war, the population explosion, worldwide hunger, and the use of torture on political prisoners.

The object of a confession is not to reiterate the already-held views of a particular constituency. It is to challenge the partial conceptions and misconceptions of people in the light of a vision given to the church by the Holy Spirit. In this sense a confession can be regarded as one means by which God witnesses to himself in a particular time and history.

The real division in the church today is not political or sociological but theological. Behind the class and ethnic barriers is a conflict of faiths. On the one hand, there is secular humanism, which can take many different forms, and on the other hand there is evangelical, catholic Christianity. Invariably opposed to the historic Christian faith is the prevailing ideology of the age. In our time and place, this means the pseudo-democratic humanism that is partially created by and that directs the technological society.

Renewal of the church will come not simply by returning to confessions of past ages. Past confessions, if they are anchored in scripture, will continue to be guidelines for correct belief, but they will not have the same power and authority that they once had. The Holy Spirit always speaks new words to his people, but these words do not negate the words that he uttered in the past.

Many free church evangelicals resist the idea of a confessional church because of their adherence to the Bible alone as the standard for faith and practice. Or they say that what matters is not doctrine but personal experience. Yet every church is confessional, if not explicitly, then implicitly. The opposite of a confessional church is a latitudinarian church, which upholds the quest for truth over a definitive witness to the truth. Pietism, with its emphasis on the experience of the new birth over orthodoxy in belief, is especially open to latitudinarianism and eclecticism. It is a historical fact that the University of Halle, founded by evangelical Pietists, became the bastion of rationalism within one generation. Personal experience is important just as is the call to discipleship. But unless these are united with right doctrine, they can prepare the way for misunderstandings of the faith that cast a shadow over both our life and our experiences.

Need for a New Evangelical Alliance

The time is ripe for a new evangelical alliance, one that will embrace Bible-believing Christians in all branches of Christendom. The burgeoning biblical renaissance that we see in the Cursillo and charismatic movements in the Roman Catholic Church can become part of this new alliance so long as we focus upon a common goal and a common enemy.

Evangelicals in Protestantism too often engage in battles against past enemies. The controversies of the past, especially at the time of the Reformation, were not unimportant, but we need to realize that in the intervening history both sides have shifted and the areas of disagreement are no longer always the same. We still need to deal with these past issues but in a new context and with the aim of convergence rather than further division in the church.

We must also be alert to the fact that new theological issues are increasingly forcing themselves upon us. At the time of the Reformation, both sides affirmed the transcendence and aseity of God, the deity of Jesus Christ, the divine authority of the Bible, and the miracles of Jesus Christ. But all of these are now being called into question—by both Catholic and Protestant scholars.

In the Catholic churches today (including Eastern Orthodoxy and Eastern rite Roman Catholicism), it is possible to discern three strands. First, there is the sacramentalist-traditionalist strand, whose orientation is focused on the past. It is in this camp that we often find exaggerated devotion to Mary and an inordinate emphasis on papal supremacy and clerical celibacy. Secondly, there is the modernist-liberal strand, which upholds a universalistic concept of salvation and which emphasizes the basic goodness of man rather than his proneness to corruption and depravity. Thirdly, there is the biblical-evangelical strand that stresses the necessity for personal faith in addition to sacramental grace, and the ruling authority of the Bible in addition to the teaching authority of the church. It is this strand in Catholicism that could form an integral part of a new evangelical alliance.

It is also well for us to consider the increasing appreciation for the catholic heritage of the faith on the part of many evangelical Protestants. A historical-confessional strand has emerged within evangelicalism, and it is mounting an effective challenge to sectarian evangelicalism, especially dispensational fundamentalism. Many evangelicals today are intent on rediscovering the roots of their faith not only in the Reformation and the spiritual movements of purification subsequent to the Reformation—Pietism and Puritanism—but also in evangelical renewal movements within the church that antedate the Reformation. There is a noticeable appreciation for the Church Fathers and the doctors of the medieval church. Even the Catholic mystics are being reappraised, though the tensions between a biblical, evangelical piety and the mainstream of Christian mysticism will always remain. Nonetheless, it is well to note that Augustine and Bernard of Clairvaux affirmed salvation by grace through faith alone and John of the Cross stressed the need to walk by faith alone. The nineteenth century French Carmelite nun, Thérèse of Lisieux, substituted for the mystical ladder of medieval piety, by which we ascend to heaven through meritorious works, the elevator or lift, by which we are taken to heaven by free grace alone.[11] Moreover, many evangelicals today recognize the place for community life within the church even where this takes the form of monastic orders. The doctrine of the saints is also being re-examined by forward-looking evangelicals. Other catholic themes that are being given new recognition by evangelicals are the role of the sacraments in our salvation, the quest for visible church unity, and the need for church authority and discipline.

If evangelical Protestants are to play a vital role in a new evangelical alliance, we will have to recover a high doctrine of the church. Too often the church is simply seen as a society of like-minded individuals, as a club for the ethically respectable, rather than a divine institution established for the salvation of sinners and founded and maintained by Jesus Christ. It is incumbent on us to recover the historical marks of the true church: catholicity, oneness, apostolicity, and holiness. We must also appropriate the two practical marks added by the

Reformers, Luther and Calvin: the faithful preaching of the Word and the right administration of the sacraments. We urge our Catholic brothers and sisters in the interest of both unity and truth to accept these marks proffered by the Reformers as bona fide characteristics of the true church.

Both Catholics and Protestants today would do well to emphasize these additional practical marks of the church that were given at least tacit recognition by the Pietists and Puritans: discipline, fellowship, and mission. Can there be a church truly catholic, truly Reformed, and truly evangelical unless church discipline is maintained and unless there is an urgency to mission? And indeed, apart from the fellowship of love (*koinonia*), all of these other marks are to no avail (cf. 1 Cor 13).

The coming conflict in the church is between the holy catholic faith and a new modernism that has in effect abandoned the old religion for a new one. It is between those who uphold the gospel as presented in Holy Scripture and those who seek to come to terms with modernity. This is a conflict that will cut across all denominational lines. It will bring together the faithful remnant present in all churches (though not necessarily to the same degree). It will call this remnant of true believers into battle against a latitudinarianism that disdains doctrinal particularity and a religious eclecticism that seeks to draw from all religious traditions in order to arrive at a higher synthesis that is tantamount to a new religion.

Liberals are not the only culprits; many conservatives unwittingly accommodate to modernity when they uncritically adopt the values of the technological society: utility, efficiency, and productivity. When method or technique preempts doctrine as the major concern of the church, this is a sign that secularism is again triumphant even if it be in the guise of the old-time religion. An emphasis on church growth that elevates organizational expansion over fidelity to truth betrays a compromise with secular, technocratic humanism.

In order to counter the secularizing trends in the church today, we need to stress contemplation over action as a reminder that prayer and devotion are the wellspring of all creative activity in the church. Similarly, it is important to emphasize the priority of being over becoming, since only those who exist in the truth ever do the truth. Finally, we need to stress the priority of faith over works, for both works of mercy and justice have their source in faith in the living God.

As I see it, the church has four options. First, there is the way of repristination by which the church seeks to restore practices and beliefs of an earlier period of history. Those who wish simply to return to past confessions of faith belong in this category. It is an approach particularly susceptible to isolationism and separatism. Secondly, there is the way of accommodation by which the church attempts to discover points of identity or contact between the message of the faith and the highest values of the culture. H. Richard Niebuhr in his book *Christ and Culture* referred to this as the "Christ of culture" position, which stands diametrically opposed to the first position, "Christ against culture."[12] Thirdly, there is the way of correlation by which we begin with the questions of the culture and then try to find in the gospel the Christian answer. This is what Niebuhr calls the "Christ above culture" position in that grace seeks to build upon what nature offers. My deepest reservation about this strategy is that too often we let the culture dictate the way we answer its creative questions. The wiser alternative is to lead the culture to ask the right questions, but it cannot do this unless it has first been exposed to the Christian answer.

Finally, there is the way of confrontation. Here the church confronts the culture with the claims and demands of the gospel and calls the culture to repentance. The purpose is not the negation of the culture (as in the Christ against culture approach) but its conversion. Niebuhr calls this position "Christ transforming culture"; its principal exponents in Christian history were Augustine and Calvin. This is also the approach I recommend, for we are called to bring the whole of creation under the dominion of Jesus Christ. Our task is not simply to preserve the doctrines and values of the past but to permeate the whole of society with the leaven of the gospel. In my Reformed perspective, this entails overthrowing false ideologies and philosophies and replacing them by the holy catholic faith. It also involves Christianizing social structures, since the ultimate goal is a holy community in which every facet of society is brought under the guidance and direction of the revealed law of God.

Biblical religion is a religion of confrontation, not mediation. It can tolerate and even encourage a pluralism in witness, but not in dogma. It can make a place for liturgical diversity but not for a variety in confessional stances. True religion will seek to redeem the world rather than make common cause with the world. It will aspire to bring the whole world under the lordship of Christ rather than unite with the world in promoting a vague religiosity. We uphold a catholic vision that seeks to include all peoples in the kingdom of Christ over religious eclecticism, which tries to reconcile disparate religions and philosophies in an overarching synthesis.

We will recover the true evangelical faith when we reclaim the apostolic mandate to preach the gospel to the whole creation, when we call all peoples to become disciples of the king. Evangelicalism and evangelism go together. The unnerving decline in the missionary personnel in the mainline churches today is an incontrovertible sign that all is not well, since only a missionary church can conquer the world for Jesus Christ. The holy catholic church will be reborn when it becomes a church in mission to a world in bondage, to a world that is crying out for the salvation that only Christ can give.

Notes

1. Charles Reich, *The Greening of America* (New York: Random House, 1970).

2. Jacques Ellul, *The New Demons*, trans. C. Edward Hopkin (New York: Seabury Press, 1975), pp. 48-87.

3. *Christianity Today* 17, no. 13 (30 March 1973), p. 7.

4. Frederick Herzog, *Liberation Theology* (New York: Seabury Press, 1972), p. 147

5. Gustavo Gutiérrez, *A Theology of Liberation* (Maryknoll, New York: Orbis Books, 1973), p. 193.

6. *The Christian Century* 89, no. 27 (19 July 1972), p. 778.

7. P.T. Forsyth, *The Work of Christ* (London: Independent Press, 1938), pp. 122-23.

8. There was a 30 percent decline in the number of American Catholic missionaries from 1968-1980. See John W. Donohue, "A Walk on the Bright Side," in *America* 143, no. 13 (1 November 1980), p. 266. The decrease in the missionary personnel in the mainline Protestant denominations has been equally if not more striking.

9. See Arthur C. Cochrane, *The Church's Confession Under Hitler* (Philadelphia: Westminster Press, 1962).

10. Arthur C. Cochrane, "Barmen and the Confession of 1967," *McCormick Quarterly* 19, no. 2 (January 1966), p. 138.

11. For an illuminating study of the evangelical dimension in the spirituality of Thérèse of Lisieux, see Ida Friederike Görres, *The Hidden Face*, trans. Richard and Clara Winston (New York: Pantheon, 1959).

12. H. Richard Niebuhr, *Christ and Culture* (New York: Harper, 1951).

Response

Peter Hocken

I am particulary glad to respond to Dr. Bloesch's paper "The Challenge Facing the Churches." The paper is admirable in its comprehensiveness, its catholicity of thought, and in its clarity of expression. I would like to thank Dr. Bloesch, not only for this paper but for the wide range of his published writings. Catholics often write about contemporary Christianity with insufficient attention to the scriptures, and Evangelicals have been known to pay great attention to the Word without enough attention to the realities of the Church. Dr. Bloesch cannot be accused of any such neglect, as is evident in his two books on new patterns of Christian community life, *Wellsprings of Renewal* and *Centers of Christian Renewal*.

My comments on the paper all involve in some way the role of the Holy Spirit in Christian life. I recognize in Dr. Bloesch's paper a real concern to hold the Word and the Spirit in proper relationship. However, I believe it is the Spirit's role that can be helpfully expanded.

My first point concerns the heart of the Gospel. Dr. Bloesch mentioned the need to reaffirm the objective, historical focus of salvation without minimizing the subjective pole. My questions are: what are the central truths of the Gospel? How do we come to know what they are? Is the heart of the Gospel as obvious as we often think it is?

It might be helpful to consider how we ourselves have come to our present understanding of the central core of the Gospel message. For myself, I know there has been a development in my understanding on this point. A few years ago, when I was teaching in a seminary in England and was active on many Church commissions, especially ecumenical commissions, I would have been very indignant had anyone suggested that I had less than a thorough knowledge of the heart of the Gospel. My deepened understanding of the basic Gospel message came about through moving from England to the U.S. to become a member of a committed covenant community. This made clear to me that we do not come to a realization of the central core of the Gospel simply by New Testament exegesis, by knowledge of the historic creeds, and by comparative liturgy, though each of these has its respective contribution to make. Rather it is the Holy Spirit who brings the Word to life in the hearts of believers. The Spirit witnesses to Jesus Christ. "The Spirit of truth who proceeds from the Father, he will bear witness to me" (Jn 15:26).

It is as the Christian community receives the Word in faith and submits to that Word that the truth of the Gospel takes on flesh and blood. The Word becomes incarnate through the Spirit. As Christians, we come to a grasp of the heart of the Gospel through its incarnation in the Christian community by the action of the spirit in each and in all.

What I now see to be at the heart of the Gospel includes all those elements that Dr. Bloesch mentioned centering on salvation through the death and resurrection of Jesus Christ. But I would make some additions. Pentecost should be included, as it is an essential part of the foundational events. It is only as Pentecost, the resurrection, and the Cross are seen in their essential interrelationship, which is implicit in the liturgical cycle of our Churches, that we have the right balance between what God has done in Jesus Christ and the consequences of that in those who believe in him. It is the Holy Spirit, poured out by the risen Lord, who applies the power of the Cross to human hearts, issuing in repentant faith. When Pentecost is neglected, the power of God for the eradication of sin is not fully realized, and the depth of God's work of salvation is lost.

I would also add a belief, a hope, and a longing for the second coming as included in the core of Christian faith. In my experience, this has come about through the revealing work of the Holy Spirit in the hearts of those living in committed community. This point adds to what Dr. Bloesch said about the future element in salvation. Not all emphasis on the future and not every theology of hope leads to a longing and praying for the second coming of Christ. However, I do not know of any authentic revival of Christian faith where the Spirit does not restore this hope and longing. This hope is one of the most effective defenses against elimination of the supernatural.

The Holy Spirit does not simply reveal a list of central truths, but the Spirit reveals these truths in their essential interrelationship. This interrelationship is not grasped by abstract conceptual arrangement but by an understanding of Christian corporate life where these truths in their organic relatedness are operative in human lives.

The role of the Spirit in bringing the Word to life in our hearts and minds is crucial, as Dr. Bloesch pointed out, for avoiding all forms of conservatism, whether fundamentalist Protestant on the one hand or traditionalist Catholic on the other hand. The Second Vatican Council's decree on ecumenism mentioned that there is a hierarchy of truths in the Christian faith. "In Catholic doctrine there exists an order or hierarchy of truths, since they vary in their relation to the foundation of the Christian faith" (par. 11). This passage, which has sometimes been used to minimize the significance of unwelcome teaching, is in fact an endorsement of this emphasis on the heart of the Gospel.

My second point concerns the nature of Christian theology. Dr. Bloesch has emphasized the theological challenge to the Churches, stressing the need for an orthodox response that is truly creative and which does not merely repeat the past. As he said, "there has to be a ferment of theology." Any theology that fulfills the traditional definition of faith—Christian faith seeking understanding—will be creative. In this colloquy, we have been hearing a great deal about contemporary theological output that does not seem to be Christian faith seeking understanding. So it is important for us to consider the role of the Holy Spirit in this process of Christian faith seeking understanding that issues in Christian theology.

Christian faith is faith in Jesus Christ, the Son of God, incarnate, Spirit-filled, crucified, dead, risen, reigning, returning.

Knowledge is only truly Christian theology when it stems from this revelation of God in Christ Jesus. It is only as human lives are submitted to the Lord that new understanding, the understanding of faith, becomes possible. Theology is not simply the sum total of the thinking of Church members or professed Christians. Christian theology is a knowledge that arises out of a lived faith that is an obedient faith seeking understanding. Just as the Christian is called on to submit his life, his habit patterns, and his priorities to God, as revealed in Jesus Christ, so has he to submit his ideas and his ways of thinking. There is a death and resurrection that has to take place in our thinking before a truly Christian theology can be thought and uttered. This death and resurrection is the work of the Spirit (cf. Rom 8:13). Each thought needs testing in the light of the basic Christian message that has already changed the life of the thinker.

At the heart of the death in the Christian's thinking is submission of our minds to God's revelation. A submission to authority is inherent in Christianity. Obviously there are differences among the Churches as to how this authority is conceived. But what we can agree upon, I believe, is that there is no real living theology without a submission of the mind to authority, to God's authority, however we differ in our beliefs as to how that authority is manifested. Dr. Bloesch mentioned that there is heresy within each one of us. In our heads, including my own, there are ideas and emphases that are not of God, that do not flow from our grasp of the death and resurrection of Jesus Christ. We have to let the Holy Spirit put our ideas and emphases through the baptismal waters. Only Christians who have truly learned to discern the will and mind of God in other areas of behavior are likely to understand what is meant by discerning the will and mind of God in our thinking, in our ideas, and what we choose to express.

My third point concerns the relationship between the condition of contemporary theology and the moral and spiritual condition of the people of God. Throughout this colloquy, we have been remarking on the significance and potential of such a coming together of Evangelicals and Catholics. But in addition to this more obvious Catholic and Evangelical dialogue, there is in this colloquy an exchange that has not been explicitly noted between people who live in covenant communities and those who do not. It is clear that there is a common concern among us about the orthodoxy and the adequacy of much that is being taught today under the name of theology. I believe that those at this colloquy who are living a committed lifestyle in these communities are manifesting a sharper awareness of the serious moral and spiritual condition of our people. It was only after I came to live in covenant community that I began to see how serious is the condition of the majority of people in our society. Lest that seem an unduly jaundiced view, I can add that I had to realize first the seriousness of my own condition. I do not believe that anything can be done to rectify unorthodox or inadequate teaching without a corresponding concern to make God's salvation fully operative in the lives of the people. It is as much an ignorance of the Lord and the power of his Spirit to transform human lives that produces off-center theology as it is erroneous doctrine that kills the spiritual life.

Finally, I would suggest the addition of the Holiness movement and the Pentecostal-charismatic movement to the movements mentioned by Dr. Bloesch at the end of his paper, namely, Puritanism, pietism, and evangelicalism. I know that anything that I am able to share about the work of the Spirit comes through the work of God in the charismatic renewal. While it is true that the Catholics here at this colloquy are not simply those that are in the charismatic renewal, we can recognize that this kind of coming together in common concern between Catholics and Evangelicals would not have been possible without the grace of God poured out in the charismatic renewal.

Response

Richard Lovelace

I too am very grateful to Dr. Bloesch for this very thoughtful and comprehensive paper. I appreciate especially the recovery of catholic wholeness which his comprehensive scholarship has sought, and also his tenacious retention of Reformation essentials. He is a convinced Protestant with thoroughly catholic sympathies. He is also, as this paper shows, gifted both in tracing theoretical problems and in offering practical, pastoral solutions.

Dr. Bloesch is primarily a systematic theologian. I am what Roman Catholics call a spiritual theologian—a historical theologian of Christian experience, specifically of renewal movements in the church. There is a large difference between these two vocations. I am hesitant to move across this distance and attempt to improve or correct Dr. Bloesch's analysis. Instead, I should like to take off from one point where I have a minor and perhaps only apparent difference, and talk about the prescription for recovery and renewal in the church.

Let me begin with a statement which I believe Dr. Bloesch and our other speakers would also affirm: *There is more involved in reforming the thinking of the Christian movement than simply attaining a perfect theology and then transmitting this to the rest of the church.* Dr. Bloesch's whole instinct as a theologian leads him to search for the clearest, fullest systematic expression of biblical truth, and then to establish this as the church's confession. But we cannot solve everything by establishing a perfect theology, because *there are relational and spiritual preconditions for the recovery and retention of live orthodoxy in the church.*

As Bible-believing Christians, heirs of the Fathers and the Reformers who laid the confessional foundations of the church, we must ask ourselves why we have failed to persuade so much of the church to believe in orthodoxy. There are many answers to that question, but among the most important is that Catholic and Protestant Evangelicals, the standard-bearers of orthodoxy, have not always met the spiritual preconditions for the propagation of biblical thinking in the church. In the church's theological warfare, there is something more subtle involved than the production of new confessions, although I do believe with Dr. Bloesch that this kind of initial step is helpful and necessary.

In the United Presbyterian Church, in 1978, we produced a kind of new Barmen Confession as we faced the crucial question of the ordination of practicing homosexuals in the church. The five Evangelicals on the Task Force studied the issue and found that it touched many vital loci in theology and provided important avenues through which to get at theological needs and promote reformation. We produced an extensive statement that, among other things, stated the normative character of scripture over the sciences; asserted the validity of biblical ethical norms and repudiated antinomian sex ethics; promised deliverance from the bondage of sin through Christ's redemptive work; rejected universal salvation; and insisted that in its mission the church should call for repentance and conversion from all forms of sin, including homosexual practice. We also balanced rather carefully the priorities of evangelism and social justice in mission. We thought we had developed the strongest body of Reformed theology to pass a General Assembly in decades. It was immediately broadcast to every Presbyterian minister, including those overseas. What was its effect? It cheered up Presbyterian Evangelicals, and it also produced a great sigh of relief in the church's center. But it did not quite produce a reformation. Instead, it provoked an angry, nervous, almost desperate counter-movement of concern among the theological secularists who suddenly saw themselves as a surrounded and decreasing minority. It may surprise some of you here in the Roman Catholic Church and other Protestant bodies, but Presbyterian liberals see themselves as cornered and dwindling, and I believe they are indeed losing ground.

But the battle is by no means over, and the conservatives could still lose it by spiritual failures under current pressures in the conflict. They need spiritual strength, and also an appropriate strategy to press their gains in ways which will educate and not alienate the rest of the church.

What posture and strategy are most suited to this task? A new confessionalism, in which an extensive confessional statement is suddenly forced like a cookie cutter upon every mind in the church by judicial authorities, is not a useful or even a practicable strategy. Beginning denominations can be unified around large documents. But the best one can hope for in dealing with large groups of Christians that are centuries old is that they will submit to the intellectual restraint of a short statement of essential beliefs garnered from the church's authentic tradition, while remaining critically open to the renovation and extension of the church's mind by more recent theologians.

In the United Presbyterian situation, theological progress toward a recovery of biblical faith took place not so much because we produced a new confessional statement, but rather because the crisis over homosexuality drove us to a deepened life of prayer and a new openness to the Holy Spirit speaking through the Word. It forced our lay people and leaders into comprehensive, continuous prayer for the life of our church at levels we had never reached before. The Presbyterian Charismatic Communion, in particular, supported the work of our Task Force, praying for each member by name at regular intervals each Friday. As a result of this prayer, during the two years we deliberated, a time of intense spiritual conflict and the endurance of torrents of blasphemy and theological foolishness, I have never experienced such a powerful enabling of the Holy Spirit in speaking and writing, and such a personal sense of his supporting presence. The other Evangelicals on the Task Force echoed this sentiment, and at San Diego, in the General Assembly which decided the matter in our favor, we saw an extraordinary outpouring of renewed Reformed theology through a large number of younger leaders rallied by the crisis. . . .

Dr. Bloesch alluded in his paper to the *Confession of 1967*. In the 1960s the United Presbyterian Church was called upon to produce a new short statement of faith which would honestly express its faith in the context of the modern world. The *Westminster Confession* was a long, seventeenth-century systematic theology on microfilm, and we felt that we needed something brief that would more honestly express the real consensus of Reformed belief in the church. But instead of getting this, we got Dr. Edward Dowey's theology spread out on microfilm, transmitted through a committee. This was an attempt to search out a new post-Barthian theological consensus which would accurately represent the church's mind. But it failed because there were alternate views both on the left and right which fell outside Dr. Dowey's statement. Currently, it has roused some opposition and occasioned some neglect, and it has not been able to prevail in the church as a theological norm or even as an educative tool. . . .

What I have been suggesting is that extensive confessional statements—which I believe are best created by prophetic individuals like Dr. Bloesch and not by committees!—are helpful in retuning and instructing the mind of the church. But what we need to guard the church's magisterium and keep its mind fixed on the essentials of orthodoxy is subscription to smaller documents (I suppose one calls them creeds) which state *the minimal circle of essential doctrines common to the whole church.* What would result from such a practice is a theological situation which I call *limited pluralism,* pluralism within the limits of an essential doctrinal consensus. John Calvin, in Book IV of the *Institutes,* notes that we must have freedom and diversity in the way we interpret scripture, but that there is a circle of truth which must be held inviolable and asserted by the church's magisterium, including items such as our Lord's deity. Unfortunately, Calvin did not fully itemize the doctrines in that small circle, and later Protestants produced huge confessional systems which were too lengthy to bind the church's mind effectively in future centuries. Today Presbyterians are being forced to go back in time and attempt to read Calvin's mind to obtain the core doctrines, but I think this will not prove too difficult.

And this process may point the way to theological solutions for the church of the future. I hope that our current situation of division in denominations can yield in some way to a reunited church, including a healthy creative diversity and at the same time retaining a steady affirmation of the essential articles of biblical faith. It is impossible to corral all the horses which have escaped from the Reformation confessional stables and get them back into the barn, at this point, and it probably would not be advisable to do so even if we could. We are dealing with a massively increased Christian movement in the center of a worldwide secular brainstorming session, in which people are generating new ideas like popcorn, sometimes with good motives and sometimes with bad, as in the case of the race for the double helix, in which the fuel was the desire for fame and fortune. This secular mind-storm is like an induction coil which surrounds the church and especially the educational systems through which Christians are processed. The mind-storm occasionally turns up some vital ideas which are part of God's Common Grace, such as many of the items of technological progress which make our lives easier today. (With all our talk about the evils of technology, I am glad that I am alive today and not in the eighteenth century, because I would not last a year without the benefits of modern medicine.) At other times, the secular mind-storm exerts a deforming influence upon the church's mind, because non-Christian minds are driven by a bias against God which leads them to construct systems which deny his existence, his commands, and his promises, and to organize human thinking against the kingdom of his Son. But it is impossible to turn off the current behind the secular humanist think-tank, nor would it be advisable to do so.

Let me say just a few more words in favor of the secularization process. Church history teaches that humanists are sometimes more humane than Christian dogmatists. Cotton Mather says somewhere, "God has a wondrous tenderness toward humane nature," and if God's people will not care for those who need care, he will reach out through non-Christians and minister to them in his mercy and his love. Some of the works of humanists are not only manifestations of God's Common Grace; they are rebukes to the Christian movement when it has ceased to care passionately for human beings, for their physical and social well-being as well as their souls. If we do not have a genuinely Christian humanism, we are going to have to put up with a good deal of non-Christian humanism, because God loves humanity! Erich Beyreuther, a good scholar specializing in German Pietism, has said that there is a mysterious coherence of early Enlightenment thought and the classical Pietist concerns; that both had world-embracing plans for the social transformation of mankind. Those two streams diverged in the eighteenth century. But the Evangelicals of the eighteenth and nineteenth centuries continued to cherish world-embracing plans of social betterment for mankind. And I believe biblical Christians must continue to promote justice, especially the redistribution of resources in a fair and equitable manner, as well as broadcasting the core of the gospel, or we will short-circuit the gospel's credibility. And in the church, we must have a genuinely biblical theology of human liberation, or else we will see bad literation theology erupting over and over again!

I believe that one key to the recovery of live orthodoxy in the church may be an ecclesiological pattern which Ralph Winter has pointed out, especially in an interesting book called *The Warp and the Woof*, coauthored by R. Pierce Beaver. Winter distinguishes between *modalities* and *sodalities*. The *modality* is the great movement consisting of the mass of professing Christians and their offspring, moving through history. The *sodality* is the small, reforming task force God raises up from time to time to labor within the modality and renew its life and mission. Some examples of sodalities: the ascetic movement of Athanasius and Augustine which reformed the post-Constantinian church and extended its mission; the Franciscan movement which preached the gospel to the poor; and the Dominican movement which fought heresy. The Jesuit Order and the Protestant Reformation are both instances of sodalities attempting to reform the church. Unfortunately, one of these orders was ejected from Western Catholicism. But both the Protestant and Catholic modalities today are generating new reforming sodalities, Evangelical and Charismatic movements which are essentially addressing similar tasks in both the larger bodies!

We are participating in a historic occasion here as these sodalities join forces theologically. I would like to see us work together toward a united church in which Augustinians, Lutherans, Calvinists, Wesleyans, and Barthians might labor together, challenging one another when this is needed, but combining forces whenever possible to inform the church's pluralism with the central core of biblical faith. I believe we need a pandenominational renewing and reforming order. And I think we see one being born today! Currently, all the major Protestant denominations have renewal groups working within them. Executives from these groups meet annually to compare notes and chart strategy, because every denomination from the United Church of Christ to the Episcopal Church is facing the same problems and opportunities.

Here in Ann Arbor we see a unique community meeting ground where Catholics and Protestant Evangelicals in The Word of God community are bearing a reforming burden for the whole of world Christendom. May we not be moving toward a future coalition, a kind of center of centers of renewal, in which we can combine forces against secular intrusions in the church's mind and life? We seem to be working in isolation against a well-unified *deforming* order, with its headquarters in one Eastern city and its interdenominational efforts well-coordinated. Theological secularists have joined forces; should we not do the same? Count Zinzendorf's Herrnhut Community offers us a pattern for this kind of Evangelical ecumenism (and let us remember that he worked with Roman Catholics and met with the Pope at a time when this was anathema for Protestants). It seems to take the kind of commitment generated by community life to produce the tenacity to fight the spiritual warfare necessary to bring the church back to biblical sanity.

Could such a pandenominational renewal order succeed? It is already having some success, although its forces are not yet fully unified. At times during this conference, I must confess, I have felt like a person on the caboose of a train that is plunging 90 miles an hour into a new future, looking backwards at a religious wasteland that we are rapidly leaving behind. We are told that technology has ruined us; but futurists and technologists are now calling for a return to religion! They tell us that we are going into a post-technological era in which people will be turning again to transcendent sources of meaning, a renewed supernaturalism in which our opposition will not be secular unbelief but pagan superstition! Our enemies in the 1980s may not be skeptical humanists, but witches and practitioners of extrasensory perception. The Bible, with its depiction of the idolatry of Baal and Ashtoreth, the horned god and female goddess of witchcraft, may again become a strangely relevant book in the 1980s.

Jeremy Rifkin, in *The Emerging Order*, suggests that in the post-technological era Christianity, and specifically Evangelical and charismatic Christianity, offer the best hope for humanity in the new age of scarcity. He asserts that a new Reformation may be at hand, in which the whole culture and society may be drawn into the Evangelical resurgence as they face the crises of the 1980s and 90s. I hope this will prove true. I have just viewed Woody Allen's brilliant new film, *Stardust Memories*, and have been startled by Allen's echoes of Rifkin's thesis in a later book, *Entropy*, which speaks of the decay of all things apart from God's renewing energy. Cultural bellwethers like Allen are now beginning to sound like the book of Ecclesiastes. They are pointing to the desperate emptiness of the ·life of technological progress and consumption. T.S. Eliot did this in the 1920s as a lone witness; but now the whole intellectual community is taking up his lament!

Philipp Jakob Spener, the great Lutheran Pietist, said that we will not be able to unite all the fragments of the shattered body of Christ until there is a comprehensive spiritual awakening of every part. Theological consensus must wait upon spiritual renewal. I believe we can see that renewal dawning today in Ann Arbor, a community in which what I call "regional ecumenical renewal" is happening. And it is happening in many other places as well. What will be the result? Certainly not instant utopia; unity will not come without a great deal of spiritual and theological warfare. But I believe the eventual result will be what Dr. Bloesch has pointed toward: a reforged unity, a catholic unity, that will include Protestants and Eastern Orthodox and Roman Catholic Christians. I hope that unity will reach out and penetrate not just a handful of the world's billion professing Christians, not just a tiny remnant, but that it will penetrate and transform the whole body of the world church.

Conclusion

In recent years, evangelicals such as Donald Bloesch, Richard Lovelace, and Howard Snyder have voiced a sense that the time has come for opening lines of communication with Catholics. Snyder, for example, wrote in *The Community of the King* that "the time may be ripe around the world for the emergence of a thoroughly biblical and evangelical movement that includes Catholic, Protestant, Orthodox, and Jewish Christians." From the Catholic side there have been calls for Catholics to turn their ecumenical sights away from mainstream Protestantism primarily and to focus instead on communication with evangelical Protestants. Ralph Martin, who was an invited Catholic observer at the 1980 meeting of the World Evangelical Fellowship, has said, "In the struggle for the gospel that is going on today in the Catholic Church, and in the midst of the manifold pressures on Christian living, increased Catholic contacts with Protestant evangelicals would be very strengthening."

It was to answer this rising sense of need for evangelical-Catholic discussion that we sponsored the colloquy. Significantly, all these men participated in it. The colloquy can thus be seen as part of a nascent movement of evangelicals and Catholics who recognize some common concerns which fall under the heading "Christianity Confronts Modernity." What we may be witnessing, then, is a movement signalling a historic realignment among Christians, bringing together evangelical Protestants, Roman Catholics, and, potentially, Orthodox around a set of pressing pastoral and theological concerns. The Anglican writer Harry Blamires, who also attended the colloquy, has written of this development:

> Surveyal of contemporary movements in religious thought leads one to the conclusion that, in the near future, the

239

dominating controversy within Christendom will be between those who give full weight to the supernatural reality at the heart of all Christian dogma, practice, and thought, and those who try to convert Christianity into a naturalistic religion by whittling away the reality and comprehensiveness of its supernatural basis. This conflict is already upon us and is pushing into the background the controversies which caused deep and bitter strife in previous ages. The old controversies over grace and free will, faith and works, authority and individualism, are of course still with us; but they no longer in themselves represent the gravest disunity within Christendom.

The message of the colloquy is that Blamires's "near future" is now. In Donald Bloesch's words, "The time is ripe for a new evangelical alliance, one that will embrace Bible-believing Christians in all branches of Christendom."

The realignment of evangelical Protestants and Roman Catholics is taking place in circumstances quite different from those in which the Protestant and Catholic modernist controversies were played out at the beginning of the century. Continuous modernization has changed the world several times over since then, and in its constant acceleration has brought the world to the point of crisis in many areas, as in the social disintegration of the Western nations and the commencement of severe struggles over dwindling resources. The challenges of modernity to Catholics and evangelicals which this book has traced come at a moment in history which presents unprecedented dangers and opportunities to the cause of Christ.

What, then, is this evangelical-Catholic alliance to be like? First, it must be concerned with pastoral issues as well as theological ones.

As Mark Kinzer's essay so forcefully demonstrates, the problems which modernity creates are not only in the realm of ideas and ways of seeing the world but equally in the realm of social structures, institutions, and patterns of daily life. We need not only to identify the points at which genuinely Christian thinking is being threatened by secular perspectives and presuppositions; we need just as much to find ways of strengthening and supporting Christians in actually living out their lives day by day in obedience to the scriptures and loyalty to Jesus Christ. As Howard Snyder commented during the colloquy, we need to give attention to the experience of Christian churches, communities, and groupings which are succeeding in building new pastoral structures and renewing old ones to meet the challenges of modernity in everyday life. The sense that the colloquy had raised this issue without adequately treating it was one of the most widely shared reflections of those who took part in the meeting.

Another way of expressing the need for pastoral as well as theological cooperation is to say that it should be constructive, not just defensive. Our attention cannot be solely on maintaining orthodoxy. It must be on finding new ways of doing pastoral work, new approaches to evangelism, new pastoral structures which will sustain a powerful Christian environment where Christians live out their values together, Christian family life flourishes, and the reality of the gospel shines out to the world around. In this context Richard Lovelace's remark comes to mind: "there are relational and spiritual preconditions for the recovery and retention of live orthodoxy in the church." We must seek the spiritual and pastoral renewal which will enable us to live out the orthodox teaching which we see the need to defend.

At the same time, defense is indeed necessary. As editors of a journal designed for pastoral leaders, our primary concern has been renewal in pastoral care. In that work, however, we have become increasingly conscious of the seriousness of the threats to Christian life which lie in the kinds of thinking which Stephen Clark and Paul Vitz, for example, analyzed in their essays. There are those within the churches whose efforts, deliberately or unwittingly, contribute to a weakening of Christians' sense of identity and speed their assimilation to non-Christian worldviews and values. Their efforts must be resisted.

A biblical scene typifies the approach which is called for; it is the picture of the men of Jerusalem repairing the city walls after their return from exile, described by Nehemiah. The work of reconstruction was threatened by their enemies, so Nehemiah prepared them for defense. Each man then labored with a tool in one hand and a weapon in the other. Their ability to combine a readiness to fight with their constructive measures is instructive for us.

Secondly, evangelical-Catholic cooperation need not seek unity directly, but neither can it ignore disunity. While responding to the urgency of the issues which are "increasingly forcing themselves upon us" and which are "pushing into the background" controversies of the past," we must not lose sight of the fact that these controversies have left the Christian people deeply and seriously divided. To recognize the important common ground that evangelicals and Catholics share regarding the essentials of the Christian faith is not to deny that the Christian people fall far short of the unity which we ought to desire because the Lord of the church himself desires it. And so we must not confuse our cooperation with unity. Rather, by mutual respect and the growth of understanding, cooperation can contribute eventually to unity. Learning to work side by side in the cause of Christ plays a practical part in the larger process of overcoming the divisions in the Christian people because it fulfills what Cardinal Ratzinger termed "the task of responsible Christians," which is "to create a spiritual climate for the theological possiblity of unity." To serve one another by helping each other respond successfully to the challenge of modernity is to promote such a spiritual climate.

Thirdly, many avenues of cooperation lie open to us. The colloquy brought together the editors of several Christian periodicals and book publishers; many of the participants were pastors—clergy and lay men and lay women—from a wide variety of church and community settings; among the participants were scholars in different disciplines—scripture, dogmatic and moral theology, history. Evangelicals and Catholics working in these various fields have yet to find ways to work together and support one another in the great task of understanding modernity's complex challenges and finding ways to deal with it. The essays presented here suggest particular areas in which they might learn to cooperate. A call for cooperation between Catholic and evangelical scripture scholars was, for instance, a significant point in James I. Packer's response to Stephen Clark's essay.

Finally, an evangelical-Catholic alliance must be hopeful and confident even as it is sober in the face of serious challenges. We are at a moment in history when more men and women fill the earth than at any time in the past, and when the opportunities for bringing the gospel to the whole world are greatly multiplied. At this moment Christianity faces one of its most serious challenges. It is locked in a struggle to maintain its true identity and way of life in the midst of modernization's shattering social and intellectual changes. The struggle is the present phase of a much older battle between God's kingdom and the dominion of his enemy.

At this moment it is crucial for us to trust in the power of God, to seek to serve him according to his mind and intentions, and to learn to work together for the defense and strengthening of his people. Then we shall see his faithfulness.

THE EDITORS